Language as Living Form
in Nineteenth-Century Poetry

LANGUAGE
AS LIVING FORM IN
NINETEENTH-CENTURY
POETRY

Isobel Armstrong

Professor of English
University of Southampton

THE HARVESTER PRESS • SUSSEX
BARNES & NOBLE BOOKS • NEW JERSEY

First published in Great Britain in 1982 by
THE HARVESTER PRESS LIMITED
Publisher: John Spiers
16 Ship Street, Brighton, Sussex

and in the USA by
BARNES & NOBLE BOOKS
81 Adams Drive, Totowa, New Jersey 07516

British Library Cataloguing in Publication Data

Armstrong, Isobel
    Language as living form in nineteenth century poetry.
    1. English poetry – 19th century – History and criticism
    I. Title
    821'.009   PR581

ISBN 0–7108–0350–8

Library of Congress Cataloging in Publication Data

Armstrong, Isobel.
    Language as living form in 19th century poetry.
    1. English poetry – 19th century – History and criticism. 2. English
language – 19th century – Style. 3. Romanticism – England. I Title.
PR585.L3A7 1982   821'.7'09   82–6694
ISBN 0–389–20293–2   AACR2

Photoset in Sabon by
Redwood Burn Limited, Trowbridge, Wiltshire
Printed by Mansell Limited, Witham, Essex

For Michael, Thomas, Ursula, Stephen.

'Exuberance is Beauty'.

Contents

Acknowledgements

While this book was being completed I was fortunate to be a member of a reading group set up by postgraduates of the English Department at the University of Leicester. The group was formed initially to consider Marx and in the course of three years ranged widely in theoretical criticism. I am grateful for the thinking and questioning we did there, which was a presence as I wrote this book, and thank the group's long-term members, Susie Meikle, Jane Nineham, Simon Dentith, Graham Mott, Rick Rylance, Paul Hoggart, Roger and Grey Stein, Roger Mitchell.

My sister, Diana Wynne Jones, A. S. Byatt (University College, London), Barbara Hardy (Birkbeck College, London), Maud Ellmann, Professor Edmund Papst (University of Southampton) and Ulrich Keller (University of Frankfurt) read parts of this book and helped me with their comments. I thank Linda Glenn and Jonathan Leslie for their thoughts on Shelley while they were third-year students in the English Department of Southampton University.

The joint-editors of the *Oxford Literary Review* have kindly allowed me to reprint a chapter on Wordsworth substantially the same as was published in Volume 4, No. 3, 1981, pp. 20–42. I am grateful to Oxford University Press for granting me permission to quote Hopkins' Notes of 9 February 1868 from *The Journals and Papers of Gerard Manley Hopkins* (eds. Humphrey House and Graham Storey), 1959.

I thank Maureen Medley, Norma Martin and Jill Bennett, who typed the manuscript, for their supportive patience and generosity throughout these last stages. My trying writing and erratic second thoughts gave them a difficult task. They performed it with good humour and meticulousness which fill me with admiration.

Preface

*... a war-like State never can produce Art. It will Rob & Plunder & accumu-
late into one place, & Translate & Copy & Buy & Sell & Criticise, but not
Make. Grecian is Mathematic Form: Gothic is Living Form, Mathematic Form
is Eternal in the Reasoning Memory: Living Form is Eternal Existence. (Blake,
On Virgil)*

In his note on Virgil, Blake sets 'Living Form' against the art
which can only 'copy ... and criticise, but not make.' With
characteristic concentration and intensity he condenses a
distinction habitual to his time to a series of aphorisms: 'a war-
like State ... Will Rob & Plunder & accumulate into one place,
& Translate & Copy & Buy & Sell & Criticise, but not Make.'
This book is about the language and structure of the nineteenth-
century poetry which aspires to 'Living Form', to make, not to
copy. What kind of language is chosen, what kind of organisation occurs, and what kind of difficulties are encountered,
when the poem asserts that it 'Makes'? For many reasons, but
primarily because it aims to make rather than copy and aspires
to 'Living Form', I call the language of nineteenth-century
poetry idealist language.

The first chapter derives a rhetoric of nineteenth-century
poetry from Romantic philosophy, notably from Hegel, and
describes the ways in which the language of nineteenth-century
poetry can be shown to be idealist. Idealist language, however,
possesses inherent problems. Gerard Manley Hopkins intuiti-
vely grasped some of these, though in escaping from them he
created other difficulties for himself. The book begins with him
and his critique of Romantic poetry. It moves subsequently to
Marx's critique of Hegelian thinking. The two figures, Hopkins
and Marx, perhaps converge oddly, but both demonstrate the
inherent strains of idealism. The strains of idealist language as
they arose for Wordsworth, Blake, Shelley, Tennyson and
Browning form subsequent chapters. I end with a short account

of the implications of these problems for twentieth-century poetry.

In deriving an account of the language of nineteenth-century poetry from the structure of Romantic epistemology, and in calling this idealist language, I mean that this language discloses a concern with the relationship of subject and object and with the nature of reality. Idealist language assumes that the object is known as a category of mind. It is not that the object has no existence, but rather the status of the way in which it is known as an aspect of consciousness which is the important problem. Two difficulties arise from this. In the first place, it requires the slightest epistemological shift for the object to be in danger of being abolished in effect if not in fact. Hegel goes to great pains to protect his thinking from this kind of interpretation, and the idea of mediation actually makes a reading of this kind impossible. Read properly, it is not possible to make the *Phenomenology* into a Fichtean tract in which consciousness sees itself as other. However, since the poets I write of are working with a more generalised form of idealist thinking, they certainly encountered the abolition of the object as a problem, and it is one which haunts their poetry. One of my reasons for deciding to use Hegelian thinking as a model with which to begin thinking about the problems of idealist language in the nineteenth century was precisely that it dramatises the incipient difficulties of idealist epistemology for the poet. Marx's critique of Hegel makes these clear enough. One might well wish to argue that he was wrong, and that there is much in the *Phenomenology* which refutes him, but it is nevertheless important historically that he could draw the conclusions he made.

The second problem involved in my approach to idealist epistemology is perhaps a problem for the critic rather than for the poets about whom I write. It is easy to confuse strict accounts of the constitutive structure of the relation between mind and objects with the debased forms of idealism which derived from it. Ruskin's account of the pathetic fallacy is one of these derivative forms. Essentially his account of the relation between the poet and external world is one which describes the poet projecting his own *subjectivity* on to the world, and finding in it, consolingly but fallaciously, an echo of his own mind and feeling in comforting analogies between the external world and himself. Hopkins' immature but intelligent response to idealist thinking shares the same confusion. This account of subjectivity debases the firm epistemological structure from which nineteenth-century poetry arose. For idealist epistemology is concerned, not with superficial subjectivity, but with the cognitive structure of mind. A Ruskinian view, in the first place, makes it difficult to make the transference from epistemology to the structure of language that I wish to make, namely that it is possible to regard the language and form of nineteenth-century poetry as a model of the structure of consciousness or being itself. Secondly, the cognitive claims for the language of poetry made by nineteenth-century poets themselves disappear in the Ruskinian view: the claim that enables the transformation of categories (including those of subject and object) and therefore brings into being the possibility of radical change. I think this sense of possibility was still present even in the more difficult conditions of Victorian poetry (part of *In Memoriam* is a critique of the Ruskinian pathetic fallacy) and that is why I have looked at the work of Romantic and Victorian poets together.

Criticism of nineteenth-century poetry often presupposes a transcendent account of the subject, in which the unity of subject and object is achieved, and in which the relationship between consciousness and the world is mystified, through the personalising and subjectivising of the free autonomous self and its agency. A study of the language of nineteenth-century poetry suggests rather that it works to de-mystify the relation between subject and object, and does not assume a primal unity on the part of the perceiving mind. Indeed, it struggles with the problem of relationship itself. The frankly affective quality of the language of poetry in this period is often misleading, and frequently leads to a reading which assumes that the poet is merely expressing his subjective life or selfhood. Hence the hostility of Hopkins and later of Pound, whom I mention in my conclusion. I believe, on the contrary, that this affective language is used with great precision and accuracy once one grants it a strict epistemological base. And if this is done, the affective and emotional resonance of the language of nineteenth-century poetry is released for very different kinds of reading than an immediate expressive account of it will allow. Perhaps it can be said that if the poetry avails itself of the easy expressive reading, it is not as uncontaminated by Ruskinian preconceptions as I maintain. Possibly not, but as with the disappearance of the object, this is one of the difficulties with which the poetry of this period contends. The poetry is to some extent in possession of its problems and this is why its language is complex and strenuous.

Finally, it is clear that for Hopkins, whose critique of idealist poetry begins this book, questions of epistemology and language elide into political and cultural concerns. Although criticisms of nineteenth-century poetry – its subjectivised nature, its prolix concern with abstraction – are often expressed in aesthetic terms by later, twentieth-century poets, and may often be based on misreadings of idealist poetry, this is a debate with political implications, as I suggest in my Conclusion, because it is concerned with language and the world. Similarly, for the earlier poets the question of the status of subject and object raised in idealist language has to do with the cognitive function of poetry, the nature of change and the possibility of relationship. If you do not 'copy' you 'make'. The stresses and strains encountered in an idealist epistemology, however, offer paradigms of relationship which threaten the activity of making and offer disturbing political and cultural implications. The language of nineteenth-century poetry registers an exhaustive attempt to come to grips with paradigms of relationship and with the nature of making.

CHAPTER 1

Introduction:
Hopkins, Hegel, Marx and the Language of Nineteenth-century Poetry

Oh, how thankful I am that my heart can feel the simple, harmless joys of the man who brings to the table a head of cabbage he has grown himself, and in a single moment enjoys, not only the vegetable, but all the fine days and fresh mornings, since he planted it, the mild evenings when he watered it, and the pleasure he felt while watching it grow.[1] (Goethe, *The Sorrows of Young Werther*).

The mind has two kinds of energy, a transitional kind, when one thought or sensation follows another, which is to reason, whether actively as in deliberation, criticism, or passively, to to call it, as in reading etc; (ii) an abiding kind for which I remember no name, in which the mind is absorbed (as far as that may be), taken up by, dwells upon, enjoys, a single thought: we may call it contemplation, but it includes pleasures, supposing they, however turbid, do not require a transition to another term *of another.kind*, for contemplation in its absoluteness is impossible unless in a trance and it is enough for the mind to repeat the same energy on the same matter.[2] (Hopkins, *Journals and Papers*, Notes, 9 February 1868)

To have your own consciousness returned to you when you eat a cabbage, so that you digest, not only a vegetable, but the history of your own experience in a single moment, transforming the cabbage and transforming the self as you do so is, perhaps, to offer a bizarre account of the 'harmless joys' of growing vegetables and the act of contemplating them. Goethe is wry enough about the over-sophisticated sentimentality of Werther's Romanticism. And yet, for all the irony, Werther's celebration of the 'organic' life delicately embodies a common proposition of Romanticism with tactful, punning wit. The cabbage, substantive enough, is digested by mind and body. Our experience is a labouring of the mind upon the objects of perception, and this labour is self-creation. Objects are constituted by human thought and become categories of it because our consciousness is reflected back from the objects of perception which are knowable as consciousness. Experience is transformation and process and being is that transitional energy, as Hopkins puts it, which moves from one term to another term *of another kind*, from subject to object, coalescing each into the other, while each maintains its separateness. The processes of mind are constantly returned to itself, digested, contemplated, generating new categories and materials for further contemplation. The joys of this experience *are* simple and harmless because the primary activity of perception is necessarily at work in the most ordinary human activities and belongs inherently to the temporal sequence of experience. A cabbage is never just a cabbage because the consciousness watches itself grow in process with it. And it is right to speak of joy and pleasure because in this activity, man and nature, the self and the world, are reconciled and do not stand over and against one another, closed out, as separate entities. They need one another and are transformed by one another.

Hopkins' is a very different account of the act of contemplation. It is not my aim to make the reader choose between Hopkins and Goethe, but it is important to observe the difference between them. 'It is enough for the mind to repeat the same energy on the same matter': to seize experience as wholeness and all-at-onceness, to grasp it as simultaneity and sensory immediacy and to defy the transitions of temporal sequence, which, with an intelligence always intensely severe on itself, Hopkins knows to be there, is the motive of this statement. To 'catch' is a verb he often uses to express a taking hold of things in their immediacy and totality, whether it is bluebells in Hodder Wood or the inscapes of snow swept by a broom.[3] 'I caught this morning morning's minion': I caught *this* morning, a particular and isolated morning, not a morning generalised out of the succession of fine days, fresh mornings, mild evenings, which cumulatively create the identity and are, as it were, ingested into the self. 'I caught *this* morning,' and with *this* morning, as a simultaneously fused experience, 'this morning ... minion', the windhover's flight in time. 'Morning' and 'minion' are so locked together by alliteration that to move from one to the other is not to require a transition to another term of another kind: morning is an attribute of minion, minion belongs to morning, is 'morning's minion'. *This* time and *this* flight are so fused and

fixed in a permanant here and now that the pastness of the verb
'caught' is almost suppressed and the flight arrested. To catch
something, as the physicality of the verb insists, is to catch in its
entirety, or not at all. To catch something is also to catch what is
outside the self, something thrown to you – again, the physicality of the metaphor insists on this, just as it hints at an
incipiently violent force in the things that come at you from
outside. The mind reaches out passionately, but it does not meet
its own image in the objects of perception, for the world is not
charged with the grandeur of mind but with the grandeur of
God, who creates all things in their unique separateness. So
there is energy of mind, and matter, or things and us, as Hopkins
puts it in the notes on Parmenides, 'the stem of stress between us
and things'.[4] Energy leaps over the gap between us and things,
absorbed, taken up by, dwelling upon, their being. It does not
dissolve, diffuse and dissipate things in order to recreate them
and itself in a successive process of transformation, for the unity
of the world is outside the self and not made by it. Objects *as*
objects are fixed and vital in themselves, Hopkins would have
maintained. This dualism is essential to his thinking.

Interestingly, the process of transition and connection by
which, for most Romantics, the mind transmutes the world and
itself, is converted by Hopkins into something suspect. Its transitions are sharply differentiated from the strenuously static
trance or contemplation which receives things as a synthesis,
and defined as mere analytical thinking, barren abstract
thought. Concepts and ideas are evolved by being successively
disengaged or 'unwound' (as he puts it later in the same notes)
from the feelings and particular concrete forms to which they
belong. Attributes are separated out sequentially from the whole
they should create and belong to. Thinking, as Hopkins
describes it, is essentially inorganic, analytic and fragmenting,
severing the unity of mind by dissociating thinking and feeling,
meaning and experience. The mind which requires successive
activity as its central experience has a predilection for 'pure dialectic'.[5]

Two very different accounts of language arise from these
accounts of consciousness and the relationship of the self and
the world. For Hopkins the word is fixed as substitution or
equivalent for a thing or classes of things in the external world
and if it cannot render the thingness of objects at least it may

become a thing in itself. Coleridge sums up the other view when he writes: 'if words are not THINGS, they are LIVING POWERS, by which the things of most importance to mankind are actuated, combined, and humanized.'[6] Actuate, combine, humanise: words are unfixed, not the equivalents of things or even things in themselves, but agents free to constitute the world in and through themselves, free to combine and transform its categories in and through their own, free to change. Above all words 'humanise', expressing relationship as one in which the subject finds itself in the object, or the object becomes an attribute of the subject. There can be no split between meaning and experience because words are not a substitute for experience. They are autonomous, the agents of change and transformation.

A dangerous autonomy, Hopkins thought, and challenged it. However much he was indebted to Romantic thinking (and it is certain that he was), it is clear that he saw the language of Romantic poetry as the symptom of an almost irremediable cultural breakdown. That is why I begin with him. He loved the poems of Keats and Shelley, and Wordsworth in particular, but the form of Romantic language caused him pain and he rejected it for a complex of reasons which were certainly personal and psychological, but mainly religious and cultural and as a corollary aesthetic.

He had so much insight into his difficulties with the idiom of nineteenth-century poetry that it is possible to understand more about the language of that poetry by understanding why he rejected it. His negative definition of it enables one to determine the nature of Romantic poetic language and its problems more precisely than at any other point in the nineteenth century. He was the first poet to make a systematic case for non-discursive poetry. It is important to see why he put the argument in these terms, why he needed a theory of non-discursive art in order to defend himself against the Romantics. The first part of this chapter charts Hopkins' early thinking on language, and his uneasy hostility to the language of Romantic poetry. I discuss his early ideas through the laconic Notes of 1868 (which are printed as an appendix to this chapter), and go on to consider the early essays in which his distrust of Hegel and Romantic culture is apparent.

The thinking in the *Notes*, written early in the year Hopkins became a Jesuit, is brilliant, passionate, succinct and stubborn. It is overwhelmingly original with the strange precocity and intensity of immaturity (Hopkins was scarcely in his mid-twenties) and seems entirely self-invented. In a few hundred lines of condensed prose it constructs a vocabulary for talking about the languge of poetry which is unique – prepossession, *scapes*, flushes, unwound. These notes represent a critical point in his thinking about poetry: also, by implication, they set out his rejection of nineteenth-century poetry and the ideas underlying it. They shift Romantic conceptions of poetry by deriving it now from the fixed and intrinsic nature of language and its activity and not from an unstable theory of consciousness. The theory of language, of course, implies a theory of consciousness but Hopkins makes language itself the prime structure. The notes reject idealism, abstraction, and the art which is created out of successive experience. They assert instead that a poem 'explodes' into meaning (an expression Hopkins uses several times elsewhere[7]) because language, even if it has to defy its nature, can express experience as simultaneity, and defeats the separation of meaning from experience by refusing to generalise and by giving form to experience as an irreducible concretion. Language respects the wholeness and otherness of things in the world, aspiring to render the '*haeccitas*' or 'thisness' of objects – a word Hopkins found in Duns Scotus. And perhaps, by an almost impossible fusing of sign with thing language may even become the thing, healing the fracture between thing and word.

The earlier lyrics, particuarly a poem such as 'Spring', even though they were written over a decade later than the Notes, explore the capacity of words to achieve such feats with rigorous and astonishing virtuosity. Hopkins' Notes represent the beginnings of a recognisably modern account of poetry, or one form of modernism. This is exciting, but it is important to remember that his polarities, distinctions and categories are often obstinate and arbitrary. He was an honest thinker, and recognised this, but he needed to construct a new poetic and critical language in so willed a fashion in order to escape the dissolution of Romantic language. However, the dichotomy between trance, epiphany, concretion, as against transitional, abstract thinking is not an inevitable one and not even a necessary derivation from the essential nature of language. Movingly, the struggle to heal the split between meaning and experience, sign and thing, reintroduces the problem in an acute form for Hopkins. His struggle against what he saw as the deficiencies of Romantic language forced him to extremity. I shall show this by looking at the *Notes* in conjunction with 'Spring', which aspires to the non-transitional language analysed as a possibility in the *Notes*.

Spring

Nothing is so beautiful as Spring –
   When weeds, in wheels, shoot long and lovely and lush;
   Thrush's eggs look little low heavens, and thrush
Through the echoing timber does so rinse and wring
The ear, it strikes like lightnings to hear him sing;
   The glassy peartree leaves and blooms, they brush
   The descending blue; that blue is all in a rush
With richness; the racing lambs too have fair their fling.

What is all this juice and all this joy?
   A strain of the earth's sweet being in the beginning
In Eden garden. – Have, get, before it cloy,

   Before it cloud, Christ, lord, and sour with sinning,
Innocent mind and Mayday in girl and boy,
   Most, O maid's child, thy choice and worthy the winning.[8]

'Nothing is so beautiful as Spring': Hopkins' earlier poems are often written to behave like an inclusive gasp or exclamation which takes in a complex of things at once, 'all in a rush with richness'. The whole poem '*strikes*' like lightning, lights up in an instantaneous flash and *hits* the sense of the reader, acting out the double meaning of strike as ignite and physical blow. The objects of contemplation in 'Spring' seem absorbed in pouring out their selfhood in static energy, in a permanent present tense, a permanent *is*ness, repeating the same energy on the same selving or act of individuation. The present tense makes them coexist in a simultaneously thronging immediacy in which no item takes precedence over any other. Weeds 'shoot', thrush's eggs 'look', thrush does 'so rinse and wring/The ear', the peartree 'leaves and blooms', these leaves and blooms 'brush', the blue *is*. Participles crush energy into immobilised presentness – the 'descending blue', the 'racing lambs'. It is in the nature of language to make transitions from one term to another but Hopkins blocks or obliterates these as far as he can, not only by arranging his words in discrete stabs of sensory description but by disguising transitions and relationship as new, autonomous sentences which yet do not progress. 'The glassy peartree leaves and blooms, they brush/The descending blue.' The leaves and blooms here hover between being things and activities, nouns and verbs. The nature of the tree is not to have extraneous objects attached to it but to *leave* and to *bloom,* and this is how the perceiver grasps its identity. The leaves and blooms belong to one congruent activity. Then Hopkins uses a paratactical construction – 'they brush': it seems as if the leaves and blooms are things again, and that the language may have failed. But this is done precisely in order to avoid the hardening of leaves and blooms into separate things which would be reinforced by using the relative and subordinate clause, '*that* brush/The descending blue'. 'They' here signifies the autonomous and equal activity of leaving and blooming which is *equally* brushing the sky, another and unsubordinated function of the tree's identity. It is not a sequential activity but simultaneous with the tree's nature. In exactly the same way as 'they brush', 'it strikes like lightnings' begins a new sentence, rather than expressing '*so that* it strikes'. Compare Wordsworth's serene acceptance of subordination, transition and sequence in the first lines of the 1805 *Prelude.* 'O there is blessing in this gentle breeze *that* blows/*From* the green fields *and from* the trees/*And from* the sky.' I shall return to these lines repeatedly as a touchstone for all that Hopkins did not wish to do, for they yield more and more. Here the contrast in syntax serves to show how Hopkins' language is forced to proceed by fiat, as it were ordering such paratactical constructions as 'they brush' in order to insist on a particular account of experience.

'All names but proper names are general while the soul is individual', Hopkins writes at the start of his Notes. He recognises that all words are arbitrary signs and that they refer to categories of things – the peartree, the weed, the thrush – except proper names, which refer to specific things or individuals. And so words cannot be like the soul, which is unique to every person and intrinsically binds concrete and abstract. If we had a different word for every item in the universe and our experience, treating words as the equivalent of things and not the culturally determined signs for classes of things, language would defeat itself and collapse into chaos. And yet, though Hopkins rigorously recognises the generalising function of words and their arbitrary relationship to things, the implicit aim of these Notes is to defeat this function and to give words a soul, to make them, as far as possible, unique things, uniquely fused with experience, not signs. 'When weeds, in wheels, shoot long and lovely and lush': if a word is quite simply the definition, or concept, it has acquired by convention or, since words rarely have a single primary meaning, the 'contraction or coinciding-point of its definitions', it will be possible, by shifting the grammatical usage of a word, to create a new coinciding point of definitions. So it is with the swathes of weeds. 'Wheels' is neither the noun 'wheel' nor the verb 'to wheel', but contracts the circularity of the wheel and the action of wheeling, swooping round upon oneself, into a new meaning incorporating at once the idea of circularity and extension. 'Wheels' is almost that impossibility, a unique word for a unique thing, a thing in itself, a rendering of experience rather than a sign for it.

Who is to say that Hopkins' word has not become Coleridge's 'living power' in itself rather than a thing in itself interchangeable with experience? It is not possible to say. It is only possible to say that Hopkins writes in theory and practice as if it might be possible for words, in T. E. Hulme's terms, to 'hand over sensations bodily'.[9] The '*glassy* peartree': radiant, shining, fragile, reflective, but, above all, you see through it, as you see through trees to the sky behind them in Spring. Hopkins goes back to the immediate sensory qualities of glass in order to create the idea of transparency. The idea emerges through the particular physical nature of glass and one might say that the notion of transparency is given a soul because it is incarnate in the specific irreducible and particular qualities of glass. 'To every word belongs a passion or prepossession or enthusiasm': Hopkins means the particular emotional resonance, the affective colouring and associative *feel* evoked by individual words, now a cultural possession through long historical process. Although this 'passion' – the term frankly drawn from the vocabulary of love, persuades us of the powerful energies of language – is akin to the soul, and creates the unique nature or 'form' of words in our minds, Hopkins ruthlessly strips prepossession away from the *essential* definition of the word in the Notes. It is connotation, not meaning. A word is a shape and a sound, and the concept called up by that shape and sound and that is all. This characteristically stringent intellectual discipline, however, which anticipates Saussurian thinking to some extent, is actually

turned on its head both in the Notes and in 'Spring'. Bare
abstract meaning is subverted. The feel of glass and its associations, the passion or prepossession of the word – clarity,
radiance, transcendence – is not extraneous because it creates
meaning. And so it does seem possible to read the word through
its prepossessions rather than its bare meaning. And to do this
not only makes the word unique in itself but forces meaning to
inhere irreducibly in particular concrete forms of words.
Meaning becomes intrinsic to the word, not an arbitrary
relation, and the word, correspondingly, is uniquely fixed to the
thing it represents. If a word in 'Spring' is insufficiently charac-
terised by its passion, the definition of the word is, as it were,
sunk back into the sensory. 'The blue', *that* blue, the sky. Wordsworth's inobtrusively generalising epithets, *gentle* breeze, *green*
fields, and the literal sky, would for Hopkins eliminate 'soul'.

Much later in his life Hopkins asked Newman if he might
make a commentary on *A Grammar of Assent*.[10] The Notes anti-
cipate the arguments of this work by two years. Newman's
distinction between notional and real assent depends on recognising two kinds of meaning in the same words. Notional
propositions appeal to the generalising, unspecific properties of
language where signs bear an arbitrary relation to concepts and
experience. Real propositions, the most intense and imaginati-
vely coercive uses of language, are 'apprehended as experiences
and images, that is, which stand for things'.

In the proposition 'Sugar is sweet', the predicate

is a common noun as used by those who have compared sugar in their thoughts
with honey or glycerine; but it may be the only distinctively sweet thing in the
experience of a child, and may be used by him as a noun singular. The first time
that he tastes sugar, if his nurse says 'Sugar is sweet' in a notional sense,
meaning by sugar, lump-sugar, powdered, brown, and candied, and by sweet,
a specific flavour or scent which is found in many articles of food and many
flowers, he may answer in a real sense, and in an individual proposition, 'Sugar
is sweet', meaning 'this sugar is this sweet thing'.[11]

This sugar is this sweet thing: this peartree is this glassy thing:
these weeds are these wheels. The language presses towards real
as against notional being. It is a form of primitivism. On the
other hand – and this is the contradiction of the Notes – the very
pressure towards the 'real' being of language is counter-
productive. It inadvertently detaches words from things by

reading words for their prepositions rather than meaning. Consider the preposessions of alliteration: 'When *w*eeds, in *w*heels, shoot *l*ong and *l*ovely and *l*ush': the naïve, almost child-like thrust of alliteration in Hopkins' poetry grants sheer sound an extraordinary autonomy. Hopkins insisted, in spite of himself, that only two things belong inherently to the word when it is contemplated as an entity or an image by the mind: its meaning, and its own particular sensory qualities made by its physical shape (structure or *scape*), form and sound, (visual and aural qualities). Each individual word has a direct 'physical and refined energy accenting the nerves'. That is, it produces a sensation, and this sensation can be detached from meaning, repeated and contemplated for itself as pure visual and aural form. A 'word to oneself, an inchoate word', inchoate because it is sensation, not meaning. It is as if words can become things in themselves as sounds and shapes if they cannot become the things they represent. They need not even call forth concepts inevitably. But this split can be turned to paradoxical use. In 'Spring' the prickly physicality of alliteration forces a contemplation of the 'inchoate word'. The words are thrust direct against the nerves, as sensation. Alliteration and internal rhyme can, paradoxically, release words from meaning by drawing attention to similarities of sound, shape and structure which are not similarities of meaning. The result is that though abstract, notional meaning may be kept at bay and subverted, a series of juxtapositions can be made, perceived as a block of sound, which bring words into non-logical relations with one another and dispense with discursive connections. The general words which no poet can help using can be tied down to sensation and action. With 'lovely', an affective, unspecific adjective like Wordsworth's 'gentle' (Hopkins was an intensely adjectival poet: it is a fallacy to suppose that he rejected a Romantic predilection for them) or with 'richness', an abstraction, the words are attracted respectively to 'long and lush' and 'rush', and coloured by them. But the leap to the particular cannot always disguise the split between sound and meaning. In Hopkins' poetry one is incipiently aware of the thrusting energies of the inchoate word, sensation anarchically severed from sense.

When the Notes reach the point at which Hopkins states his preference for the untransitional experience of trance (although he carefully recognises that 'contemplation in its absoluteness' is impossible) they wheel round upon themselves. It may be that works of art 'like words utter the idea', and that the energies of trance and transition 'are not incompatible'. Impressions must be successive or spatially distinct, the psychology of reading insists upon this. But the work of art must be a complex synthesis, a highly organised whole, and the mind must be encouraged to 'keep making' an instantaneous comparison between the 'whole and the parts, the parts and the whole', and defeat succession. The way to enable the perceiver to receive that synthesis is to make the uniquely individuating passion or prepossession of each item of language belong so inseparably to it that meaning cannot be 'distinguished and unwound' from prepossession, and the winding of prepossession and meaning together integrates and unifies the work. (Significantly 'unbound' is the word Hopkins uses later for the terrible dissolution of 'Spelt from Sibyl's Leaves'.) The more highly organised the work 'the deeper the form penetrates, the prepossession flushes the matter'. 'Flushes' finely express the idea of feeling physically penetrating, not superficially colouring, an object. The mind is forced to 'effort' and 'comparison' of likeness and difference when it is confronted with the complex particularities and concretions of prepossession, but it is from this activity, and from attention to prepossession rather than meaning, that it recovers the sense of the whole and with it a new prepossession belonging to the whole. This I take to be the meaning of the condensed eleventh paragraph of the Notes. It is a sophistication of the earlier dialogue on beauty, in which relationship in unlikeness and likeness discovered through non-progressive parallelism, is the source of beauty, and, one may add, the cognitive power of metaphor. What is new in the Notes is the idea that the individual 'feel' of words, whether conveyed through their associative power and connotation or their sensory qualities and physical shape (for Hopkins talks of words and the elements of a work of art interchangeably), is responsible for unity and meaning. Prepossession wins, even though it is not, on Hopkins' own admission, an essential part of the 'meaning' of a word. What Hopkins has done is to redefine Romantic unity, multeity in unity, as Coleridge called it, as non-discursive language, the 'sane way of contemplation': there is a radical distinction between what is felt and concrete when words are things, and what is meant when words at best call forth concepts and ideas, not experience.

Thrush's eggs 'look little low heavens', the 'blue' descending: heaven meets earth and earth meets heaven (as it was in Eden, the sestet amplifies) and is *seen* to do so. The thrush's song comes 'through the echoing timber', the pear tree shows the sky through its leaves and blooms. The song rinses or purifies the sense and touches, strikes, the being; the pear tree brushes, touches and sweeps clean the sky. The concrete particularity of things on earth, an unexpected but typically Hopkinsian reversal, clarify what is spiritual and, indeed, fuse with it. Weeds shoot, low, like thrush's eggs, lambs have fair their fling towards the *descending* blue, on either side of thrush and tree, testifying the energy and fullness of Eden. Varied and disparate things, thrush and tree, do 'brush' one another, as the rhyme words assert, brush, thrush, like and unlike, unified in their separate identities by energy and richness, rush, lush. The rhyme words assert the new prepossession to be recovered from the independent prepossessions of the discrete things in the poem.[12]

What need of the sestet if the first part of the sonnet implies so much? The bald answer is that, for all the virtuosity of the language, we would not be on the lookout for these implications if Hopkins did not tell us to be later in the sestet. The sestet is an explication of the octet. It is expressed in the form of urgent questions, imperatives and invocation or prayer: 'What is all this juice?': 'have, get': 'Most, O maid's child, thy choice and worthy the winning'. The intensiveness of these forms does not disguise the fact that they are statements of a very different kind from those in the first part of the poem; transitions to different terms. The poem is split between prepossession and meaning. Two kinds of writing are at work, prepossessional and discursive.

Here is the moving spectacle of a poet straining to climb back into his poem. There is agony and strain even at the greatest moments of ecstasy in Hopkins' work as the movement from one term to another of a different kind alienates him from the first. He has to move from 'juice' to 'joy', from the sensory to the abstract, to relate and connect them, to force them together, so that his joy and the joy of things correlate. The explication of the sestet, however, forces them apart as much as it brings them together. The things in the octet are given a rich and autonomous being, and are described as much as possible as if they exist independently of the poet. Peartree, sky, lambs, fling out their curiously transfixed energies, straining to maintain their separate being. The poet's emotion and rapture is strongly enough present – 'Nothing is so beautiful as Spring' – but things are arrested in their individual identities and energies, acting quite externally to him, becoming almost accidentally his own experience, a lucky striking, an unexpected seizure. 'Thrush's eggs *look* little low heavens': Hopkins's interpretative act is disguised by this verb and by the contraction of the syntax. Thrush's eggs could *seem* to the watcher as low heavens, or they could themselves appear, or they could look out independently of him as low heavens or from them. 'What you look hard at seems to look hard at you,' Hopkins wrote in his *Journals*, expressing the 'seems' which is suppressed in 'Spring'.[13] But even here the world exists as inalienably other, as object. The mind does not belong to the world, but, through intense concentration, forces the gaze of the world upon it. The things that give Hopkins most joy are cut off from him. For all its rapture the poem is a poem of severance. 'Thrush does so rinse and wring/ The ear': the thrush wrings the senses (and rings against the ear), those things which respond to external stimuli, and not the heart, that customary Romantic word for the centre of self. Keats's vocabulary – 'My *heart* aches' – is inappropriate to this song. 'Spring' has an estranged intensity. In spite of its 'brilliance, margaretting, quain' (Hopkins's terminology for the sharpness and sensory individuation he wished for[14]) its passion is over-anxious, awkward: 'And thrush/Through'. The syntax here is blocked and congested by the need both to conceal and achieve the act of transition. The emotion can be precious – 'thrush's eggs look little low heavens' – with that muscular (or musclebound) preciousness that sometimes intrudes into a Hopkins poem. At least some of this blocking comes about because he was caught in a theory of discursiveness which separates things or experience from our interpretation of them – the very thing he did not wish for – and so was locked out of his own poems. Wordsworth, the poet he found so puzzling, better out of context and in short extracts, comes to mind again as a touchstone against which to test Hopkins. 'O there is blessing in this gentle breeze/That blows from the green fields and from the trees/And from the Sky. It beats against my cheek/And seems half-conscious of the joy it gives.' The breeze 'seems', not looks:

seems itself and seems to the poet. Wordsworth acknowledges
the activity of his own consciousness in interpreting experience
and the flow of his selfhood into the world. Blessing and breeze,
the syntax allows, blow as one, a physical and a spiritual agent,
a physical experience and its psychological and spiritual
meaning together. And as the ambiguity of 'there is blessing'
acknowledges that the blessing is bestowed by the breeze upon
the poet, and by the poet upon the breeze, the poet's blessing
blows from fields, trees, and sky and is returned to him from
them, as other but as an aspect of his consciousness too – it,
breeze and consciousness, 'beats against my cheek'. This poetry
does not need that separating out of explication and experience
which is to be found in 'Spring'.

The virtuosity of Wordsworth's lines is inconspicuous in comparison with that of Hopkins, who found the unemphatic,
'casual' quality of Wordsworth's poems so strange.[15] The first
lines of *The Prelude* are an example of the poetry he did not
want to write. It is idealist poetry. It recognises the transforming
power of mind and expresses this in the structure of its language.
What 'flushes' the matter of such poetry is the consciousness of
the perceiver in external things, which must take place as
process, and not the brilliant individuating of objects in themselves perceived in a moment of oneness. Hopkins was the first
nineteenth-century poet to refuse idealist poetry who was
capable of constructing a theoretical justification for his procedure. He made a consistent distinction (he was a congenitally
binary thinker) between two kinds of poetry in a series of
remarkable undergraduate essays from 1864 to 1867. These cul-
minate in the Notes of 1868. The essays were written before he
began to use the words inscape and instress in his writings, and
represent the thinking behind those terms. 'Inscape', the unique,
individuating particularity of the object which creates not only
its identity but its unity, and 'instress', the specific energy with
which its being is charged and which renders a particular
emotion to the perceiver, are words which require a good deal of
de-coding. They are clearly related to Hopkins' concern with the
soul or passion of words, but by the time he used them regularly
his ideas had hardened and the terms contract within themselves
a whole series of earlier assumptions and phases of thinking
which need to be explored in some detail. These earlier phases
are most useful for my purposes, and I have chosen to use the

words inscape and instress rarely.

I now turn from the Notes to the earlier essays and consider the opposition they make between what Hopkins called chromatic and non-chromatic art, or what we might term idealist or non-idealist art. It is in these essays that his distrust of Hegel and Hegelian thinking becomes apparent. The distinction between two kinds of poetry, or art, occurs in musical terms as a polarisation between chromatic and intervallery or diatonic art, between the art which is formed on the principle of gradation, transition and succession (the chromatic scale sounds tones *and* half-tones) and the art which juxtaposes a series of fixities which do not merge into one another and require an instantaneous reference between them on the part of the perceiver. In 1868 the distinction takes the form of discursive and non-discursive art and all that it implies. He found chromatic art profoundly disturbing. It is clear that chromatic poetry is transitional poetry, idealist poetry, Romantic poetry.

Hopkins' struggle to invent a new vocabulary in which to describe two kinds of poetry and the extraordinary originality of his terminology demonstrates the problems that the distinction between discursive and non-discursive writing created for him. Interestingly, this distinction, though expressed in a different vocabulary, is one of the truisms of some twentieth-century thinking and modernist accounts of poetry. Hulme's insistence that words should try to 'hand over sensation bodily', Pound's preference for the metaphor which releases a multiple meaning 'in an instant of time', based on Fenollosa's belief in the concreteness of metaphor, Eliot's dislike of 'rumination' and his celebration of the poetry in which a thought could become a sensation, have obvious affinities with Hopkins. The poem must fuse thinking and feeling or, if possible, thought and sensation in an irreducibly concrete configuration of particulars seized as epiphany and oneness. One is led to the aesthetic of the short poem, in which the poem becomes a thing and not, as for so much Romantic poetry, a model of the structure of consciousness. What is striking about some modernist thinking, perhaps, is its crudity in comparison with the discipline and subtlety of Hopkins' thought. But like his, the assumption that thought and sensation, meaning and experience, sign and thing should be fused actually reintroduces the fracture between them in an extreme form. (Perhaps this is endemic to twentieth-century thinking: Freud's assumption that latent dream-thoughts are encoded in the concrete images of the manifest dream, Saussure's account of the sign in which the signified is encoded in the signifier share the paradoxical tendency to split through the very attempt to unify.) In fact, though the distinction between non-discursive and discursive is frequently made in theory it is difficult if not impossible to distinguish them in practice except, perhaps, in such an extreme case as Hopkins himself. Indeed, abstraction in itself is surely not particularly alarming: if it means that we talk about what we have talked about, have thoughts about thoughts, experiences about experiences, thoughts about experience abstracted from it and returned to the consciousness *as* experience, then it is fundamental to the activity of consciousness and the growth of knowledge. It is that reflexive act of understanding which is coextensive with the activity of mind and by which we apprehend ourselves and the world.

Abstraction and discursiveness, as Hopkins fractured them from experience, seem to be a problem he created for himself. And the more one looks at this and other distinctions of the same kind it seems that some more difficult and haunting problem is behind it. Hopkins' essays provide an answer. The very act of cognition is threatened by what he thinks of as a Hegelian chromatic culture and a chromatic language in a condition when words are unfixed from things. What is at stake is not merely an impoverished imaginative apprehension of things, but a state in which language is radically unstable, where words unbind or unwind from their tethering to the things in the world and float free in a constant slippage of reference. Configurations of sound no longer call up concepts and the things they represent as language moves towards the self-referential. 'Sweet' can never be related to 'this sweet thing'. 'Chromatic' is a term he used to describe cultural and historical situations, and what is responsible for the language of flux is a chromatic philosophy of flux. 'On the Probable Future of Metaphysics' (1867) describes and rejects nineteenth-century philosophy as a chromatic philosophy of flux and invokes Hegel as its representative thinker. The reference is brief but significant. It may be that Hopkins' view of Hegel can help us to derive an account of nineteenth-century poetry, and by extension its language, from within Romantic epistemology itself. The corollary is to ask if there is any sense in which his fears about Romantic language are justified.

Hopkins' strenuous search for terms in a series of three essays written over 1864 and 1865 maintains the distinction between the art of 'interval' and 'continuance'.[16] The striking fact about them is that the account of the art of interval becomes more and more precise, while specific description of chromatic art is steadily eroded. By the end there is little left discussable about chromatic art. At first the division is 'of *abrupt* and *gradual*, of *parallelistic* and *continuous*, of intervallery and chromatic, of quantitative and qualitative (a significant distinction) beauty' (1864).[17] The difference is between, for instance, deepening colour and a collocation of separate colours, a *continuously* held note on a violin which yet changes ('or a strain of wind', a characteristic Hopkins insight) and the distinct notes sounded on a piano.[18] In the essay on poetic diction (1865), interestingly, though both kinds of art achieve parallelism (the repeating figure which for Hopkins structures the main relationships in a work), only the formal devices we can point to precisely belong to 'abrupt' art – 'metaphor, simile, parable, and so on, where the effect is sought in likeness of things, and antithesis, contrast, and so on, where it is sought in unlikeness'.[19] The means of cognition, and by implication a precise, cognitive language, belong to abrupt art. Only the distinctions of abrupt art enable us to make and create fixed and precise relationships. To chromatic art belong far less definable things, and the terminology is vague and groping, using words from the analogy of music and painting – 'gradation, intensity, climax, tone, expression (as the word is used in music), *chiaroscuro*, perhaps emphasis'.[20] By the 'Essay on the Origin of Beauty' (1865) parallelism, those structures and devices which create the wholeness and relationship of a work of art by composing it of an infinite number of agreements and differences, is firmly associated with abrupt or diatonic art. Parallelism, to which metaphor belongs intrinsically, has gone over to the other side, and there is almost nothing left for chromatic art to be. It seems to be deprived of language.

The devices of diatonic art are abrupt, and sharply distinguished and non-progressive, but even more important they are *fixed*. The essentially conservative need to fix is everywhere in Hopkins' thinking. 'On this walk I came to a cross-road I had been at in the morning carrying it in another "running instress". I was surprised to recognise it and the moment I did it lost its present instress, breaking off from what had immediately gone before, and fell into the morning's.'[21] Hopkins is scrupulously distressed and puzzled that the same landscape can *feel* different as he moves through it on different occasions during the same walk. He describes the experience with his usual awareness of complexity and the moving stubbornness so characteristic of him. What is significant is his *relief* that the instress 'fell back into the morning's'. Instress, even a running instress – an instress on the run, while you move from place to place – has to be fixed, absolute, unalterable. He dismisses as negligible the idea that a landscape can be modified by feeling 'imposed outwards from the mind', which is a superficial change, and decides that in effect one can have a deceptive or approximate memory, the wrong recall, a false memory, like getting hold of the wrong word when you are groping for the right one. The significance of 'disremembering' in the evening out or flux of evening in 'Spelt from Sibyl's Leaves' becomes clearer. To have the right, precise, fixed memory of experience is essential for our sense of the stability of things. The world collapses if experience cannot be guaranteed by this fixity. The notes on Parmenides base the stability of our relationship with the world on the permanence of memory.[22] This obstinate, defensive clinging to fixedness is there in the passionately laconic intensity of Hopkins' objectivity in the Journals. Waves harden into glass and gems, water turns into solid metal as moonlight roughens, dints and tools its surface, skies are held still by becoming architecture, massive, heavy structures overburdened with vocabulary of weight.[23] The language holds a fluent world still.

And in philosophy, too, it is necessary to achieve fixity. The nineteenth century is in the third 'season of Philosophy', a Hegelian 'philosophy of development in time', which was preceded by Baconian or scientific philosophy, and before this by a Platonic or metaphysical era. 'To prevalent philosophy and science nature is a string all the differences in which are really chromatic but certain places in it have become *accidentally* fixed and the series of fixed points becomes an arbitrary scale' (my italics).[24] One could as easily read '*language* is a string ... really chromatic but certain places in it ... *accidentally* fixed'. The horror of arbitrary, accidental fixing which is 'rife' in Hopkins' time may be attributable to Darwin and evolutionary ideas, but Hegel is named as the philosopher of this science because he is the philosopher of process, 'of continuity and of time'.[25] If the axiom of this philosophy is that all things are constantly trans- forming themselves, then nothing can be absolute, and all values will be arbitrarily fixed, including the axioms of that philosophy itself. And so it is a philosophy not merely of chromatic relativ- ism, but of 'flux' and contradiction: 'It must contradict itself whether it claims to be final or not.'[26] Hopkins attributes to chromatic Hegelianism two other important ideas to which he is hostile. He writes elliptically, but what he says refers first to the idea that a species is not fixed but maintains 'development in one chain of necessity': that is, knowledge evolves and changes, is not static but is 'the history of growth' from parts to the whole. Knowledge is its own history, a process of becoming. Secondly, predominant in this philosophy is the idea of 'personality', meaning, I think, subjectivity (and here Hopkins is sketchy and superficial), an obsession with the self as the determinant and creator of experience. We are back with Werther's cabbage. By now the conservatism, in the broadest sense of the word, in Hopkins' thinking about religion, science, nature and language should be seen congruently as a reaction to cultural dissol- ution.

Hopkins is talking about Hegelianism (we must remember that Oxford originated 'Hegelians') not Hegel, and even then his hostile account of it is specious in strictly philosophical terms.[27] He returns to Hegel much later in the extraordinary meditation which starts from his sense of the 'taste' of himself, but he may not have known much about him, telling Bridges again much later that he had never had time to read his work.[28] But the mis- reading, or incomplete reading of Hegel is indirectly helpful. Hopkins' accuracy or his knowledge is not so important as his intuitive leap to the notion that Hegel is his anti-philosopher (just as Wordsworth is his anti-poet), the philosopher of all chromatic thinking and, it follows, of chromatic poetry too. What we can interpret as the chromatic element in Hegel's thinking may offer, then, an inward account of the nature of Romantic poetry. It may serve as model or analogue for the way that poetry behaves, suggesting a model of the structure of con- sciousness which may by extension become a model of language and of form. It may offer, too, a way of understanding the strains of this poetry and of placing Hopkins' fears about it and his cultural despair. Hopkins' response to Hegel enables us to use Hegel in order to understand more about 'chromatic' thinking.

I turn to Hegel's *Phenomenology of Mind* (1807), the work in which Marx saw the essence of his thinking, and to the ways in which it can illuminate nineteenth-century poetry. In the second part of this chapter I suggest the form which a rhetoric of nineteenth-century, chromatic or idealist poetry could take. Then, with the help of Marx's critique of Hegel, I look at the strains from within idealist language and return to reassess Hopkins' fears in the light of it. My aim here is not to use philosophy to 'explain' or account for poetry as a prior and authoritative structure of ideas. Nor is my discussion of Hegel in any way exhaustive. Of course, there are many areas of Romantic thinking – Coleridge's writings, for example – where one could begin to find the basis of a rhetoric of Romantic poetry. My choice of Hegel followed from my attention to Hopkins and produces coherence in this context. It is a starting point for interpreting chromatic thinking and chromatic art, and for a reading of Romantic poetry. If my argument moves rapidly, it is because the subsequent chapters of this book are intended to amplify this preparatory essay. I stress that my enterprise is to consider a structure of poetic language and how it behaves in relation to an epistemology concerned with the structure of consciousness. Our words for consciousness – mind, thought, self, selfhood – often suggest self-expression and subjectivity as well as designating an analytic relation between subject and object. There are good reasons for this and in practice a reading of nineteenth-century poetry rightly involves paying attention to both the affective and analytic designations of words such as self and mind. However, the act of constituting and transforming relationship and what this implies is the central problem of nineteenth-century poetry, and one from which the 'chromatic' nature of its language follows. A reading of the expressive qualities of nineteenth-century poetry in the affective sense of the word depends on an understanding of the constitutive nature of mind with which the poets were concerned. The second part of this chapter addresses itself to the language which arises from this concern.

'Knowledge is from birth upwards, is a history of growth' (Hopkins).[29] Being is 'the process of its own becoming'

(Hegel).[30] The self, Hegel says, is 'unrest';[31] to constitute an other, a not-self, in order to see itself as an independent entity and separate identity it has to negate itself. On the other hand, the act of construing what is outside the self brings it into a living relationship with externality. And the living relationship with externality which has been created by the self's act of negation, the construction of a not-self, the 'labour of the negative'[32], re-instates the self in its sense of autonomy, and cancels the negation of the self by reaffirming its freedom. Being is media-tion or transition; it is the continual and reciprocal construction and deconstruction of self and other. It is the perpetual movement between subject and object. It is neither static subject, nor static subject against static object, but the continual movement by which one recreates the other. Reality is not outside the self; it *is* the act of relationship. Without mediation the self would be incapable of becoming 'objective to itself', in-capable of 'reflection into itself' and therefore incapable of creating relationship with the other.[33] The principle of being is movement, a 'Bacchanalian revel'. 'True reality is merely this process of reinstating self-identity, of reflecting into its own self in and from its other and is not an original and primal unity as such... It is the process of its own becoming.'[34] Mediation, therefore, presupposes both an active interaction between subject and object, and a condition in which the subject does not come into being without an object. The subject is not placed in an autonomous or prior existence to the object.

To return to Wordsworth. Romantic syntax is fluid, coalesc-ing, a syntax of transition, because it restructures its own elements and discovers ambiguous relationships as it forms. Coleridge talked of 'the modes of connections ... the breaks and transitions' in Wordsworth's poetry.[35] We watch Romantic syntax happening. Parts of speech transform themselves as you read, and the meaning of a sentence *is* the transition, the movement which transforms, not the sum of its ambiguities. Line breaks shift the relationship of parts of a sentence, subjects duplicate or coalesce with objects, subject and object change places, concord is ambiguous, tense changes transform temporal relationships; prepositions, the minute particles which denote relationship, have multiple functions. All these elements interact together. The syntax is the process of its own becoming.

O there is blessing in this gentle breeze
That blows from the green fields and from the clouds
And from the sky: it beats against my cheek,
And seems half-conscious of the joy it gives.
O welcome messenger! O welcome friend!

With limpid, unostentatious subtlety, the syntax here is constantly reordering relationships. It discovers that breeze and blessing – the breeze's blessing or Wordsworth's blessing, or both – blow together: and the blessing is *in* the breeze, fused with it. The mild, self-effacing virtuosity reverses the expected sequence: blessing and breeze blow from the earth upwards and outwards until they blow from the clouds and sky which include them and the earth so that blessing and breeze include themselves in themselves. The gathering of 'from … from … from' and its expansive movement intensifies one sense of 'from': blessing and breeze blow directly out of, as if from their sources; fields, clouds, sky and consciousness include and are included by the gathering energy. But another application of 'from' establishes a simultaneous countermovement. Blessing and breeze also blow from the direction of fields, clouds, sky, towards the poet, and the movement outward returns upon itself, consolidated by 'it beats against my cheek'. His blessing returns to the poet. *My* cheek, not *the* ear: characteristically Wordsworth uses a possessive pronoun, Hopkins, the impersonal definite article. The wind beats invasively against, infused with physical life, not distantly 'strikes … to hear'. Wordsworth's own awareness is allowed to partake of the objects of perception and, more importantly, his awareness of his awareness. For he experiences himself as an object, as other to the wind, even though the syntax simultaneously establishes the breeze as an aspect of his own consciousness. And with 'And seems half-conscious' the movement is reversed: the wind is other to the poet; and yet with the doubleness of 'seems' – appears or seems to *me* – the poet himself invests the breeze with half-consciousness. The breeze is almost conscious, but also precisely *half*-conscious: consciousness is shared between breeze and poet. Again, the action and interaction is reversed, for the breeze seems half-conscious of the joy it gives. The joy is the wind's possession, and yet other to it because it is the poet's joy. 'O welcome messenger! O welcome friend!' if 'welcome' is a verb, the onrush of emotion is towards the messenger or breeze. If it is an adjective, the welcome faces towards Wordsworth, a gift of the breeze, welcome, joyous, to *me*. The action and reaction of the syntax here has created the rhythms of a reciprocal, reflexive experience in which the consciousness is reflected back from the objects of perception, and in which the world is included within the self but is simultaneously other to it. The backwards and forwards movement is there in the flow, hesitation and flow, of the verse. Wordsworth is doing what Theseus says of the poet in *A Midsummer Night's Dream*, feeling or apprehending joy and comprehending the bringer of that joy; blessing the breeze, expressing the life of feeling, but also moving outwards to comprehend or include the breeze which blesses him as part of himself.

Hegel goes on to develop further his notion of the dialogue with experience. Being is 'a process of splitting up what is simple and undifferentiated, a process of duplicating and setting factors in opposition'.[36] If the external, or the other, becomes a possession of the consciousness and not something standing irrevocably outside it, it is changed by this process. The dialogue with experience becomes a dialogue with the self, and the positing of otherness becomes a duplication of the self because things are constituted by thought. 'It must be its own object in which it finds itself reflected.'[37] It is necessary, in fact, to propose a multiple self. Hegel expands and enriches the plurality of selves in his section on 'The truth of self-certainty'. Consciousness can only be consciousness if it sees itself in its otherness, the 'Ego that is "we".'[38] Perceiving poet, breeze, fields, clouds, sky, messenger, are 'we' at the beginning of *The Prelude*, aspects of Wordsworth's consciousness. Growth is inherently self-moving because it is a continual process of reflexive self-reduplication. If the self is externalised as other to the self this is acknowledged by the self as a reflexive act, and so is set up again as self-consciousness, externalised once more as self-consciousness so that 'A self-consciousness has before it a self-consciousness'.[39]

A *double* reduplication takes place, and the self-production continues, for both self-consciousnesses are capable of mutual self-externalisation and so on, in a continual play of energy – 'And seems half-conscious of the joy it gives'.

The continued flux of self-separation goes on in unity with itself because the externalised selves which are the objects of consciousness, are as much ego as the experiencing consciousness itself. This manifold and creative reflexive activity has to be emphasised because the self will always see itself in the other. Self and other will be continually remade in the act of self-production and all things will be categories of thought. We can never get directly at the world or at the unique particular sensory otherness of objects because what is knowable is our constitution of them, and it is a primitive assumption that we can do anything else. For when we talk of *this* morning's minion, *this* breeze, *this* tree (Hegel's example) as if they are specific and irreducibly concrete things, we are actually talking in the most general way possible, because the idea 'this' is constituted by thought; a concept not a thing. (Hegel would probably have placed Hopkins' thinking at a primitive incomplete stage of self-certainty.) What is important for Romantic language here is a corollary that Hegel does not make: we know things as language. Moreover, it suggests that the shifts and conflations of language will work towards the transformation of its categories: of subject and object, internal and external, space and time. Though we may point to what appears to be sensuous language in Romantic poetry it will not be sensuous in the cause of rendering the sensory directly. Its aim is not to be 'concrete' (whatever this may mean) but to render the processes of a mind-created world, a world creating mind, through its processes. [I have suggested the way in which the language of nineteenth century poetry differs from that of Augustan poetry in *Tintern Abbey*: from Augustan to Romantic,' *Augustan Worlds: Essays in honor of A. R. Humphreys*, J. C. Hilton, M. M. B. Jones and J. R. Watson eds., Leicester, 1978, pp. 261–79.]

To take the poem by Tennyson which Hopkins most admired, section cxxi of *In Memoriam:*

> Sad Hesper o'er the buried sun
> And ready, thou, to die with him,
> Thou watchest all things ever dim
> And dimmer, and a glory done.

Tennyson's finished, fastidious lyricism meets a disjunction in the line break 'ever dim/And dimmer'. The last line seems to take the poem a whole gradation further into darkness, and the strongly perceptual sense of a peering, hesitant attempt to make relationships comes about because 'dimmer', a comparative adjective, seems elliptical, as if it has missed out a stage in grammatical relationship. It is preceded by 'And', which may be co-ordinate or sequential and throws the status of dimmer into question. It unexpectedly dissolves the concord that 'dim' encourages and makes the status of 'dim' ambiguous, an ambiguity which is then passed on yet again to 'dimmer'. 'Dim' could be a verb, but 'dimmer' makes it oscillate between being a verb and an adjective and even an adverb. For 'dim' as an adjective could belong to 'things' or 'Thou', to both subject and object, and could even belong to the verb 'watchest'. The effect of this multiplication is to make 'dim' envelop perceiver, perceived and the activity of perceiving. Or if 'dim' is a verb, Hesper would not be watching all things which are static and dim for ever; it would be watching all things perpetually changing, *always* dimming. Correspondingly, 'Dimmer', pulled towards 'dim' as an adjective, could signify 'and all things more dim still', or pulled towards 'dim' as a verb, it adjusts to signify 'all things *becoming* progressively dimmer'. There is a pull between fixity and movement, between what is static and what is changing, even if change means death. The pull is not resolved but reinforced by 'and a glory done'. For 'done' in one sense is finished, over, and in another is made, *created*. If the glory is over it is not there, and Hesper is watching nothing, or watching the darkness that has inevitably succeeded the history of the Sun's setting (as in a sense Tennyson, contemplating death in the poem, has watched nothing, a darkness). If the glory is being made the nothing is a something, a glory. This immediately suggests the radiance of sunset; but deeply embedded in the process of sunset is the cyclical process of renewal, so that the 'glory' could be the rising sun which follows cyclically upon darkness and which Hesper, the evening star, also watches as Phosphor, the morning star. Even the perceptual significance of 'dim' undergoes a change, for light can dim into darkness and darkness can dim into light. The delicate indeterminateness of 'a glory', implying both radiance and *feeling* as spiritual experience, reinforces the pull between negative and positive possibilities that the adjustments of this fluid, open syntax exert – that the categories of life and death are shifting in relation to one another, re-defining one another. Fixity (for the sun *is* 'buried', the glory absolutely 'done') may partake of change, a nothing may be a something, darkness may be light, so that as perception changes, the very nature of the categories of 'reality' are transformed. What is required is not a superficial adjustment to changing phenomena, or a revaluation of the same phenomena as altering from bad to good or good from bad; the structure of experience itself is profoundly altered.

In the same way the dispersed, nearly deranged syntax of this fifth stanza from Browning's 'Love Among the Ruins' jolts the lines from one undiscovered relationship to another. A series of discrete subordinations, indeterminately related to different items in the stanza, melts away the categories of past and present, time and space, just as the dusk 'melts away' the landscape in 'undistinguished grey'. 'I know,' the poet says,

> That a girl with eager eyes and yellow hair
> > Waits me there
> In the turret whence the charioteers caught soul
> > For the goal,
> When the king looked, where she looks now, breathless, dumb,
> > Till I come.

'For the goal', 'breathless, dumb': the two short phrases swing equally between the girl-lover of the present and the king of the primitive, war-like society of the past. Both wait for a goal, the climax of a game or race, the climax of a lovers' meeting, and are alive in the speaker's imagination. And yet both are 'breathless, dumb', the charioteers, of course, literally breathless and dumb in the dead ruins of the past. The insistent words of place and time – 'waits me *there*', 'In the turret *whence*', '*When* the king looked, *where* she looks now' – struggle to keep history away from the present. But in the last full line the adverbs are curiously reversible: '*when* the king looked, *where* she looks now'. The coincidence of space makes a convergence of time: history invades the present, catches soul and lives in it, appropriating the syntax of the present. But the double syntax is resolved by 'Till I come'. That resolving clause, however, is the bathos of history's syntax. An immense expenditure of energy and spirit waits for the solitary figure of a lover: history has been working towards the bathetic goal of romantic love. The clause may be a climactic resolution for the girl living in the present, but the certainties surrounding an assertion of the totality and self-sufficiency of romantic love begin to be questioned. By the end of the stanza the poet 'know[s] ... till I come': he knows his objectified self in the private certainties of passion, but he knows also the pressure of the critical and mocking energies of history upon this privacy, that past and present struggle to re-evaluate one another. So that by the end of the stanza history is undistinguished from, bound up with, the present, by virtue of having waited for it, like the girl, and the present may be 'undistinguished', bathetic and difficult to 'know', when history is bound up with it. The transformation of categories transforms knowledge and may well *be* knowledge itself.

The labour of the negative and the transformation of categories should be most apparent in the work of metaphor. Metaphor transposes qualities between its two referents, synthesising not merely a comparison between existing categories but a new meaning. Hopkins was very clear about the nature of metaphor, though, interestingly, he talks mainly in terms of parallelism. It established that leap to likeness in difference, difference in likeness, which enables us to relate the swarming distinctnesses of the universe. This means that literal and figurative have to be sharply apart and specific in order that analogy can be made with the maximum of precision. For Hopkins analogies are pre-existing in the world, ready to be apprehended – glass, peartree. For Romantic language analogies are made in and through the process of perception and the creation of categories.

To return, for the last time, to the opening of *The Prelude*: 'O welcome messenger! O welcome friend!' In this utterance the poet discovers a metaphorical possibility in the wind, transforming a relic of eighteenth-century personification (compare the frigid 'visitant' of the 1850 *Prelude*, which, in comparison with the 1805, which I use, reinforces the personification) by an onrush of feeling which makes the metaphor delicately apt. A messenger *comes* to us, brings news, making us aware of things we did not know before, is exciting and strange. A friend is known, an intimate, a familiar who brings with him familiar joy. The two words reflect the double nature of the wind, which is both an object to the poet and included in his own subjectivity. Unlike the placing of 'visitant', which establishes an immediate and explicit analogy between visitant and breeze, it is not until the word 'messenger' occurs that we are aware of the wind's metaphorical status, or that it is one side of a metaphor. The similitude, wind/messenger, emerges out of the *process* of the wind's activity: it is not stated as a prior analogy. To look closer at the word 'messenger' is to see that it is easier to describe it as an attribute of the wind, rather than as an analogy of it, for it is only possible to see what qualities of messenger are relevant by deriving them entirely from the activity of the breeze itself. The figurative qualities of the messenger are defined by the literal term 'breeze' which does all the work, and 'messenger' brings very little to the image of its own account. In fact, at first sight, messenger is an exiguous figurative term. The similitude between wind and messenger is quickly exhausted if one tries to give equal and parallel weight to the nature of messenger and wind. The conviction grows that the messenger is there, as it were, in deference to a figurative term, to alert us to conceiving the wind in metaphorical relationship with something, rather than on its own account as messenger, and that the metaphor is really 'about' something else. To go further with the messenger/wind analogy is to move towards tautology and circularity. The relationship between wind, poet and messenger is such that the energies and joy the wind gives are like the energies and joy a messenger gives. The wind is *like* energy, joy, animate life, and yet the wind *is* energy, animate life, generating vitality as all animate life does. It seems that literal and figurative change sides, that the wind is a figurative term for 'life', rather than a literal term by which we interpret the figurative messenger. The dormant, or hidden side of a Romantic metaphor is frequently and simply the inclusive totality, life, experience, being – vitality itself. And yet this must necessarily include the first term within itself. If the wind is like life, life includes the wind, and the wind cannot include it. What the wind can do, however, as one side of metaphor, is to render the experience of livingness autonomously, as the wind does here, by the processes it goes through, and by creating an ever evolving, self-transforming cycle of activity. The wind blows, beats (the intensification here redoubles its energy), always in transition, generating energy, which in turn reciprocally generates energy in an ever-expanding cycle of vitality. It is as if the meaning of the metaphor evolves parthogenetically, out of the transformation of one side of itself within itself. Romantic metaphor is implicitly *about* metaphor because it is about the nature of transformation. I owe much here to Wimsatt's classic essay on the structure of Romantic Metaphor in *The Verbal Icon* and to Paul de Man's critique of Wimsatt.[40] In an impressive essay, de Man claims that Wimsatt and others have a misplaced and 'mystified' emphasis on symbol or metaphor. Symbol, a part of the totality it represents, is 'tautegorical', in Coleridge's words. It is the figure which enables the poet to assert the fundamental unity of subject and object, to read meaning into nature which are analogies of his own state of mind and thus to claim a privileged subjectivity which at the same time has power over nature or at least a reciprocity and oneness with it. De Man thinks that to give priority to symbol is to neglect the strong allegorising, emblematic tendency of Romantic poetry. Allegory, now divested of the inherited typologies which formerly anchored it, reasserts a dualism which establishes a distance from, not identity with, the world or its origins. It is thus free from the myth of organic totality, and constructs its categories in and through time, dependent, neither on subject nor object but on its own anteriority. My own belief is that Romantic symbol or metaphor is concerned with questioning categories, including those of subject and object, and with transforming and creating new categories. Its importance lies in its capacity to ask questions about the process of transformation through its structure. Thus it approaches the freedom de Man attributes to what he calls allegory. Wimsatt makes the point that in Romantic metaphor analogy is unstated, and that tenor and vehicle are wrought out of the same material in double process. An extension of this is to say that Romantic metaphor is about the nature of mind, at work simultaneously on the universe and itself, and including everything within itself. It proposes its 'tautegorical' structure as a problem. Further, Romantic metaphor is about the capacity of language to transform itself, a problem consequential on the first.

Consider the transformations in this passage from Wordsworth's *Prelude*:

> As one who hangs down-bending from the side
> Of a slow-moving boat, upon the breast
> Of a still water, solacing himself
> With such discoveries as his eye can make
> Beneath him in the bottom of the deeps,
> Sees many beauteous sights – weeds, fishes, flowers,
> Grots, pebbles, roots of trees, and fancies more;
> Yet often is perplexed and cannot part
> The shadow from the substance, rocks and sky,
> Mountains and clouds, from that which is indeed
> The region, and the things which there abide
> In their true dwelling; now is crossed by gleam
> Of his own image, by a sunbeam now,

And motions that are sent he knows not whence,
Impediments that make his task more sweet;
Such pleasant office have we long pursued
Incumbent o'er the surface of past time
With like success, nor have we often looked
On more alluring shows (to me, at least,)
More soft, or less ambiguously descried,
Than those which now we have been passing by (iv. 247–67)

The slow-moving boat is a more expanded example of Wordsworth's imagery and of the one-sided activity of Romantic
metaphor. A simile, it works in the same way as the first lines of
the poem. (Our twentieth-century scrupulousness about the difference between metaphor and simile is not always relevant to
Romantic poetry.) The analogy is tautologous. The literal side
of the comparison is in fact metaphor drawn from the substance
of the figurative term – 'Such pleasant office have we long
pursued/*Incumbent o'er* the *surface* of past time'. Here is that
activity with which Wimsatt has familiarised us, in which tenor
and vehicle are wrought in parallel process out of the same
material; so much so as to make the distinction between tenor
and vehicle virtually superfluous in that it is not possible to
make it. This is the paradox of Romantic imagery. This time it is
the literal side of the similitude which is the deference or token
term, suspended for nearly twenty lines, discovered almost by
accident in the long search of the image for its meaning. The
meaning turns out to be created through, and is – the search –
the process of its own becoming. It is not about gazing into one's
past consciousness, as the deference terms would have it, but
about the processes of perception and its objects which change
with the movement of perception itself. It is about things 'ambiguously descried', and Wordsworth's masterly conflating
syntax suggests simultaneously that things seen are ambiguous,
and that seeing is ambiguous as well.

'Sees many beauteous sights – weeds, fishes, flowers,/Grots,
pebbles, roots of trees, and fancies more', sees more fancies or
fantastic objects and *imagines* more. So far the integration of
perception is reassuring, following the visual ordering of experience from height to depth, penetrating further into 'the deeps'.
The psychological order here glances back to and radically redefines an ordering process in Book III, the arrangement of the
'museum' of Wordsworth's Cambridge education, where the

juxtaposition of things is an arbitrary, random collection of categories with no necessity about them and no organic relationship between them. The only relationship is one of contiguity, the mechanistic, superficial ordering of the Enlightenment. 'Carelessly/I gazed, roving as through a Cabinet/Or wide museum (thronged with fishes, gems,/Birds, crocodiles, shells)' (iii, 651–4). The second list has the same formal pattern as the first, but the discrepancy of kind and size in the list of dead things is beautifully re-adjusted in the perception of living order in Book IV, where fishes, gems and shells reappear in another form and necessary sequence – 'fishes... Grots [shells], pebbles [gems]'. The poet's roving gaze in Book III is very different from that searching from the slow-moving boat, which moves in process with the water it is on, and cannot move without it, and where the water is almost a maternal, supportive medium – 'Upon the *breast*/Of a still water'. Yet Wordsworth is 'perplexed': not merely puzzled, but actually tangled up with (so the Latin root allows) the things he tries to 'part'. The deceptive pairings, *rocks* and *sky*,/*Mountains* and *clouds*', which follow the words 'and cannot part/The *shadow* from the *substance*', suggest momentarily that it is difficult to separate solid rocks and mountains, substance, from shadow, sky and clouds. But Wordsworth means that the external landscape as a whole becomes shadows, inverted as reflections in the water, that it cannot be parted or unperplexed from the substance of the water or from the internal landscape of grots, pebbles, roots of trees, which have their true dwelling in the water. Yet the clarity is momentary, no sooner established than dissolved, because the relationship between shadow and substance is unstable; it can be transposed and inverted. The external landscape could be shadow, the syntax allows, the water substance. But it also allows us to read the water as shadow, the landscape as substance. How substantive, how shadowy, are internal and external worlds? And where *is* the 'region', the true dwelling' of things, if the water may be shadow to the subtance of the landscape, or the landscape shadow to the substance of the water? In one case the landscape is inverted and included in the world of water, in the other it includes the water by making it an extension or reflection of itself. The problem is compounded when the self is 'crossed', puzzled, or literally crossed over by its own reflexive image, reflections inside or shadow outside the water, or both, and by 'motions' in the air, or in the water, or both. He knows not 'whence', from which, or *to* what, things come or go. The poem uses metaphor almost to dissolve metaphor. For if you cannot 'part' the categories of things ('part', of course, is a term of rhetoric as well as meaning 'separate'), you cannot discover the two terms of metaphor. And if the distinction between external and internal is eliminated by the fact that both are aspects of consciousness because nothing lies outside the self, then all categories are wrought out of mind which subsumes them. What comes out of the metaphor, however, is puzzlement rather than certainty. It is a puzzlement which seeks to de-mystify the relations between mind and world, rather than to mystify them, but it draws no conclusions.

Even if Romantic metaphor does not directly raise the great epistemological questions, it raises them implicitly by using the one-sidedly self-productive structure I have described. 'My soul is an enchanted boat', Asia addresses the singing Voice in the Air, in *Prometheus Unbound*, a boat which floats on the silver waves of beatific sound created by the Voice.

> My soul is an enchanted boat,
> Which, like a sleeping swan, doth float
> Upon the silver waves of thy sweet singing;
> And thine doth like an angel sit
> Beside a helm conducting it,
> Whilst all the winds with melody are ringing.

The Voice, as soul and angel, gets into a metaphor which begins by being a metaphor simply for the 'silver waves' of its singing (the delicate analogy between sound waves and watery waves initiates the metaphor), so that the voice is on the waves it has itself created, within the landscape which was a metaphor for it. The river of sound, derived from the airy undulation of the voice, naturally generates its own landscape – mountains, woods, abysses, and its own *atmosphere* of winds and air, and the metaphor of sound expands to incorporate them.

> It seems to float, ever, for ever,
> Upon that many-winding river,
> Between mountains, woods, abysses,
> A paradise of wildernesses!
> Till, like one in slumber bound,
> Borne to the ocean, I float down, around,
> Into a sea profound, of ever-spreading sound.

Landscape and atmosphere are 'music's most serene domin-
ions'. 'Whilst all the winds with melody are ringing': the wind is
melody and fans the boat which in the second stanza is 'by the
instinct of sweet music driven'. The metaphor breeds on itself
(airy waves of sound suggest water waves of sound) and the top-
ography of that landscape suggests the reduplication of airy
waves of sound, the internal winds of melody which drive the
boat, so that air or wind identified as sound impels Asia's soul
on a river or sea identified as sound. Literal and figurative
become interchangeable and redulplicate one another, creating
a world within a world within a world in which everything
becomes part of everything else. Words almost dissolve as they
spread to include meanings within themselves, meanings which,
paradoxically, are their own meanings. The Angel-Soul of the
Voice in Air sits at the helm of Asia's soul-boat, 'conducting it'.
It is 'conducting' the boat, and simultaneously 'conducting' the
music of its own singing, even though the singing has originally
been metaphorised as the boat-water figures in the first place.
Ever-spreading, the metaphor includes itself within itself. 'The
sea profound, of ever-spreading sound', which ends the stanza,
reaches towards a pun on 'sound', which is music and, more
remotely, *water*. The 'sea' meets itself again in 'sound', and
again one discovers the conflation and virtual collapse of terms
and categories. The similitude established between sound and
waves is less important than the structure of the metaphor in
which distinct terms are blended and subsumed into one-ness,
unity, totality. The process itself is a metaphor for achieved
bliss. The metaphor is given new applications in successive
stanzas, and yet it is always turning back on itself: the air or
winds which are music are love which harmonises earth and air
which are music, love: the river which is sound is also a journey
back through time into the recesses of the self, towards a primal
experience of unity. But it is a perpetual movement towards.
Unity is never achieved, for experience again reduplicates
singing, voice, and 'shapes' which walk upon the sea of sound,
and 'chant melodiously'. The movement of the stanza is
winding, retarded, expansive, and winding again, non-
progressive and progressive, just as the journeys of the three
stanzas move forwards, 'Borne to the ocean', by music 'driven',
and yet nowhere, 'down, around', 'without a course'. The three
successive journeys are really repetitive analogies of one

another, and the movement is that of ever-spreading inclusiveness, 'ever, for ever,' a phrase which equally signifies time and
eternity. The metaphor images an ego-free (the floating soul is
borne, driven) and ever-repeated serene movement towards bliss
which is fulfilment itself, a condition which collapses categories
by including everything within itself.

If the language of Romantic, chromatic, idealist poetry
renders the processes of a mind-created world, one can expect to
find that the form of Romantic poetry will also do this. Like its
language, it will be a model of the structure of consciousness.
Quite simply, poems will have to be long. A poem of this kind
has to be long enough to have a past on which it can reflect, long
enough to contemplate itself, to interpret itself to itself, to transform and create new experience out of its own elements. The
poem's past is essential because there will be a dual process in
which the past of the poem is modified by and itself modifies the
subsequent experience of the poem. It is only by this mutual
backwards and forwards transformation that new experience
can be created and the poem achieve its necessity. The living
form of Romantic poetry needs the temporal process, but this in
itself does not give the form necessity. The poem is not an imitation of time, but imitates the self-comprehension of the mind
which goes on simultaneously with conscious life. Since consciousness only terminates with death there is a real sense in
which such poems will always suggest beginnings before their
beginnings, and endings after their endings. However long, they
will be, paradoxically, fragments. What is important for the
internal organisation of these self-evolving poems is the
sequence of their transitions, their capacity to enable us to make
the act of relationship between their parts, the mediation of the
parts with one another. The meaning of the poem is not the progressive movement from one stage of experience or argument to
another (the poem never *arrives*), but in the transitions from one
part of the poem to the next. Transition is both a break and a
joining and both exist so that the poem can create new relationships within itself. One thinks of Byron's digressions or Keats'
dreams within dreams. When Wordsworth rejects the dead inorganic list which signifies knowledge for Cambridge and
explores a new ordering of experience in the subtle, perceptual
ordering of the river image, the new list cannot be understood
without the first. Its full meaning is in the relationship between

them, and not the two lists taken separately, one abandoned, one accepted. The new list, indeed, incorporates and transforms the first. And it creates the possibility for further transformation. The shells and gems, transformed by relation to the aqueous grots and pebbles, reappear in the dream of Book V, carrying a weight of symbolic significance. The stone and the shell, Euclid's geometry and the human imagination, the knowledge transmitted through tradition, the abstracting and the image-making power, both have to be redeemed from the destruction of civilisation, the fleet waters of the drowning world.

This reflexive activity is accomplished by the simplest of things, repetition, within the line, the sentence, the paragraph, between episodes. The Romantic poem is built up by, or builds itself out of, repetition, because this is the way it can meet its own image and grow by making itself other to itself. For repetition acquires a new meaning in the very act of being repetition. Hopkins thought of repetition as a fixed and static thing, the '*oftening*', '*over-and-overing*', 'aftering', of a pattern which will 'detach' to the mind a form and not a meaning. It is 'over and above' meaning, at least 'the grammatical, historical and logical meaning'.[41] Repetition in a Romantic poem aims not to be a copy but a new thing every time it occurs: it *works* in the poem as Keats describes the discoveries of repetition when he talked of 'the repetition of its own silent Working coming continually upon the Spirit with a fine suddenness'.[42] The movement of Romantic poetry is one of slow, cumulative growth through repetition which can take many forms. One repetition is always contemplating redefining, a prior form of itself. Or else there is a cyclical movement forward, where repetition successively readumbrates and enriches itself, carrying itself further with every repetition. Another form of duplication is the swing between opposites, a drama of contraries which is really a kind of repetition because the opposites are inverted forms of each other. In all these ways the poem *discovers* itself through repetition.

Repetition is a way of repossessing and transforming knowledge, and to see how this functions we can remember Hegel's insistence that a theory of consciousness collapses into fatal one-sidedness if we believe that 'anything lies outside the self'. If we are aiming for a triumphant account of mind 'that does not have mediation outside it, but *is* this mediation itself', that is the process of its own becoming, we shall have to find a way of explaining how knowledge grows, how the mind is origina- tive.[43] If objects are aspects of consciousness the astonishing 'energy of thought' must in some way work on itself, and it does this by making itself other to itself. 'It externalises itself and then comes back to itself from this state of estrangement, and by so doing is at length set forth in its concrete nature and real truth, and becomes too a possession of consciousness.'[44] When the object is possessed and repossessed by consciousness, it is changed by the very act of repossession, and this in turn engen- ders a new cycle of externalisation and repossession. The act of perception alters the object and mind itself, and in this way the mind can proceed to a new content, new forms of awareness which evolve out of preceding forms. What 'at first appeared as object is reduced, when it passes into consciousness, to *what knowledge* takes it to be [my italics: i.e., in the act of interpret- ation it becomes a form of mind] ... this latter is the new object, whereupon there appears a new mode or embodiment of con- sciousness, of which the essence is something other than that of the preceding mode. It is this circumstance which carries forward the whole succession of the modes or attitudes of con- sciousness in their own necessity'.[45] Growth comes from within. The mind is always able to move forward because its reflexive, self-contemplating activity makes this contemplation the content of further contemplation and creates a living knowl- edge, capable of dealing with the 'sheer restlessness of life' because it is part of it, and not outside it.[46]

Hegel saw repetition as a way of making growth to include the principle of its own development within itself and of enabling the process of abstraction. A look at the living repetition which meets its own image and transforms its content prepares the way for this larger argument. Blake's six lines here are constructed out of actual and virtual repetition in the form of synonym or the same forms are transposed from verbs to adjectives to ad- verbs. Repetition evolves out of itself without being redundant.

> Sundering, darkening, thundering,
> Rent away with a terrible crash,
> Eternity rolled wide apart,
> Wide asunder rolling
> Mountainous, all around
> Departing, departing, departing. (*The First Book of Urizen*, 96–101)

A single 'departing' would not have done Blake's work here. The tripling prolongs the anguish of lament for an ever-retreating eternity and makes this an infinite regret, a departing which is a departing which is a departing, an endless vanishing. The departing is a continuous series, never final, as the continuous acting of the participles suggests. The repetition evolves a further and more terrible meaning. 'Eternity rolled wide apart', separating from itself. Eternity is de-parting, continually divided from itself, continually multiplying its fragmentation in an eternal fission, an inverse creation. The triple sounding of departing, now defined as perpetual severance, and amplifying not only 'apart' but also 'sundering' is necessary in order that we can possess this meaning. 'Sundering' and 'apart' provide the further content of departing and this in turn develops that meaning. The intransitive participles make what is happening perpetual and self-acting. Eternity can have no transitive re-lationships, only everlasting relationships of severance within itself. Hence the repetition 'Eternity *rolled* wide apart,/Wide *asunder rolling*,' for Eternity severs itself not once but always. And 'rolling' is generated out of 'rolled' because it is of the nature of the action to turn on itself and be without end. 'Rolling' revalues the other particples; the sundering, darkening, thundering, are perpetual, as in the 'Rent away'. The terrible crash is not a single noise but an endlessly reduplicated recur-rence. Repetition transforms meaning and this new content enables us to see why Eternity is 'rolling/Mountainous all around' and simultaneously 'all around/Departing'. It is vanish-ing, destroying itself 'all around', and yet this endless destruction takes place within itself and is paradoxically re-doubling fragmentation continuously, so that it is 'rolling/Mountainous'. Reduplication here is both destruction and addition. As with metaphor, Romantic repetition is often about the contradictory nature of repetition itself.

Repetition, then, is not formalism, but a way of making form – and here I return to Hegel – 'the indwelling process of the concrete content itself'.[47] If we are to have 'a living experience of the subject matter itself' which rejects an external view of knowledge as standing outside the materials on which it works we must conceive of knowledge as continually developing its content anew.[48] We may have, for instance, 'in a flash and at a single stroke' an idea 'of the form and structure of the new world' but 'just as little is the attainment of a general notion of the whole the whole itself'.[49] For 'the real subject matter is not exhausted in its purpose, but in working the matter out; nor is the mere result attained the concrete whole itself, *but the result along with the process of arriving at it*'.[50] Knowledge must be 'the process of its own development', a carrying out or a *going through* of meaning, not a terminal generalisation.[51] Living experience of subject matter and our enquiry into it is necessarily tied to the temporal process: for 'the temporal process would thus bring out and lay bare the necessity of it, nay, more, would at the same time be carrying out that very aim itself'.[52] It is only through the process of discovery in time that we understand experience and that understanding is itself a carrying out of meaning – as well as an exposition of it. Experience is sequential and our collective analysis of it is sequential too, and the process of externalising and repossessing experience is not merely the analysis of a prior process ready to create further experience but the *subject* of a further one. Through the temporal process analysis is returned to the self as *experience*.

This account of knowledge, perhaps, may seem to condemn us to an unending 'working the matter out' or 'process of arriving' exhaustively readumbrated and developed anew but never finally comprehended. But Hegel's point is that repetition creates the possibilities for abstraction, and abstraction reciprocally generates repetition. There can be no doing without abstraction because the processes of experience must be reducible by the mind, not only so that they can be abbreviated but so that they can be transformed and perpetuated. The self knows by making its experience other to itself and reabsorbing it, and it absorbs the reabsorbtion, reducing it to a 'moment' or simple form. But the moment can only come into being if the experience it absorbs has a fully 'evolved content' otherwise there would be no history of experience for the mind to reduce, nothing which 'passes over' into another form. But the 'struggle and effort'[53] of abstraction does not cease here, for if thinking is to be knowledge rather than the pursuit of something outside itself the meaning of abstractions will always have to be developed anew and rediscovered in their fullness, and there will be a cyclical self-reproducing activity of constant readumbration.

It is a whole which, after running its course and laying bare all its content, returns again to itself; it is the resultant abstract notion of the whole. But the actual realisation of this abstract whole is only found when those previous shapes and forms, which are now reduced to ideal moments of the whole, are developed anew again, but developed and shaped within this new medium, and with the meaning they have thereby acquired.[54]

Experience, abstraction, abstraction returned to experience, not only *as* experience but as experience transformed by the very act of having been reduced to the moment from which its fullness is redeemed, ready to form a new moment in its turn. This is the iterated movement which brings knowledge into being and experience can never be the same. In the act of being repetition it is new. This may or may not be an adequate account of thinking (and Hegel, of course, sophisticated his ideas by allowing that forms of abstraction were subsumed into other and higher forms), but it is a marvellous justification of Romantic form and of art itself. The Romantic poem struggles to give content to the abstraction towards which it strives, it must repeat as much as it must generalise, but these things will not be severed from one another; they make each other necessary. The Romantic poem will aim to be 'the result along with the process of achieving it'; it will aim to be the living process of its generalisation not an *illustrated* generalisation.

> Wisdom and Spirit of the universe!
> Thou Soul that art the eternity of thought,
> That giv'st to forms and images a breath
> And everlasting motion, not in vain (*Prelude*, 1, 428–31)

Wordsworth is explaining something. One might say that he is dealing with ideas, 'moments, of the whole' *Prelude*, thinking about thinking or 'the eternity of thought', although in saying this I would not like to deprive the lines of their feeling. They are experienced as thought which involves the poet in feeling about them. They seem, perhaps, rather like the statements in the sestet of Hopkins' 'Spring', but are really less straightforward. 'Wisdom and spirit': the universe is personified here, or else wisdom and spirit are attributes of it, or they may be the things out of which it is *constructed*. The ambiguity leaves the source of thought either with the universe or with the poet. Wisdom, spirit, universe, are 'soul', the syntax allows, and these or the personified spirit and soul are the eternity of thought; they *are* everlasting thought or they *make* our thought everlasting, and give to 'forms and images', inside or outside the mind, or both, 'a breath/And everlasting motion' – the energy of being. Wisdom, spirit, soul, breath, motion could be described as 'moments' in the living experience of the poem's subject matter because they conflate, reorder and contain within themselves the vocabulary of earlier experiences, 'previous shapes and forms', as Hegel puts it, the woodcock-hunting and boat-stealing episodes in particular. 'I heard among the solitary hills/Low breathings coming after me, and sounds/Of undistinguishable motion' (*Prelude*, 1, 30–1). Low *breathings* and undistinguishable *motion* are reduced from the particulars of their panic and intensity and reordered in 'a *breath*/And everlasting *motion*': 'everlasting' displaces 'undistinguishable', but this has not been lost, for the syntax of the abstracting passage, making the source of thought the universe or the self, paradoxically clarifies through ambiguity the ways in which perception found motion 'undistinguishable', difficult to identify, and difficult to distinguish as belonging to the self or outside it.

The boat-stealing episode takes up the vocabulary of the woodcock-springing and reorders it. The huge cliff 'With measured *motion*, like a living thing,/ Strode after me' (*Prelude*, 1, 411–12). Low breathings 'coming after me': '*Strode after me*'. The breathings and sounds of motion, the paradoxically silent steps, coalesce in the words 'With measured motion ... Strode'. The *undistinguishable* motion is internalised in the brain which 'Worked with a dim and *undetermined* sense/Of *unknown* modes of being) (419–20). The external world falls away: 'No familiar shapes/Of hourly objects, images of trees... But huge and mighty forms, that do not live/Like living men, moved slowly through my mind' (422–6). The later abstracting passage collapses the lost 'images' of external reality ('that giv'st to forms and images') and the threatening 'forms' which moved through the mind, and conflates them indissolubly with the vocabulary of the earlier woodcock-springing passage, which has already been reordered in the vocabulary of the boat-stealing episode. It is no surprise to find the poet saying that the universe 'didst intertwine' the passions two lines later. The 'eternity of thought' reorders, conflates and abstracts these earlier passages and gives them breath and motion as new forms and images of themselves. It allows the suggestion that they belong to the eternity of thought and that they are life-giving both in spite of and because of the fear and desolation of the earlier experiences.

Beauty and fear, the things which fostered the poet's childhood, become inseparable here. By reducing the earlier passages to moments it has assimilated and celebrated the experiences of guilt – forms, images, breath, motion, come together as 'moments' of past experience, and the 'notion'[55] which evolves from them at the same time as it creates them, transforms without obliterating their inexplicable psychological horror by abstracting them as forms of energy and forms of mind. They are indeed 'not in vain'.

This enables Wordsworth to go forward yet again and re-develop the 'notion' of energy and mind in the skating episode. The children's activity is 'imitative of the chase', a boisterous, cathartic re-enactment of the activity of pursuit – 'Strode after me', 'coming after me' – which the child exultantly controls. The solitary cliffs (a conflation of the solitary hills and huge cliff in the two earlier passages), not with indistinguishable but with '*visible* motion' reciprocally chase the boy – 'wheeled by me' – who provokes them into doing so by the trick of a sudden pause. The release and interchange of energy here is exuberant and joyous. Terrified flight from the universe is superseded by an easy flow of self-hood towards it – 'When we had *given* our bodies to the wind' (479) – '*reclining* back upon my heels' (483). The cliffs, however, are those same precipices and icy crags which 'tinkled like iron' with the sound of echoes. While 'the distant hills/Into the tumult sent an alien sound/Of melancholy not unnoticed' (469–71). The tumult sends echoes to the hills which return the sound to the tumult which, circularly, returns it again. But the superadded '*alien* sound/Of Melancholy', a sound which is a *feeling*, returns as well, seemingly made by hills and tumult interacting. The echoes of the horror of the earlier passages are 'not unnoticed', assimilated but alien (the double negative suggests their subliminal presence), constantly present in the joy of the redeveloped moment which contains their histories within itself. We remember Werther's cabbage again, and the peasant who enjoys his history in 'a single moment', the fine days, mornings and evenings when he watered his plant. *The Prelude*, like other Romantic poems, digests its history, in-corporating a succession of forms and images into an episode or even a phrase in order to release new content.

What I have done in this section is to offer the grounds on which a rhetoric of Romantic poetry might be evolved. I have given particular attention to syntax, metaphor and the nature of repetition, for these aspects of language and form gain a central significance once they are made meaningful by the analogy with Romantic philosophy. Up to this point I have said little of the strains and difficulties of this poetic discourse because it first seemed necessary to establish the nature of Romantic idiom. Now, however, in the next section, I turn to the inherent difficulties of Romantic language.

The chromatic nature of Hegel's thought then, can be a model for, or a commentary on the forms and movements of Romantic or idealist poetry. All such poetry encounters what Wordsworth called the 'abyss of idealism' whether it is confessedly idealist or not. (I have used Wordsworth's poetry so frequently and so unapologetically because he is not confessedly an idealist poet, but nevertheless does not always avoid idealist thinking and language.) But there is another commentary, Marx's, which detects the strains in Hegel's thought, and the structure of Hegel's thinking cannot be an analogue for the language and organisation of Romantic poetry unless we see what these are. That 'Nothing lies outside the self', and that man and nature belong to one another because the self, acting on the universe, incorporates it as object which incorporates it, and is protected from solipsism because of this, is an axiom which Marx simply turns inside out. 'A being which does not have its nature outside itself is not a natural being.'[56] Man and nature belong to one another because they are *objects* for one another, each reciprocally confirming one another's externality and independent being, enabling the self and other to *act on* one another. We must conceive ourselves as *acted* on, not as self *acting* on the world. Interestingly, Marx replaces *desire*, that state of yearning and emptying out which Hegel conceives as the self's continual need to create an other for itself, with *passion* as man's essential nature: passion is aroused, generated creatively from without, when the self is acted on in relationship with something else and, in the proper sense, *suffering*.[57] Marx takes the word back to its Latin root, *passio*, suffering, and expresses relationship as suffering, being acted upon.

Hunger is the acknowledged need of my body for an *object* which exists outside itself and which is indispensable to its integration and to the expression of its essential nature. The sun is an *object* for the plant, an indispensable object which confirms its life, just as the plant is an object for the sun, an *expression* of its life-awakening power and its *objective* essential power'.[58]

Hegel's thought, on the other hand, tries to do the impossible by making mind conceive itself as the opposite of itself, the sensuous world. Therefore, Marx argues, Hegel's thought inevitably sees to it that 'the object as such presents itself to consciousness as something disappearing', constituted not as object but as mind.[59] The object postulated like this is 'only a confirmaion of the act of postulating' and has a fleeting apparent life as independent being before dissolving.[60] It can be argued that Marx is unfair to Hegel here. In the body of the *Phenomenology* Hegel begins with life rather than with the subject in order to establish the pressure of the world on the subject. The subject does not stand over and against nature any more than the world over the subject. But Marx refuses to see this.

The aim of Marx's critique is not simply to show that Hegel dissolves as object the real sensuous world, and destroys 'the inexhaustible, vital, sensuous, concrete activity' of both nature and himself:[61] nor is it that the end of Hegel's thought is solipsism, though Marx does claim this – 'such a being would be the *only* being; no other being would exist outside it, it would exist in a condition of solitude';[62] his main attack is on the grounds that if the mind postulates itself as object, if it denies that it is fundamentally nature and not mind to which man and the world belong, then every encounter is an encounter with itself'.[63] *All* activity is reduced to a formal, contentless abstraction of self-production which resolves itself quite outside and irrelevant to the world of nature. Man is therefore irrevocably deprived of *relationships* and thus of the capacity for *action* in a living human and social world. Man cannot create himself in terms of a meaningful and *evolving* relation with externality; he can only create himself repeatedly anew as an entity of thought, as barren self-consciousness. The patterns and forms of relationship might be embodied in the processes of thought but will not resolve themselves in and with reality. His thought will be 'fixed phantoms' existing outside the world of 'nature and man', and man will be driven by a 'longing for a content'.[64]

The disappearance of the object, the collapse of relationships: how does Marx's stress on these things redirect us to the language of Romantic poetry? It might be that the coalescing transitions of Romantic syntax and those forms which express the transformation of categories and which impress us so by their synthetic and magical power, 'fusing each to each' as Coleridge put it, actually move towards a state in which no distinctions can be made, melting away relationships by melting things into each other. I have already suggested that there is an incipient collapse in the terms of Romantic metaphor. The fertile, self-enlarging growth of repetition might regress into a closed and eternally reduplicated contentless succession. Relationships might be eliminated, not restructured. The importance of Marx's critique is that it *can be made*, whatever steps one takes to protect idealism and its forms. If language fails to make relationships, the possibilities of meaningful discourse fail too. These *are* the possibilities that are struggled with in Romantic poetry.

Consider a passage from Shelley's *Prometheus Unbound* with the attack on idealist forms in mind:

> It feeds the quick growth of the serpent vine,
> And the dark linkèd ivy tangling wild,
> And budding, blown, or odour-faded blooms
> Which star the winds with points of coloured light,
> As they rain through them, and bright globes
> Of fruit, suspended in their own green heaven,
> And through their veinèd leaves and amber stems
> The flowers whose purple and translucid bowls
> Stand ever mantling with aërial dew,
> The drink of spirits: and it circles round (III, iii, 135–44)

The liquid syntax of Shelley's description here disperses relationships by fusing each object into each. The indefinite 'it', the breath, odour, or 'exhaltation' of Earth's secret love which feeds simultaneously budding, blown, or odour-faded blooms, fuses circularly with the words 'blown' and 'odour-faded', aided by the duplicity of 'blown' and the ambiguity of the compound. 'Odour-faded': dead or dying, either faded by odour, worn out by the play of air, breath, exhalation, upon it, or faded as a result of giving out and exhausting its perfume. The air feeds a dead bloom irrespective of its deadness or it has accomplished the fading. Feeding and fading are drawn together by their sounds and it is as if the whole temporal and causal cycle has collapsed so that no beginnings and endings can exist in relation to one another, just as budding and blown blooms coexist (simultaneously at their prime or past their prime). The blooms, as if they are physically dissociated, dispersing, 'star' the winds with points of coloured light 'As they rain through them'. The winds rain through the blooms, and, the syntax allows, rain through the points of coloured light which are, strangely, scattered over the winds themselves. Or the blooms, points of coloured light, might rain through the winds, each inextricably involved with each, also allowed by the syntax. The blooms are scattered over the winds, but as the verb 'star' implies – prick, fix, print – they are *fixed* to what is mobile, impaling the winds or impaled *on* the air which itself blows through them. Again, the hurrying, merging coalescences leap ahead of themselves and a series of re-lationships is collapsed into the single verb, 'star'. The isolated, free-floating sentence which follows, suspended like the 'golden globes', makes relationships and concord uncertain yet again. And 'bright golden globes/Of fruit, suspended in their own green heaven'. The exhalation, seemingly, feeds blooms, golden globes, and also, '*through* their veined leaves and amber stems' the 'flowers mantling with aërial dew'. The conflation of air and water in the metaphorical verb 'rain' makes the wind partake of spirit and fluid *substance*. Appropriately enough, since air *does* feed leaves, passing into or through them in the process of pho-tosynthesis, and they in their turn give air out, 'aerial dew', which has been taken in through the 'rain' of wind. But the second 'through' is also attracted to 'As they rain *through* them' and the winds might also rain through blooms, globes, flowers alike. The initial ambiguity of 'they' and 'them', subject and object, is still maintained; *blooms* may also rain through winds, globes, flowers, leaves, stems. Everything is moving through everything else and the kinship of exhalation and winds, rain and aerial dew, which are all offered as separate entities and actions, is such that forms and functions merge, reverse and exchange. With 'it circles round', 'it' is not merely either the original exhalation or the aerial dew but *every* element in the passage. Exhalation, winds, blooms, fruits, flowers, stems, leaves, dew, as a totality, a unity, circle round. The rapidity, the flux of syntax, the capacity of Shelley's words to make things dematerialise into aery thinness, is extraordinary. We must remember that even the guidance given by the punctuation is Mary Shelley's and not Shelley's own, which is no more helpful.[65] Is it virtuosity or is it confusion?

The same question might be asked of the metaphor in Tennyson's 'Go not happy day' lyric in *Maud*. The triteness of 'Rosy is the South,/Roses are her cheeks', where rosy and roses are conventional figurative terms for sunset and blush, is violently converted into a universal suffusion of colour when Maud's literal blush crosses over into a figurative term for the spread of sunset-colour over the world – 'Pass and blush the news'.

> Go not, happy day,
>   From the shining fields,
> Go not, happy day,
>   Till the maiden yields.
> Rosy is the West,
>   Rosy is the South,
> Roses are her cheeks,
>   And a rose her mouth
> When the happy Yes
>   Falters from her lips,
> Pass and blush the news
>   Over glowing ships;
> Over blowing seas,
>   Over seas at rest,
> Pass the happy news,
>   Blush it thro' the West;
> Till the red man dance
>   By his red cedar-tree,
> And the red man's babe
>   Leap, beyond the sea.
> Blush from West to East,
>   Blush from East to West,
> Till the West is East,
>   Blush it through the West.
> Rosy is the West,
>   Rosy is the South,
> Roses are her cheeks,
>   And a rose her mouth.

A blush is a betrayal. Maud's blush and the blushing sunset become intermingled and move contagiously outwards over glowing ships and seas which reduplicate and fuse with blush and sunset, spreading outwards to the mysterious, primitive 'red man' who leaps 'beyond the sea'. A fitting description, for it is in the nature of blushes to breed, to 'leap' into further pulsations of colour. The lurid obsessiveness of this poem, so strange for such a fragile lyric, comes from the fact that the figurative blush persuades the sunset to take on a febrile, autonomous energy of its own, moving in perpetual circles, sunset becoming sunrise, 'Till the West is East'. The poem comes to rest where it began, with a delicate shift from cheek to mouth. 'And a rose her mouth.' But the figurative blush has a quality not shared with natural blushes. It never ends. The ceaseless transition from West to East commits the blush, sunset's blush and Maud's blush interfused, to an eternal closed circle of continuity. It is caught there, relating to nothing but itself. The poem halts but it does not. Again, one wonders if this may be a brilliantly charged rendering of erotic experience or a hectic derangement of categories.

Such poetic language and the problems it creates must make us ask questions (for its formal elements force them upon a reader), about the construing of the human energies and activities which go to creating the act of relationship. If the poem appears to conjure objects merely as 'phantoms', if the language fails to construct the external world as anything but a fleeting, disappearing entity, if the poet fails to construct a 'sun', as it were, which acts on him as he reciprocally acts on it, he is left with a poetry which is without a content, or which can only take mind as its content. He is left with a poetry which cannot *act* in the sense that it cannot create relationships, with a poem that can only be about itself, caught in its own reflexiveness, and an unstable language which dissolves reference and can only be about that instability. This is the most pessimistic account of the possibilities. If the poet constitutes the world as mind he may be caught in an epistemology which only enables him to talk ceaselessly about epistemology.

It is precisely this question, however, that nineteenth-century poets themselves recognise as the important and central one. The whole effort of Romantic and post-Romantic poetry goes into struggling with it, and into a struggle with language, which is both its consequence and its cause. The dilemma Marx offers to Hegel is a variant of the dilemma of Romantic poetry. It is significant that at moments of choice and decision in this poetry – the unbinding of Promtheus, for instance, the revelation of Snowdon, the suicide of Empedocles, to take some moments where the same metaphoric language is used – the poem offers an image of relationship which is both confirmed and questioned: structurally, if not overtly, it is an image of the relationship between mind and world. Which is the prior or the stronger entitiy? 'The Sea, in storm or calm/Heaven's ever-changing shadow, spread below' (*Prometheus Unbound*). The same image reappears in Arnold's *Empedocles on Etna*, when Empedocles talks of the 'Living Clouds' round Etna (which draws him to the Dionysian destruction of suicide) which are echoed by 'the fainter sea below'. Arnold's image has its precedent not only in Shelley but in Wordsworth's *Prelude*. The mist round Snowdon doubles 'the real sea' below it. In Shelley's sea the qualities of the sky as shadow, weightless, flimsy, have crossed over into the sea's nature. It is a shadow because it is responsive to the climactic conditions of the sky, because it reflects it, and because the lower world is the *double* of Heaven itself. Double or reflection? The status of sea and cloud is implicitly questioned in *Empedocles* and the *Prelude* and perhaps even more by the silent reversal of priority from one poem to another. In the *Prelude* the material sea is 'real': in *Empedocles* it is 'fainter' than the clouds, which are the stronger 'sea'. Whether to deem 'reality' as a real or a fainter sea: this is the problem of interpretation endemic to nineteenth-century poetry. The structure of the metaphor seems to commit the poets to offering a split between self and world, and to deciding upon which is stronger. These images suggest the problems which are at the core of the nineteenth-century poetry. And from them follow questions of relationship and action. The work of a nineteenth-century poem is to discover paradigms of relationship and action, models of the nature of knowledge and transformation which ceaselessly disclose and encounter the mediation of subject and object.

If the struggle of nineteenth-century poets is either implicity or directly a struggle with what knowing and its implications are, the poet will never be immediately and, as it were, naïvely, in the grip of experience as Hopkins. 'Nothing is so beautiful as Spring': he will always be trying to see what is going on behind his back in the processes of consciousness even though by its very nature the vision is incomplete. He will have to try to be the phenomenologist of his own poem. For Hegel self-comprehension could not come into existence without absorbing the prodigious labour of the world's history, for phases of consciousness are embodied in cultural forms and his history is digested as moments in the life of every individual self. The poem likewise will have to be epistemology, psychology, history, cultural analysis, and these will be inherently necessary to it. That is why so many Romantic poems begin with the act of cognition and move 'from birth up', as Hopkins says, though this is only one way of evolving a form which will enquire into the nature of knowing. Certainly such poetry will never be either straightforward narrative of the literal, or discursive philosophical debate or symbol, but, in order to catch itself at it, it will be something half way between all of these. Narrative of the literal or discursive philosophical debate in a pure form, offered as they are in themselves as ostensible content, have an authoritative status which is too rigid and closed for the writing which is an investigation of its own processes. They can avail themselves to the process of inspection only by being contemplated as a phase of feeling or thought which is part of the experience of contemplation and modified by the act of contemplation itself. Symbol, likewise, in its pure form is as absolutist as the narrative or the discursive in its pure form. It stands apart as an entity, declaring itself to be what in itself it is, resisting interpretation and the reflexive activity which would reabsorb and transform its meanings for further contemplation. In fact, the poem can only catch itself at it and become self-conscious in time, and through succession, in which one thing modifies another.

De Quincey has a valuable insight here when he says that

far more of our deepest thoughts and feelings pass to us through perplexed combinations of *concrete* objects, pass to us as *involutes* (if I may coin that word) in compound experiences incapable of being disentangled, than ever reach us *directly* and in their own abstract shapes. (*Suspiria de Profundis*)[66]

An involute is an *experience* as it happens to us. It is a developing configuration of often contradictory things, events, happenings, feelings, thoughts which accrete new associations, feelings, thoughts, in time. It becomes more complex with each successive recurrence of similar or analogous experiences, and these in turn are absorbed into the involute's 'compound' of experiences, thoughts, feelings, continuously enriching and deepening its significance throughout the history of our lives. These compound experiences are not autonomously released from temporal succession but depend upon it and evolve. And the way in which the involute compounds itself by repetition, converging with and attracting new experiences, is part of its significance. It is not the equivalent of another experience, nor does it point to an experience beyond itself but develops a complex of interacting relationships through time. It is a way of constructing experience. The compound of concrete objects does not stand symbolically *instead* of or replace thoughts and feelings. The thoughts and feelings discovered by it are, indeed, taken back into the involute, 'incapable of being disentangled' from it. One of De Quincey's experience-clusters was the convergence of death, a sunny day, and guilt, but an involute for him can be a book and its associations, like *The Arabian Nights*.

Because it pays attention to the uniqueness and continuity of experience the involute is a sufficiently inclusive term to describe the recurrent ascent of mountains in *The Prelude*, the repeated configuration of groves, bowers, trellised and flowered retreats in *Endymion*, the invasion of Rome in *Amours de Voyage*, sexual encounters in *Don Juan*, Los's furnaces, dawn in *In Memoriam*, the yellow book and the murder case in *The Ring and the Book*. The important common element in all these things is the accretion of significance which is slow and quiet, the making of relationships which are unstated and implicit. At the same time they can avail themselves to overt commentary and interpretation within the poem, commentary which is part of the meaning of the involute itself. Wordsworth's mountains, Arnold's Etna, gather significance silently as the poem proceeds, a significance not exhausted by the commentary and interpretative passages within the poem, which are nevertheless themselves incorporated as aspects of the involute. They allow the poem to investigate experience implicitly and explicitly and that investigation to be compounded as experience. Such investigation never remains as 'abstract' shapes which stand over the against the 'real' content of the poem. The involute allows the poet to struggle with what knowing is by experiencing knowing, which must imply the experience of knowledge as knowledge, knowledge self-consciously known as such, and in doing so to struggle with form and language. Yet, even as the form of an involute allows this struggle it is itself vulnerable. The subtle compounding of relationships by which it has its being is open to dispersal. Its unity can fragment and fail to assimilate the disparate things it holds together. Its repetition need not be meaningful and it can fail to reabsorb the abstract shapes of ideas as experience. And so the nineteenth-century poet has on his hands a struggle with the form which expresses form. The collapse of form, the disappearance of relationship into a fleeting 'phantom' world created and recreated out of the poem's own materials, is a constant threat to the writer of this time, as the involute threatens to become involuted.

In the following chapters on Wordsworth, Blake, Shelley, Browning and Tennyson, I explore this compound struggle and its different forms as it is expressed in the work of individual poets of the nineteenth century as they attempt to explore paradigms of the nature of self and world, to see what knowing is and to find a language and an organisation creative of it.

I end this chapter as I began it, with Hopkins and his dread of idealism. The evasion of idealism or 'chromatic' poetry contains as many problems as the embracing of it. Hopkins' dilemma is the dilemma of late nineteenth-century poetry and by extension the dilemma of modernism. It is as well to complete Hopkins' story before looking at the poetry with which he struggled in such a lonely, puzzled and intransigent way. The work of his poetry was a sustained attempt to prevent the world of objects from disappearing in the fleeting attempts of mind to construct an other from or for itself. He wanted to separate out the world and the consciousness, as Marx did, releasing objects in their rich substantiveness from the entanglement of mind, giving back not only to nature but to God (as Marx did not) their full autonomy and authority. It is an attempt of great cultural and ideological importance. It is an attempt to re-establish a concrete referential world, a world that can be acted on and in and which acts on the subject independently of him.

Did he find a solution to the coalescing language and the collapse of relationships incipient in idealist or chromatic poetry by submitting to what one critic has called the moral duty of accurate sense-perception?[67] Partly. But Hopkins' difficulty is that his world is fixed and static, never dynamic. The terrible flux of evening in 'Spelt from Sibyl's leaves', in which sounds and forms merge into one another, 'all throughther in throngs', 'dismembering, disremembering', epitomises the chromatic annulment of individuation which he dreaded. The poem both encounters and defends itself against that dissolution. The stable fixities of language dissolve, and with them the reciprocal separateness of self and world. Subject and object are dispersed into one another, and since there can be no fixity and separation there can be no memory or identity – 'disremembering' – and no continued moral life.

Earnest, earthless, equal, attuneable, vaulty, voluminous, ... stupendous
Evening strains to be time's vast, womb-of-all, home-of-all, hearse-of-all
 night.
Her fond yellow hornlight wound to the west, her wild hollow hoarlight hung
 to the height
Waste; her earliest stars, earlstars, stars principal, overbend us,
Fire-featuring heaven. For earth her being has unbound; her dapple is at end,
 as-
tray or aswarm, all throughther, in throngs; self in self steepèd and pashed –
 quite
Disremembering, dismembering all now. Heart, you round me right
With: Our evening is over us; our night whelms, whelms, and will end us.
Only the beakleaved boughs dragonish damask the tool-smooth bleak light;
 black,
Ever so black on it. Our tale, O our oracle! Let life, waned, ah let life wind
Off her once skeined stained veined variety upon, all on two spools; part, pen,
 pack
Now her all in two flocks, two folds – black, white; right, wrong; reckon but,
 reck but, mind
But these two; ware of a world where but these two tell, each off the other; of a
 rack
Where, selfwrung, selfstrung, sheathe- and shelterless, thoughts against
 thoughts in groans grind.

The way in which the noun 'evening' is preceded by a series of generalising adjectives, unusual for Hopkins, each partaking of each other's sounds, initiates the gradation or evening out and 'waste' of the chromatic experience which the poem explores – 'Earnest, earthless, equal, attuneable, vaulty, voluminous, ... stupendous/Evening'. Darkness, intent, pure of the material and not *of* the earth, an interloper, invading with consistent gradation and harmonious with itself, encompassing, all-inclusive, overwhelming, is invasive. It can only be encountered by wresting a new identity for evening out of the contrast between darkness and what it is not, and a series of rigorous moral and spiritual antitheses: 'black, white; right, wrong'. And, one must add, self, world, the antithesis which is prior to these and to the meaning and value they reconstitute. This can only be made by an agonising recreation of identity and memory which acknowledges the being of God in the nature of darkness. The cost is appalling mental anguish and isolation – 'selfwrung, self strung ... thoughts against thoughts in groans grind' – for the poet in acknowledging relationship acknowledges that he is at the mercy of this simple, remorselessly punitive relationship offered to him from outside himself by God.

Hopkins wrote increasingly of living inside his mind, or minds, a multiple mind inalienably cut off from God and the world. This 'tormented mind/With this tormenting mind tormented yet' (69), 'cliffs of fall' (65), is estranged from the outer world of God's 'Betweenpie mountains'. The antithesis between self and world is so rigorous and complete that there can be no spring of energy from one to the other. Hopkins' solution to the Hegelian flux of mind-constituted universe is so extreme that it falls into one-sidedness. It leads to that very isolation within the self which he tried so hard to avoid. It refutes idealism by splitting the autonomous external world away from the feeling, perceiving, suffering self so inexorably that the two fall apart as disjunct entities. It reintroduces the solipsism of which Marx accused Hegel. He, the poet, is 'the *only* being'. The estranged poet is left to beg pity from his own heart in his isolation. *Everything* lies outside the self, who feels so painfully the taste of his intense but isolated identity. The almost unendurable strain of these last poems comes from the sense of a mind moving about in its mind where God's 'smile' cannot even be 'wrung' but accidentally and arbitrarily impinges on the poet, 'unforeseen'. The 'skies/Betweenpie mountains', where the smile of the sunset 'lights a lovely mile', might in their form unify mountains and skies, but they do not incorporate the poet in that relationship. They lie irrevocably outside him. Hopkins is not an object for the skies, the skies are not an object to him. Neither expresses its life in the other. This is a world without relationships except those between physical objects, and where the self is enclosed in mind. In that isolation and in its struggle with the implications of Romanticism is the 'lonely began' of modern poetry.

NOTES: 9 February, 1868

(From Hopkins' note-book headed 'Notes on the history of
Greek Philosophy etc.')

All words mean either things or relations of things: you may also say then substances or attributes or again wholes or parts. E.g. *man* and *quarter*.

To every word meaning a thing and not a relation belongs a passion or prepossession or enthusiasm which it has the power of suggesting or producing but not always or in everyone. This *not always* refers to its evolution in the man and secondly in man historically.

The latter element may be called for convenience the prepossession of a word. It is in fact the form, but there are reasons for being cautious in using form here, and it bears a valuable analogy to the soul, one however which is not complete, because all names but proper names are general while the soul is individual.

Since every definition is the definition of a word and every word may be considered as the contraction or coinciding-point of its definitions we may for convenience use word and definition with a certain freedom of interchange.

A word then has three terms belonging to it, ὅροι, or moments – its prepossession of feeling; its definition, abstraction, vocal expression or other utterance; and its application, 'extension', the concrete things coming under it.

It is plain that of these only one in propriety is the word; the third is not a word but a thing meant by it, the first is not a word but something connotatively meant by it, the nature of which is further to be explored.

But not even the whole field of the middle term is covered by the word. For the word is the expression, *uttering* of the idea in the mind. That idea itself has its two terms, the image (of sight or sound or *scapes* of the other senses), which is in fact physical and a refined energy* accenting the nerves, a word to oneself, an inchoate word, and secondly the conception.

The mind has two kinds of energy, a transitional kind, when one thought or sensation follows another, which is to reason, whether actively as in deliberation, criticism, or passively, so to call it, as in reading etc; (ii) an abiding kind for which I remember no name, in which the mind is absorbed (as far as that may be), taken up by, dwells upon, enjoys, a single thought: we may call it contemplation, but it includes pleasures, supposing they, however turbid, do not require a transition to another term *of another kind*, for contemplation in its absoluteness is imposs-

---

*That is when deliberately formed or when a thought is recalled, for when produced by sensation from without or when as in dreams etc it presents itself unbidden it comes from the involuntary working of nature.

ible unless in a trance and it is enough for the mind to repeat the same energy on the same matter.

Art exacts this energy of contemplation but also the other one, and in fact they are not incompatible, for even in the successive arts as music, for full enjoyment, the synthesis of the succession should give, unlock, the contemplative enjoyment of the unity of the whole. It is however true that in the successive arts with their greater complexity and length the whole's unity retires, is less important, serves rather for the framework of that of the parts.

The more intellectual, less physical, the spell of contemplation the more complex must be the object, the more close and elaborate must be the comparison the mind has to keep making between the whole and the parts, the parts and the whole. For this reference or comparison is what the sense of unity means; mere sense that such a thing is one and not two has no interest or value except accidentally.

Works of art of course like words utter the idea and in representing real things convey the prepossession with more or less success.

The further in anything, as a work of art, the organisation is carried out, the deeper the form penetrates, the prepossession flushes the matter, the more effort will be required in apprehension, the more power of comparison, the more capacity for receiving that synthesis of (either successive or spatially distinct) impressions which gives us the unity with the prepossession conveyed by it.

The saner moreover is the act of contemplation as contemplating that which really is expressed in the object.

But some minds prefer that the prepossession they are to receive should be conveyed by the least organic, expressive, by the most suggestive, way. By this means the prepossession and the definition, uttering, are distinguished and unwound, which is the less sane attitude.

Along with this preference for the disengaged and unconditioned prepossession in these minds is often found an intellectual attraction for very sharp and pure dialectic or, in other matter, hard and telling art-forms; in fact we have in them the two axes on which rhetoric turns.

NOTES

Notes on Texts
Where there are no Longman's annotated editions of the works of the poets discussed here I have quoted from Oxford Standard Authors editions except in the case of Hopkins and Wordsworth. Quotations are taken from the following: William Wordsworth, *The Prelude: A Parallel Text*, J. C. Maxwell (ed.), London, 1971; *The Poems of William Blake*, W. H. Stevenson, (ed.), text by David V. Erdman, London, 1971; Shelley, *Poetical Works*, Thomas Hutchinson (ed.), G. M. Matthews (second edn.), Oxford, 1970; Browning, *Poetical Works 1833–64*, Ian Jack (ed.), Oxford, 1970; *The Poems of Tennyson*, Christopher Ricks (ed.), London, 1969; *The Poems of Gerard Manley Hopkins*, W. H. Gardner and N. H. Mackenzie, (eds.), Oxford (fourth edn.), 1970. In quotations from poems in chapter 1 all italics are mine, unless otherwise stated.

1 Goethe, *The Sorrows of Young Werther*, Hermann J. Weigand (ed.), London, (Signet Books), 1962, p. 43.
2 Gerard Manley Hopkins, *Journals and Papers*, Humphry House and Graham Storey, (eds.), London, 1959, pp. 125–6.
3 *Journals and Papers*, p. 230–1; p. 331. 'All the world is full of inscape and chance left free to act falls into an order as well as purpose: looking out of my window I caught it in the random clods and broken heaps of snow made by the cast of a broom.' 'Bluebells in Hodder Wood, all hanging their heads one way. I caught as well as I could while my companions talked the Greek rightness of their beauty.'
4 *Journals and Papers*, p. 127.
5 *Journals and Papers*, pp. 125–6. The Notes of 9 February 1868 are reproduced on pp. 54–6.
6 S. T. Coleridge, *Aids to Reflection*, London, 1836 (third edn.), p. XV.
7 e.g. *The Letters of Gerard Manley Hopkins to Robert Bridges*, Claude Colleer Abbott (ed.), London, 1935, pp. 90, 98, 125.
8 All quotations from the poetry of Hopkins are taken from *The Poems of Gerard Manley Hopkins*, W. H. Gardner and N. H. Mackenzie (eds.), (fourth edn.), Oxford, 1970.
9 T. E. Hulme, *Speculations*, London, 1924 (second edn.), 1958, p. 134.
10 In 1883. See Paddy Kitchen, *Gerard Manley Hopkins*, London, 1978, pp. 208–9.
11 John Henry Newman, *An Essay in Aid of a Grammar of Assent*, London (third edn.), 1870, p. 38, 39.
12 For an important account of 'rhyming' in the poetry of Hopkins see J. Hillis Miller, 'The Univocal Chiming', in *Hopkins: A Collection of Critical Essays*, Geoffrey H. Hartman (ed.), Englewood Cliffs, N. J., 1966, pp. 89–116.
   J. Hillis Miller has another essay relevant to my argument, his 'Nature and the Linguistic Moment', in *Nature and the Victorian Imagination*, U. C. Knoepflmacher and G. B. Tennyson (eds.), Berkeley and London, 1977, pp. 440–51.
13 *Journals and Papers*, p. 204.
14 Ibid., p. 290
15 Ibid., p. 98. See also ibid p. 97: 'I must say that Wordsworth often disap-

points me when I come upon a passage I knew by quotation: it seems less pointed, less excellent, with its context than without.'

16 'On the Signs of Health and Decay in the Arts', 1864, *Journals and Papers*, p. 76.

17 Ibid.

18 Ibid.

19 'Poetic Diction', 1865, ibid., p. 85.

20 Ibid.

21 14 September, 1871, ibid., p. 215.

22 Ibid., p. 128: 'for absence cannot break off Being from its hold on Being.'

23 Here are two characteristic accounts of seas and skies. 'I saw the waves well. In the sunlight they were green-blue, flinty sharp, and rucked in straight lines by the wind; under their forelocks the most beautiful bottle-green beam, as bright as any gems; when the wave had passed this same part – upon the turned-over plait of the crest – neighboured by and sometimes broken by foam, looked like chrysophase' (17 July, 1867).

'At sunset and later a strongly marked moulded rack. I made out the make of it, thus – cross-hatching in fact... Those may have been scarves of cloud bellying upwards but often I believe it is, as it looks in the perspective, downwards, and then they may be curds or globes and solid, geometrical solids/that is, for all clouds are more or less cellular and hollow (24 May, 1871). *Journals and Papers*, pp. 148, 210.

24 'The Probable Future of Metaphysics', ibid., p. 120.

25 Ibid., p. 119.

26 Ibid.

27 The source of Hopkins' knowledge of Hegel is probably Jowett and J. H. Stirling's *The Secret of Hegel: being the Hegelian System in origin, principle, form and matter*, 2 vols., London, 1865. This is an unreliable guide.

28 For the meditation on selfhood see *The Sermons and Devotional Writings of Gerard Manley Hopkins*, Christopher Devlin (ed.), London, 1959, p. 125. But the entire meditation (pp. 122–8) is relevant. In a letter of 20 February, 1875, Hopkins wrote to Bridges: 'I have had no time to read even the English books about Hegel, much less the original, indeed I know almost no German. (However I think my contemporary Wallace of Balliol has been translating him)... After all I can, at all events a little, read Duns Scotus and I care for him more even than Aristotle and more *pace tua* than a dozen Hegels... I like to hear about you and how glad I am you are as you say, nearer the top than the bottom of Hegel's or anybody else's bottomless pit.' *The Letters of Gerard Manley Hopkins to Robert Bridges*, Claude Colleer Abbott (ed.), London, 1935, pp. 30–1.

29 *Journals and Papers*, p. 120.

30 *Hegel's Phenomonology of Mind*, J. B. Baillie, (trans.), London, 1910, vol. I, p. 16. I have quoted mainly from the Preface. The argument described here is readumbrated in many places but particularly in Section B, 'Self-Consciousness', pp. 163–219.

31 Ibid., p. 20. 'The realised purpose, or concrete actuality, is movement and process of development. But this very unrest is the self.'

32 Ibid., p. 17. The 'portentous power of the negative' paradoxically re-instates selfhood. It is the energy of thought, pure ego. 'Death, as we may

call that unreality, is the most terrible thing, and to keep and hold fast what is dead demands the greatest force of all . . . But the life of mind is not one that shuns death, and keeps clear of destruction; it endures its death and in death maintains its being.' pp. 30–31.

33 Ibid., p. 22, 23.

34 Ibid., p. 44, 16. An alternative translation is: 'Only this self-*restoring* sameness, or this reflection in otherness within itself – not an *original* or *immediate* unity as such – is the True. It is the process of its own becoming, the circle that presupposes its end as its goal, having its end also as its beginning.' W. F. Hegel, *Phenomenology of Spirit*, A. V. Miller (trans.), Oxford, 1977, p. 10.

35 *Biographia Literaria*, J. Shawcross (ed.), Oxford, 1907, vol. II, p. 83.

36 Baillie, p. 16. The truly living is realised 'solely in the process of positing itself, or in mediating with its own self its transitions from one state or position to the opposite. As subject it is pure and simple negativity, and just on that account a process of splitting up what is simple and undifferentiated, a process of duplicating and setting factors in opposition'. A. V. Miller has 'being . . . is in truth actual only in so far as it is the movement of positing itself, or it is the mediation of its self-othering with itself. This substance is, as subject, pure, *simple negativity*, and is for this very reason the bifurcation of the simple; it is the doubling which sets up opposition'. *Phenomenology of Spirit*, p. 10.

37 Baillie, p. 22. The following is the context in which this sentence occurs: 'This means, it must be presented to itself as an object, but at the same time straightaway annul and transcend this objective form; it must be its own object in which it finds itself reflected . . . In this way it is aware of itself as an object in which its own self is reflected. Mind, which, when thus developed, knows itself to be mind, is science.'

38 Ibid., p. 174. 'With this we already have before us the notion of *Mind* or *Spirit*. What consciousness has further to become aware of, is the experience of what mind is, this absolute substance, which is the unity of the different self-related and self-existent self-consciousnesses, in the perfect freedom and independence of their opposition as component elements of that substance: Ego that is "we", a plurality of Egos, and "we" that is a single Ego. Consciousness first finds in self-consciousness – the notion of mind – its turning-point, where it leaves the parti-coloured show of the sensuous immediate, passes from the dark void of the transcendent and remote supersensuous, and steps into the spiritual daylight of the present.'

39 Ibid. A. V. Miller has 'A self-consciousness exists *for a self-consciousness*'. *Phenomenology of Spirit*, p. 110.

40 W. K. Wimsatt, 'The Structure of Romantic Nature Imagery', *The Verbal Icon*, Lexington, 1967, pp. 103–16. The essay was first published in 1954. Paul de Man, 'The Rhetoric of Temporality', *Interpretation, Theory and Practice*, C. S. Singleton (ed.), Baltimore, 1969.

41 *Journals and Papers*, p. 288.

42 Letter to Benjamin Bailey, November 22, 1817, *The Letters of John Keats 1814–21*, 2 vols., Hyder E. Rollins, (ed.), Cambridge, 1952.

43 Baillie, p. 31.

44 Ibid., p. 34.

45 Ibid., p. 88. It is important to realise that Hegel is not concerned here with *self-awareness* but with the dialectical structure of consciousness in which the movement to a new content can be observed or analysed by the phenomenologist but not immediately by the mind which is 'in the grip of experience itself'. For consciousness the dialectical process necessarily goes on 'behind its back'. A. V. Miller's translation clarifies this point: 'the *origination* of the new object, that presents itself to consciousness without its understanding how this happens, which proceeds for us, as it were, behind the back of consciousness'. *Phenomenology of Spirit*, p. 56.

46 Baillie, p. 43.

47 Ibid., p. 55.

48 Ibid., p. 5.

49 Ibid., p. 10, 11.

50 Ibid., p. 3. My italics.

51 Ibid., p. 17.

52 Ibid., p. 5.

53 Ibid., p. 11.

54 Ibid.

55 These words are best understood in context. The moment is the act of repossessing knowledge as other without which a new content cannot evolve dialectically from within. 'Science can become an organic system only by the inherent life of the notion. In science the determinateness, which was taken from the schema and stuck on to existing facts in external fashion, is the self-directing inner soul of the concrete content. The movement of what is partly consists in becoming another to itself, and thus developing explicitly into its own immanent content; partly, again, it takes this evolved content, this existence it assumes, back into itself, i.e. makes *itself* into a moment, and reduces itself to simple determinateness.' Ibid., p. 50.

56 *Karl Marx: Early Writings* Lucio Colletti, (ed.), London. 1974, p. 390.

57 Ibid.

58 Ibid.

59 Ibid., p. 388.

60 Ibid., p. 389.

61 Ibid., p. 396.

62 Ibid., p. 390.

63 Ibid., p. 385.

64 Ibid., p. 398.

65 Shelley's punctuation is
> It feeds the quick growth of the serpent vine,
> And the dark linked ivy tangling wild,
> And budding, blown, or odour-faded blooms
> Which star the winds with points of coloured light
> As they rain through them, and bright golden globes
> Of fruit, suspended in their own green heaven,
> And, through their veined leaves and amber stems,
> The flowers whose purple and translucid bowls
> Stand ever mantling with aerial dew,
> The drink of spirits. And it circles round, ...

See *Shelley's Promethus Unbound: the Text and the Drafts*, Lawrence John Zillman (ed.), New Haven and London, 1968.

66 Thomas De Quincey, *Suspiria de Profundis, Confessions of an Opium-Eater and Other Writings*, Aileen Ward (ed.), New York and London, p. 130.

67 Geoffrey Hartman, *The Unmediated Vision*, New Haven and London, 1954, p. 53. *The act of sight has become a moral responsibility.*

CHAPTER 2

Wordsworth's Complexity: The Prelude VI, 1805

> O'er paths and fields
> In all that neighbourhood, through narrow lanes
> Of eglantine, and through the shady woods,
> And o'er the Border Beacon, and the waste
> Of naked pools, and common crags that lay
> Exposed on the bare fell, was scattered love,
> A spirit of pleasure, and youth's golden gleam. (VI, 239–45)

This is one of the earliest journeys in this book, or involute of journeys and travel and journeys within journeys. It is a remarkable feat of idealist language, performing the creative imaginative act which it describes. Surprisingly, and against all expectations, the postponed verb here is 'was scattered love,/A spirit of pleasure and youth's golden gleam'. It retrospectively transforms the contours of the sentence from the rear, lighting up new possibilities in the syntax as if it were conferring on it the 'gleam' of fresh experience which belongs to love, to spirit and to youth – those states which so unexpectedly enter the end of the sentence. Unexpectedly and yet appropriately, for this is a book about youth and restless maturation. Initially the syntax modestly proposes a progressive physical movement as the sentence starts out on a walk, as it were, with the insistent pressure and thrust of prepositions moving sequentially through a substantive landscape, from woods to waste – 'O'er ... In ... through ... through ... o'er'. The shape of the sentence at first suggests a delayed verb of physical action, sought for rather like the terminal point of a journey. But when that verb discovers itself as a metaphor which has nothing to do with physical action it acts on and changes the proposal of the sentence almost in the moment that proposal is made. 'Scattered' over the landscape are feeling and emotion, love, spirit, pleasure, and while these are offered emphatically as pure categories of affective experience the gently quiescent metaphor of seed allows them the physically generative power and propagative properties of organic life. It allows that love as pure feeling can take root in physical objects. The intangible 'golden gleam' of the subsequent metaphor is governed by the suggestion of seed activated in the first metaphor – 'scattered' – and so light, the gleam, that modifying, transforming agent, is also scattered over the landscape with the same largesse, and shares the fertilising possibilities offered in 'scattered', for both light and seed can be 'cast' on things.

Like a landscape which alters *behind* one as one's movements change, the syntax changes its value. 'O'er', 'through', no longer possess the immediate sense of physical passage, but their energies are transferred to the meaning of diffusion and organic penetration of feeling *into* external objects. One's mounting dismay as the description of the landscape moves from pastoral to barren surroundings is redeemed when the metaphor brings into prominence 'In *all* that neighbourhood', for 'neighbourhood', insisting on kinship, replaces the strongly progressive sequence from one unlike area to another and it suggests that the disparate elements belong to one another because they stand in mutual relationship in a humanly defined area and are included in its unity. 'Neighbourhood', glancing towards an analogy with 'brotherhood' even suggests a unified group of friends and friendly feeling in addition to its meaning as physical area. Pastoral and barren landscape belong to one another because they are equally in possession of the largesse of scattered love, and Wordsworth quietly challenges the parable by allowing that the seed of love falls both on fertile and stony ground and takes root in both. Feeling bestows living passion on the inorganic stone of common crags, bringing the dead to life and reclaiming the barren landscape. The penetrative metaphor of seed counteracts the accounts of the landscape as obstinate matter, an inorganic resistant surface, 'naked', 'exposed', 'bare' – the barren crags lay *on* the fell in contrast to the seed which can penetrate beneath it.

The language here seems to guarantee for Wordsworth that transforming act of feeling which enables him to make the bold and simple idealist claim that the mind has dominance and power over sense, is 'lord and master' (xi, 271–2) and is its own object, 'the consciousness/Of Whom they are, habitually infused/Through every image and through every thought' (xiii, 108–11). The subject is the object of itself. 'Love', multiplying itself appositionally as 'A spirit', 'youth's golden gleam', is the passive subject of this sentence, but the verb '*was* scattered' abstains from denoting the source of the scattering. Love might be the subjective feeling scattered by that notional band of friends who gleam momentarily in 'all that neighbourhood', and who are only grammatically present as a *state*, youth, which is an *attribute* of love, the real subject of the sentence. Or 'love' as autonomous feeling, possessed of external objective being, acts on landscape and the human beings included in it alike, and is returned to them from outside themselves, as something other to them. The passive verb enables 'love' to be the subject of the sentence and yet to be strangely independent of an agent. 'Love' is its own agent, acting upon itself, and thus 'youth's golden gleam' is equally cast on the world (the delicately appropriate connections with what is fertile are still here, as we *cast* looks, light, seed) and refracted back to itself as 'golden gleam', as other to itself.

The 'running in stress' of Hopkins' walk, which 'returned to the morning's' when he realised where he was, is useful here by way of contrast. Wordsworth's metaphor is quite different. It revalues the sentence by transforming it from a physical to a qualititative experience, and so we cannot return to the first experience. For the sentence, in restructuring itself, offers the process of transformation itself *as* experience, *as* 'running in stress', rather than two successive interpretations of the same thing. Metaphor here transforms experience as it is happening, just as it argues that love transforms life as it is being lived.

And yet, though the spiritual progress of the second 'walk' can never be 'returned' to the first physical journey, which actually turns out to be a grammatical illusion, it would be wrong to say that the earlier expectation *is* entirely eliminated. It is there in the second qualitative experience, palimpsestically layered under the new experience which is superimposed and which supersedes it. And because the first 'walk' is not eliminated, language maintains two different kinds of externality simultaneously. On the one hand there is the solid physical externality of woods and crags, substantive but estranged until it is acted upon and reclaimed by the mind's feat of transformation. On the other hand *mind* is its own externality. The subject as love is its own object, construing the world as an aspect of itself. The triumph of the sentence is to have enabled the two forms of object or otherness to be powerfully co-present without antagonism, but potentially they disagree; for one proposes a severance between the mind and the world and the other maintains that the world is constituted as mind. The threat of proposing a dualism of mind and object is that the self and nature are always in danger of falling apart, and the threat of proposing the self as its own object is the obliteration of relationships as mind acts on itself. The sentence represses these dangers partly by invoking each *form* of object to redress the problems created by the other. If love redeems the landscape and sees itself reflected in it, the landscape is there for love to root itself in, and Wordsworth can claim both the reflexive, self-creating powers of mind which makes the world categories of itself, *and* a reciprocal relationship in which the self is an object for the landscape as much as the world is an object for the self. The contradictions are disguised because the sentence offers the vital process of feeling as the primary joy, a *running* instress, shared in relation to both forms of object or otherness. It is quietly miraculous in its avoidance of the strains of incompatibility.

But elsewhere the strain is not always suppressed, and the kind of double syntax I have described recurs throughout *The Prelude*, constructed in infinitely varied forms. An under-syntax, making its claims for reciprocity as a reflexive syntax proceeds, or the other way round, maintains an openness of language which seems to have been vital to Wordsworth. Both possibilities are kept in play, and one does not take priority over the other. In his discussion of 'the mystery of words' (v. 619–29), a declaration of belief in language which forms a triumphant preface to Book VI, the same openness is present. The words allow either a reciprocal or reflexive meaning to the same elements because almost every item can be read in more than one relationship to the others.

> Visionary power
> Attends upon the motions of the winds,
> Embodied in the mystery of words:
> There, darkness makes abode, and all the host
> Of shadowy things do work their changes there,
> As in a mansion like their proper home.

Even forms and substances are circumfused
By that transparent veil with light divine,
And, through the turnings intricate of verse,
Present themselves as objects recognised,
In flashes, with a glory scarce their own. (v, 619–29)

The nature of language is seen ambiguously. Words construe the world '*with* a glory', '*with* light divine', but whether the structure of language actually determines the way in which we see the world and relationships, or whether it is a transparent medium, seen through, by which given relationships express themselves, is not clear. Shadowy things work their changes '*there*' – in words themselves or in visionary power or both, the syntax allows. 'As in a mansion like their proper home': a mansion, a construction, a containing building; the implication is that they can't get out, that neither mind nor world can be released from the structure of language, which is their 'proper home', their origin and source and the place where they have their being. But language is also, in another metaphor, a 'transparent veil', enabling things to 'Present themselves' 'through the turnings intricate of verse'. The multiple possibilities of 'through' here – that self-effacing preposition – contain astonishing contradictions. 'Through' as *seen* through, or 'embodied in', or as 'by means of', or as 'throughout', a temporal sense, all offer different accounts of language. But 'turnings' is the vital word. The meaning of verse is to turn, of course, but the word here not only denotes the turn and return of rhythm and cadence, but the 'turnings' or transformations of metaphor and, above all, the 'turnings' of syntax. For words 'turn' in different relationships towards one another, simultaneously face in different directions, and therefore 'turn' the relationships they construct. The nature of language, therefore, allows for not merely the transformation of relationships, but for more than one possibility between relationships. This is just what the passage itself does. And so it is proper for Wordsworth to speak of 'visionary power', a way of seeing, a way of transforming, as actually 'Embodied' in 'the mystery of words', for visionary power is given form, comes into being and is expressed through the *physical* structure of words and the mysterious and miraculous capacity of language to reorder and create multiple constructions of the world.

Accordingly, visionary power 'Attends upon', works on or

waits dependently upon, 'the motions of the winds', an active and a passive agent, facing towards the winds or faced by them. The 'host of shadowy *things*' are ambiguously insubstantial and substantive, indeterminately of the mind or outside it, just as darkness is. Shadowy things work their changes 'there', in language, and the openness of 'changes' allows them the possibility of working upon something other than themselves, or of working upon each other, or of reflexively acting on themselves, *their* changes, in transformations that are wrought in and by themselves. '*Even* forms and substances are circumfused': forms, both physically solid and *abstract* things, things in the mind and things outside it, substances, substantive and *fluid* things, are 'circumfused' by language. True to the nature of the possible meanings of that word, which denotes both a blending together in circular relationship of things with themselves or the fact of being surrounded and fused with something else, the syntax offers a causal relationship between separate entities and yet so fuses prepositions and their relationships that things are bound together in one identity. 'Circumfused' serves first both forms and substances, blending their different existences, and then serves 'that transparent veil,' the 'veil' of language, which here both covers and is seen through, with the possibility that language enables the objects of its discourse to be themselves transparent. For forms and substances are circumfused *by* language, *by means of it* and *with* language, so that in this last case forms and substances are in one identity with words. But finally, 'circumfused' serves 'with light divine', and language becomes the agent by which forms and substances are fused, either with God-like insight from the consciousness or irradiated with divine light which participates in their being. Again, 'forms and substances' and 'light divine' are both, the syntax allows, mediated by language. The source of the divine is left open, as is the metaphorical meaning of light (of the mind, or of God) and as by this stage the syntax has offered and fused cause and effect, entity and identity, subject and object, the 'light divine' moves freely between two possibilities. It might come from God or from the self.

The sentence continues in its complexity: by means of the turnings of verse, the intricate transformations of metaphor and syntax, even 'forms and substances' are endowed with glory. Again, a double syntax allows a reading of 'forms and substances' (despite the 'Even', which declares their physicality in the act of stating that they are transformed) as objects, as independent things, autonomously *other*, substantive and external, *and* as extensions of mind. Two structures are at work: 'Even forms and substances ... Present themselves as objects ... In flashes, with a glory.' Alternatively, 'forms and substances ... Present themselves as objects *recognised*,/In flashes, with a glory.' The ambiguity turns upon the open movement of 'In flashes', upon whether objects present themselves 'In flashes' or whether they are *recognised* 'In flashes'. Language allows us a world of objects which impinge upon us with startling immediacy, light *themselves* up, indeed, with an independently self-generating illumination. It also allows us a world of objects recognised, a world of objects *perceived* as objects in flashes of immediacy and mental illumination, in which objects are created by the perceiver's recognition. The perceiver's recognition is returned to him as his own awareness of recognition. Again the language 'turns' relationships in two ways, to a world of objects separate from mind, or to a world construed as the mind's self-consciousness. 'In flashes', intermittent but instantaneous, allows a momentary and astonishing illumination to both relationships. But the subtlety of the convergence of 'objects' with 'recognised', delicately isolated at the end of a line, momentarily suggests a world in which objects *enable* us to recognise them, and here Wordsworth is able to say that while the consciousness of the perceiver is returned to him as consciousness or mind, the perceiver is also an 'object' for the object, which enables his recognition and returns it to him as his. The reflexive and the reciprocal notions of relationship quiver together here, converging on one another, but not quite resolving one another. Objects may present themselves 'with a glory', but also objects may enable us to confer on them a glory scarce their own, just as we may enable them to possess this glory. And further, 'glory' may not be our own or that of objects, but from some other source. For there *is* a mystery in words, an uninterpretable 'darkness' which may even be the darkness of the consciousness, but which Wordswororth leaves unpenetrated. To resolve the opposition between two ways of seeing the world would be, finally, too dangerous.

The dangers of deciding for one syntax rather than another, for one account of the world rather than another, are the subject of this chapter. Wordsworth maintains the ambiguity of syntax with remarkable rigour. The subtle and simultaneous pressure of one syntax upon another can be found everywhere in Book VI. Each syntax asks questions of the other. Like imagination itself, each comes 'athwart' the other. Since the preoccupation of the book is with freedom and its possibilities and dangers, I shall look at three moments where the syntax asks questions about freedom and domination before returning to the significance of the 'golden gleam' passage to Book VI and to the whole of *The Prelude*.

The first sentence of Book VI describes the poet's return to Cambridge: a liberated return, or a restriction? 'The leaves were yellow when to Furnace Fells. ... I bade adieu, and ... Went back to Granta's cloisters.' The ostensible narrative, composed of free, successive, ongoing clauses, which leave the main sentence and Furnace Fells behind, is steadily deprived of its assertive *progressive* sequence by an alternative co-ordinate and *consequential* syntax attached to the casually accumulating 'and' series. The main sentence, 'The leave were yellow ... and ... and' has to be layered into the following clauses with the recurrence of each 'and'. There is a causal and a temporal relationship between the yellowing maturation of autumn, faintly admonitory, and the young man's departure. The yellow leaves are not left behind but are carried along in the grammar, pressing in much more closely upon the defensive autonomousness of the speaker than he realises, as if they are entering in ambiguously to his mental life. 'The leaves were yellow when ... and ... and (The leaves were yellow when) ... I bade adieu'. The landscape left behind 'enters in' insistently rather as the beauty of autumn 'enters in' ambiguously in the next sentence, coming into being in the external world or in the mind. The under-syntax constitutes another narrative which asks questions about the complexities of freedom ignored by the defensive mock-heroic and the insistence on being 'gay and undepressed'. It imposes a check on 'the lightsome mood', and forces an awareness of a half-formed, unregistered antithesis between that and 'my *own* unlovely *cell*'.

Again, another model of relationship is shifted, questioned, revalued, by a syntax which is 'exquisitely wreathed' about itself. The Cambridge ash, which holds a mysterious authority for the 'foot-bound' poet, is 'green with ivy' (95), and as the sentence proceeds it is impossible to say whether it describes the profuse 'outer spray' of the master tree or the ivy (it so happens that both ivy and ash can possess sprays 'that hung in yellow tassels and festoons'). 'A *single* tree' (90), '*this* lovely tree' (101), Wordsworth calls it. The inseparable intertwining of the ash's syntax and the ivy's syntax persuades the following questions. Does the ivy take from or define the tree's vitality? Does it form the tree or the tree form it? Is it 'trimmed out' (98), a decorative external, or is it one organic identity with the ash? These are questions appropriate for a poet who, like the ivy, is weaving imaginative fictions round the tree, and thinking of the authority of a literary tradition. 'Foot-bound', rooted in one life with the tree and yet creating an image out of it, the poet implicitly asks in what sense the image-making power is 'bound'.

In just the same way the 'rapid river flowing without noise' (417), which impinges on the 'boisterous' company in France, noticed by the unnotice of its presence, raises questions about the nature of awareness. How does the physical world impinge on us if we do not notice it? What was not heard 'without noise', paradoxically 'Spake with a sense of peace, at intervals/ Touching the heart' (419–20). Either the sense of peace, equally the river's suggestion of peace or the poet's 'sense', sensation or intuition of it, touched the heart (both sense and peace, a subtle interaction of feeling with feeling, *touch* the heart), or, the syntax allows, the flowing river itself, unmediated by ideas or feelings, *touched* the heart. The sensory aspect of sense and 'heart' and the quiescent physical implications of 'touching' come alive in this reading and begin to challenge the more abstract and mental reading of 'sense' and 'heart'. In what ways does the world work on us or we on it? Is the self or the world privileged as 'lord and master'?

The breaks and transitions, the modes of connections which Coleridge noticed as the life of Wordsworth's verse consistently create two syntaxes which press upon one another and ask questions of one another. It is in these questions that 'darkness makes abode'. There is indeed a 'mystery' in words which does not finally resolve the struggle between two syntaxes with the equanimity expressed in the account of mind in Book II, 'creator and receiver both'. As the structure of each syntax implies alternative epistemologies they silently construe contradictory accounts of human possibility and maintain them concurrently. Wordsworth seems so much the innocent writer of his own poem: that self-abosrbed intentness, the equanimity which appears to be steadily synthesising, cohesive, reconciling by letting connections emerge, unnoticed almost by the writer himself, tempts a reader, as it often does Wordsworth himself, to accept all that goes on in the poem as already resolved. But what the poem assumes its premises to be, are in reality its problems. The relation of subject and object is constantly struggled with. In fact, the poem has an immense patience with itself, an extraordinary way of letting its inconsistencies emerge from its 'pure' transparent diction and, as it were, letting them be. The ordering of Book VI is as much in terms of breaks and transitions as its syntax, and these disjunctions ask the same questions. There are ellipses, junctures which do not join, connections which do not connect and often invert the ostensible meaning of their relationship. The clefts in the poem are like the chasm of Snowdon in Book XIII, breathing places from which the energies of horror and desolation emerge, just as they are also 'hiding places' of power. The passage on imaginaion which erupts inexplicably out of the centre of the book 'unfathered' by anything in it, its confidence unjustified by what precedes it (the crossing of the Alps unawares) or by the ominous energy of the apocalyptic descent which follows it, is one of these hiding places of power. It is one of the most flagrant non-sequiturs of the poem and dramatises the problems inherent in the double syntax. Just as it describes imagination itself its 'power' comes 'athwart' the poem, disrupting it, at once celebration and threat, unwilled, self-derived, 'unfathered', 'lifting up itself', engendered without antecedent or *authority*. 'To my soul I say – I recognise thy glory'. The syntax allows what is 'recognised' to be either the glory of the soul itself, or an autonomous external power.

Power, usurpation: transcendental and political, prophetic and social meaning converge in the vocabulary. It is not strange that the problems of epistemology and revolutionary politics converge in Book VI. The usurping power of the imagination and the heady rush through liberated France, both mock-heroic (Nature had 'given a charter to irregular hopes') and paradisal, go together. The political metaphor is not simply transferred to the rival epistemologies offered by the syntax but the structure of the syntax itself generates the metaphor. Each syntax exerts a pressure on the other and requires the other to ask whether power is to be located in the subject as agent, as lord and master over outward sense, by construing the world as attributes of itself and making it 'the servant of her will', or whether the subject is truly subject, truly constituted by what is outside it. 'Now I am free, enfranchised and at large.' The successive relationships expanded in these synonyms in this line from the first section of *The Prelude* effectively ask what *to be* free is. To be enfranchised is to be set free by something other to you, a political franchise: to be at large is to constitute yourself as free (like a criminal? a thief?), to make freedom and to constitute the other as restriction and bondage. This sentence condenses the complication of the double syntax of the poem.

One of the underground researches in the first half of Book VI before the crossing of the Alps seems to offer a reconciliation of the two syntaxes in the notion of the image. The word image (and variants of it) is recurrent in the book and its use depends on another contraversion of itself. When the poet speaks of himself almost casually as 'happy in the strength and loveliness of imagery and thought', presenting these as coequal and harmonious activities the two things, in fact, become antitheses of one another. Progressively, 'imagery' and 'thought' come to be seen in opposition to one another. The poem subtly opposes the stone and the shell from the Quixotic dream of Book V, pure thought against the prophetic imagination – something of more worth. The image-beset poet with a mind haunted almost by itself, the pure intelligence and universal sway of geometry, the passionately courteous contrast between the poet and Coleridge, reverse their relationships, as the pure intelligence of geometry begins to share something with the airy wretchedness of Coleridge who is 'debarred from nature's living images'. *Living* images are not only an alternative to pure thought, but subsume it; images make thought possible. Images, 'lifting up' themselves, testify to the free, constitutive power of mind, and yet they are dependent upon sense-derived experience. As a result, they compound 'sensuous and intellectual' knowledge and allow for a precarious double account of experience as a world of self and objects and a world constituted by thought. In them the light of sense 'goes out', both extends itself and is obliterated in the mental abstraction of image-making. Creation and self-creation seem reconciled. In the process of image-making we might say that the mind is 'working but in alliance with the works/Which it beholds' (ii, 274–5) or that Nature works with the transforming mind which is 'Willing to work and to be wrought upon' (xiii, 100). Image-making, as I shall show, is the hidden subject of Book VI.

The golden gleam passage with which I began, one of the mute, astounding ironies of *The Prelude*, is one of the 'hiding places' of image-making power, as I shall show. On the other hand, the hopeful possibilities of the golden gleam passage are counterpoised by the descent of the Alps. In it image-making fails. The two syntaxes collapse into one another. It answers the redeeming golden gleam passage with disintegration. In it we remember the precarious contradictions of the word 'works', open enough to denote both the works of nature or of God and the creation of the mind which contemplates or receives its own power and activity. 'Willing to work and to be wrought upon' allows that the mind is open enough to be wrought upon but brings that process into being. The descent of the Alps is an inexplicable breathing space of destructive power, approached but uninterpretable. The movement into apocalyptic prophecy and then into a conflation of Milton's Hell with Coleridgean dream in the journey in which night is mistaken for morning, wrecks the more urbane genres of the earlier part of the Book and brings the poem down upon itself. The civilised debate about the poet's life in Cambridge, tradition, authority, learning, the image-making as against the abstracting powers of mind in geometry, comes to an end. The movement from mock-heroic, biography, epistle, comparing the minds of Wordsworth and Coleridge, the progressions to the journey through liberated France, at once travelogue, guide-book, pastoral idyll and mock-heroic, where references to Spenser's Colin Clout and to Prince Hal still exist in uneasy contiguity, all these are halted in the descent. The journey is a fine model for the activity of the mind in image-making, a projection which depends on a movement through space and time, but the book is full of failed projections, like the disappointment with Mont Blanc. It is a journey without a climax. The crossing of the Alps is made unawares. The displaced centre of Book VI is a descent, not a peak. Book VI itself, virtually at the centre of the whole poem, looks back to its past and forward to its future, a transition rather than a centre.

Before turning to the crossing of the Alps we need to know

more of the process of image-making and the connection between images and the golden gleam passage. In the crossing of the Alps experience happens unawares, and this is an involute which is given living form in the golden gleam passage which itself crosses obliviously over an earlier consciousness which the *poem* betrays no knowledge of until five books later. This is characteristic of the 'turnings' of the poem upon itself in repetition. The words 'A spirit of pleasure and youth's golden gleam' recur as '*The* spirit of pleasure and youth's golden gleam' as one of the high points of the poem in Book XI. They follow the account of Wordsworth as a child ('not six years old') losing his guide in the landscape of the Border Beacon. The child stumbles upon a murderer's gibbet and experiences that sense of desolation and 'visionary dreariness' which as a mature poet he counts as one of the saving 'spots of time', 'invisibly' nourishing existence. The child's landscape of the Border Beacon in Book XI is the same landscape, the same 'spot', as in Book VI, which is traversed by an older Wordsworth and his companions. Appropriately enough, buried 'invisibly' beneath the words of Book VI, which proceeds as if unawares, unconsciously traversing the tragic landscape of this very 'scene', is the geology of the poet's past, an experience as well as a landscape. Spots of time, moments of intensity, Wordsworth says in Book XI, just before the 'visionary dreariness' passage are 'scattered' through life, germinative and seed-like, as love is scattered in the first golden gleam passage. The turnings of the poem upon itself reversing the order of mature and early experience, embody the way in which past and future experiences act and react, creating one another, repairing one another. Feeling comes in aid of feeling. The 'power' experiences leave 'behind' is the power of extremity which releases the possibility for further extremity – the 'spirit of pleasure' which turns, redeems the loss and desolation of the child even as it is enabled by it.

And yet these are *spots* of time. Particular spaces, areas or sequences of time, but also moments of time which belong to particular areas and places. The categories of time, place and space are strangely fused. While the structure of *The Prelude* appears to release the poem into a world in which mind as past and memory acts on and transforms mind as present and future and mind as present acts on mind as past, freeing mind, as the reversal of the order of adult and childhood experience implies, the process in which mind makes itself other to itself is absolutely dependent on the categories of time and space and cannot take place without going through the temporal sequence.

The phrase 'spots of time' returns upon the passages on geometry in Book VI. The permanent forms of geometry enable the poet to construct 'An image ... of the one/Surpassing life which – out of space and time,/Nor touched by welterings of passion – is,/And hath the name of, God' (154–7). The 'one surpassing life' is 'out of space and time', and so, the syntax allows, is the image which enables us to 'name' it as God. But again, the syntax has the double structure so familiar in *The Prelude*, for it allows that while an image transcends time, and while geometry transcends time, they are both *constructed out of* space and time. The constructions of geometry were pleasing and liberating to a mind 'haunted almost by itself', a mind 'beset with images', besieged and *rooted* with images as a plant is 'set'. We remember that the poet was 'foot-bound' when he gazed at the mysterious ash and created images from it, rooted in one identity with the tree. For there is a radical difference between image and geometry. Geometry, in a later passage, is a 'clear synthesis' a free and 'independent world', created out of 'pure intelligence' (186–7); *out of* pure intelligence because it is out of space and time, as the earlier passage states (both passages owe much to Plato's discussion of geometry in *The Republic*). But the constructions of geometry stand over and against experience, abstracted from it and incapable of self-movement and growth simply because they are free from 'the welterings of passion'. For all its beauty geometry is fittingly a stone. Images may create impure syntheses but they are living ones, creative of further experience because they have experienced the dimensions of space and time with passion, as geometry does not. Moreover, the image transcends geometry because, created out of space and time in both senses, it can interpret the significance of geometry by making an image out of it, which geometry itself cannot do. Perhaps we can name the *image* of geometry as God indeed.

An image requires the categories of space and time in order to be made and yet because it is an image, a thing of the mind, it can be released from them, but it always depends upon pre-existing things in the world. And so the 'spots of time' are rooted in 'space and time' even as they are liberated from them. The abstractions they will create will be different from those of 'pure intelligence' because they derive from the 'impure' intelligence of sense experience but it is this which makes them important. In the sentence which follows the golden gleam passage in Book VI, Wordsworth salutes Coleridge in a generous and creative act of image-making – 'I seem to *plant* thee there'. To be 'be-set' with images is fruitful here. The youthful walks took place before the two friends had met, but Coleridge can be 'with us in the past', which he did not inhabit, because of the conflating and combining powers of mind. The poet's very consciousness of the limiting conditions of space and time enable him to escape from them even as he depends on them for his escape. The image partakes of sensuous and intellectual knowledge. It allows for the pressure of the world on the self and for pure mind as its own object. Wordsworth uses the word 'image' in several senses so far as one can see. An image is an object or form in the external world *seen* as a form, or it is a representation or picture of those forms, or it is a mental representation and can be a synthesis of mental forms or it is a symbol. The shifts of meaning allow for the maintenance of that precarious double account of experience, a world of self and objects and a world constituted by thought. The image belongs to both.

To turn, then, to the moment of visionary dreariness which underlies the golden gleam passage is to understand that the account is about the process of constructing imagery, the drama of a creative act of abstraction and the source of symbol.

> forthwith I left the *spot*
> And, reascending the bare common, *saw*
> A naked pool (xi, 302–4)

The spot of time which underlies but *succeeds* the narrative of the poet's youthful roamings over the spot of the Border Beacon is offered hardly at all as direct description. What is described is the construction of an image 'out of' it. Like the letters which record a murder in the community's past, kept 'fresh and visible' (299) by 'superstition of the neighbourhood' (297), here emphatically the *community* and not the *area* designated in Book VI, the account of visionary dreariness is an attempt to 'enshrine the spirit of the past' (342) through words. The metaphor for language is apt. A shrine contains but conceals its contents, or testifies to a presence or an event which it cannot reveal because the event is absent, past. Words are like the ivy on the ash, given form by what is concealed. Colours and words 'unknown to man' would be required to 'paint' (311) – the mimetic word stresses the paradox, shifting the 'colours' of rhetoric towards the material of paint – a *feeling*, visionary dreariness, or the seen experienced as feeling. The passage accepts the impossibility of finding a new or unknown language and constructs itself out of itself by repetition. And the triple account of the experience (for the 'spot' is given three times in succession) gives another sense of 'turnings', the return of words upon themselves in repetition and the transformation of meaning through repetition. Wordsworth makes it clear that the passage is a recreation of experience in the present moment of writing and thus virtually a new experience – as all memory is. 'I should need/Colours and words that are unknown to man,/To paint [now] the visionary dreariness/Which ... Did *at that time*'. The procedure of the narrative embodies 'future restoration', the way in which experiences restore us (that is replenish) and are restored (regained) to us. It is built out of itself, using its own materials to grow. The building of the image is the process of its own becoming.

The first construction is nakedly literal and marks bare circumstantial and *spatial* relationships, making great use of the force of prepositions and adverbs.

> ... saw
> A naked pool that lay *beneath* the hills,
> The beacon *on* the summit, and *more near*,
> A girl who bore a pitcher *on* her head,
> And seemed *with* difficult steps to force her way
> *Against* the blowing wind. (xi, 303–8)

Here is a 'difficult' world in which self and nature fall apart, a world of objects and an estranged self who 'saw' as an outcast, 'bewildered and depressed' (ii, 261). The girl who forces her way 'Against the blowing wind' is set in opposition to a resistant element, like the child who watches her. All the negative aspects of a universe of self and things are present. But even here, in this stark, uncompromising antithesis, the world is construed with feeling – 'And *seemed* with difficult steps'. It was an 'ordinary sight' (309), and in the words of the *interpreting* Wordsworth, construing his image here in the act of writing, the transition from 'saw' to 'sight' already anticipates the coalescing of mind with its objects, for a sight is what is seen outside the self and what you *have* as your possession. Appropriate to the word 'visionary' the second account of the scene constructs itself out of the first. It fuses and transfigures its elements, eliding them and eliminating the spatial and circumstantial detail, moving out of space and time but still dependent on 'that time' and on the naked pool, the beacon, the woman, which now share the solitary power and symbolic feeling of the 'lonely eminence' on which the beacon stands.

> To paint the visionary dreariness
> Which, while I looked round for my lost guide,
> Did at that time invest the naked pool,
> The beacon on the lonely eminence,
> The woman and her garments vexed and tossed
> By the strong wind. (xi, 311–16)

If 'visionary dreariness' cannot be described directly the relationships it transforms can be, and what is now described is not a landscape, not visionary dreariness itself abstracted from space and time, but the way in which it enables the poet to construe the landscape with feeling. The 'visionary dreariness' itself is offered with that openness habitual to *The Prelude*. It occurs 'while I looked round for my lost guide', while the child is doing something else, searching for what is not present. It occurs as if independently of him, a dreariness he experiences as visionary from outside himself, or a dreariness he creates as visionary through the process of his subjective looking. It 'did invest' pool, beacon, woman: clothed, but also Wordsworth must have in mind the sense of invest as to give *power* to, a sense lost in the 1850 *Prelude*, where the verb becomes 'Invested' (258). The earlier 1805 form, 'did invest', not normally used with a direct object, allows the reflexive possibility of the verb, generating power through and out of itself. Visionary dreariness is self-acting, but here so fused with objects – pool, beacon, woman, that it belongs in one existence with them. The openness of 'visionary dreariness' allows that it is given to the landscape and returned from the landscape as awareness of feeling. The child both acts upon the landscape with feeling and is acted upon by it. And the mature poet, constructing this past out of space and time in his own moment of writing, is repossessing this experience as a new creation.

This, surely, is the way in which we can be 'strong', repossessing our experience by recognising its power to act on us as an object to ourselves and recognising that it is a new creation. But just as the meaning of 'invest' as 'clothed' hints at a more separate relationship between consciousness and the world, so the 'woman', heroically transfigured from the 'girl' of the first passage (and bathetically turned to a 'female' in 1850), with her garments 'vexed and tossed/*By* the strong wind', also asserts a dualism which the passage is working to abolish. In the first passage she is an image of struggle, in the second an image of *suffering*, because she moves from an active to a passive relationship with things. This image itself becomes an image – an image of an image which actively renders the construction of experience out of experience – for the way in which we are acted on by feeling and our own consciousness, 'vexed and tossed' by our 'own creation' (1, 47). Yet this reflexive reading of the girl/ Woman transformation contains within itself another account of the world. The woman is vexed by the resistant *physical* forces around her and so Wordsworth maintains that pressure of the world on the self which is the source of images.

This dualism is virtually lost on the third iteration. Just as the second account is at a remove from the first by repetition, so the last is at a remove from what precedes it. The landscape is a spiritual one, possessed by subjective feeling, contracted to a series of abbreviated affective signs. As

> Long afterwards, I roamed about
> In daily presence of this very scene,
> Upon the naked pool and dreary crags,
> And on the melancholy beacon, fell
> The Spirit of pleasure and youth's golden gleam. (319–2)

The concrete forms become abstracted into or fused with forms of emotion – 'Deary crags', 'melancholy beacon'. They are derived out of the words and feelings which went before and yet they are new forms, new feelings, ready to be aided by and come in aid of further feeling, 'the spirit of pleasure and youth's golden gleam'. In all the descriptions (including that of Book VI, which pluralises it) only the 'naked pool' remains as a resistant, unchanged element as the passages evolve experience out of experience, compounding and recompounding it. Perhaps this emphasises an important quality of these passages. Pool,

beacon, crags, woman, become symbols only in the strictest
sense that they are signs for earlier and more expanded forms of
themselves. They do not stand for or substitute themselves for
feelings or meanings external to them. The metaphorical force of
the passage is in the process of the transformation of relationships, not in anything outside them. The symbols are not split up
into concrete forms with equivalents. This is a true involute. It
refers to nothing but itself but establishes meaning through the
accretion of new relationships, a mediation or a process of
becoming, which is its meaning.

As if to elaborate the creativity of repossessed feeling the
golden gleam passage in Book VI modulates from epiphany to
epistle, from memory to the present, in the address to Coleridge
absent and ill in Malta. 'Speed thee well! divide/Thy pleasure
with us; thy returning strength,/Receive it daily as a joy of ours;/
Share with us thy fresh spirits, whether gift/Of gales Etesian or
of loving thoughts' (256–60). The earlier phrase, 'spirit of
pleasure', is divided up and shared between 'divide/Thy pleasure
with us' and 'share with us thy fresh spirits' and the syntax
makes 'the spirit of pleasure' not merely divided up but multiplied because it is the reciprocal creation of Coleridge and his
friends. 'Thy pleasure' is 'thy returning strength' and pleasure
and strength are received back to themselves and redoubled as 'a
joy of ours'. And so 'thy fresh spirits' are the gift of a renewing
environment (the gentle affinity of gales and spirits is silently
asserted here) and of loving thoughts, loving thoughts which –
the syntax makes no distinction – are Coleridge's own and those
of his friends, redoubled and redoubling each other. The reciprocal and reflexive accounts of the world are momentarily held in
perfect balance here, to witness the benign *creativity*, both
passionate and urbane, of a human and social affection.

The descent of the Alps, so ambiguously a triumph and an
entry into chaos, answers the redeeming golden gleam passage in
Book VI. The troubled sleep of the walkers which follows it, in a
way characteristic of *The Prelude*, suggests an unease and guilt
which does not seem to have a causal relationship with the
descent. It is another of the disjunctions I have mentioned. The
noise of waters, Ezekial-like, makes '*innocent* sleep/Lie melancholy among weary bones' (580) – the bones are described as if
already scattered and dispersed in some inexplicable upheaval.
The golden gleam passage declares the using and creative

mastering of visionary dreariness. The image binds power by
enabling us to repossess feeling. By making an image the mature
poet knows about power. The vestigial affective forms, 'dreary
crags', 'melancholy beacon', are like the Hegelian moment, containing within themselves the processes of their becoming and
enabling the mature poet to be lord and master of his experience.
This poise is disrupted in the descent of the Alps, in which
syntax falls apart, and which cannot be comprehended by
images. It is an eruption of unbound power.

The inexplicable guilt can be partly understood by remembering again what is beneath the golden gleam passage I have just
discussed – the hiding place of fear. The adult's equanimity there
in Book VI should not dissipate the fierceness of what is being
said in Book XI. Wordsworth beautifully maintains concurrently the adult's control in constructing an image and the child's
terrible loss of self-hood and fear. The horror is generated partly
by loneliness but also by the contemplation of punishment for
murder. The child is vexed and tossed by a fear which takes him
see himself as an outcast. One might say, remembering that the
child is 'not six years old', that the gibbet reawakens profound
unconscious experience, so the gibbet becomes symbolically displaced on to the landscape as an image of castration – 'the
beacon on the summit'. The totality of the involute is, of course,
too complex to reduce it in this way, and what matters most is
the intensity of the child's anxiety. Wordsworth is certainly
writing about a ruthless process of psychogenesis by which a collective morality is internalised. The gibbet has a potency for the
community, its history commemorated 'by superstition of the
neighbourhood'. To know about fear is to be liberated, but fear
also *trains*, exerts a punitive discipline through the imagination
by appropriating the power of its usurping energy. The poem
does not let the mature poet's triumph in self-creation through
memory forget the brute pressure from outside upon the child.
The image which is lord and master has been created out of a
pressure on the self of the external things of sense – gibbet and
beacon – and by the pressure of guilt and fear.

The descent of the Alps is part of a massive involute of fear
and destruction which also erupts again in Book X at the description of the September Massacres. The punitive fear
underlying the golden gleam passage looks forward (because it
belongs to Book VI) and backwards (because it belongs to Book

XI) to Book X and has a second birth there. The ruin and energy of the descent of the Alps also converges on Book X in a second birth. The September Massacres are another hiding place of power. They become another gibbet which both represents and punishes unbound power.

Macbeth's 'sleep no more', which culminates the prophetic insight of Book X, conflates with the sleepless and inexplicably guilty night in Book VI after the descent of the Alps, and the horror of the September Massacres reduplicates the 'spot' in Book VI. The sleepers lie in a '*dreary* mansion, large beyond all need/With high and spacious rooms' (577–8): in Book X the sleepless poet lies in a 'high and lonely' room, near the roof 'of a large mansion or hotel, a *spot*/That would have pleased me more in quiet times'. (58–9). Just as the sleepers in Book VI are 'close upon the confluence of two streams' (576), Book VI itself is at the confluence of the past and future of the poem, looking back and looking forward. In Book X Wordsworth writes as if he had committed the crime of massacre himself, as Macbeth killed Duncan, reaching back to the time when as 'a fell destroyer' he massacred woodcocks as a child, and to the suspect freedom of being 'at large' (like a criminal, like Macbeth) in Book I. Book X confronts the energy of unbound power as it was confronted in the descent of the Alps.

Book X makes a supreme prophetic effort to reappropriate the imaginative energy of fear, to 'read' the massacres which are like a book written in a tongue the poet cannot read. Images and sense-experience of the past (Remembrances', 69), the art and history of his civilisation ('tragic fictions,/And mournful calendars of true history' (68)) conjure substantial dread. The fear '*pressed* on me almost like a fear to come' (63). Wordsworth likes to think of emotion and images as possessing substance and weight in the mind, partaking of their origins in things of sense in space and time. This passage 'remembers' but cannot altogether use the shell/book of Book V, written in an 'unknown tongue,/Which yet I understood' (94–5), and the 'characters' or writing of 'the great Apocalypse' from Book VI, in order to make a reading of the destruction of civilisation. The descent of the Alps is embedded in the language of destruction in Book X, the power that comes 'athwart': 'winds thwarting winds'; the wind/Of heaven wheels round and treads in his own steps' (X, 70–1). It has a second birth there as the poet realises that de-

struction can be reborn. The language of Book VI looks back to
the prelude to the Quixotic dream in Book V which contemplates the destruction of the earth – 'should earth by inward
throes be wrenched throughout' (V, 29) – and the fragility of
human thought – 'Oh! why hath not the Mind/Some element to
stamp her image on/In nature somewhat nearer to her own' (V,
44–6). That retrospection of Book VI to Book V is also present
in the return of the prophetic dream upon the September Massacres.

In the descent of the Alps the world can be neither read (to
read is to construe, connect, to see an eye and progress in the
sequence of language which is independent of you) nor can the
mind stamp its image on nature. Readings of relationship fall
apart and fail, as they do later in Book X. And both accounts of
the world collapse, the world as self and objects, exerting reciprocal pressure on one another, and the world as constituted
by mind as an aspect of itself. They thwart one another. The
world can neither be read as a pre-existing image or made into
an image.

> The immeasurable height
> Of woods decaying, never to be decayed,
> The stationary blasts of waterfalls,
> And every where along the hollow rent
> Winds thwarting winds, bewildered and forlorn,
> The torrents shooting from the clear blue sky,
> The rocks that muttered close upon our ears,
> Black drizzling crags that spake by the wayside
> As if a voice were in them, the sick sight
> And giddy prospect of the raving stream,
> The unfettered clouds and region of the Heavens,
> Tumult and peace, the darkness and the light –
> Were all like workings of one mind, the features
> Of the same face, blossoms upon one tree;
> Characters of the great Apocalypse,
> The types and symbols of Eternity,
> Of first, and last, and midst, and without end. (VI, 556–72)

The displaced climax of Book VI, the descent of the Alps, is
offered as one huge sentence of seventeen lines, a sentence which
simultaneously holds everything it describes in one unitary experience and yet allows each clause to fall apart from the others
as discrete items – 'The ... The ... The ... The' Wordsworth's
antitheses insist upon an inclusive relationship, even if it is a re-

lationship of opposites. 'Tumult and peace, the darkness and the light – /Were all like workings of *one* mind, the features/Of the *same* face'. But there is something queer about these antitheses: one cannot see where he gets the opposites from. Tumult, but where is peace? it seems an odd way of describing the *stationary blasts* of waterfalls, or 'winds thwarting winds'. Darkness, but where is light? Unless it is in the brief reference to the torrents shooting 'from the clear blue sky'. It is as if the sentence wrestles to exact reconcilement and resolution out of itself; it tries to save itself from chaos by wresting – the great saving activity of the mind as Book VI has already shown – an image out of the land-scape: '*Characters* of the great Apocalypse,/The *types* and *symbols* of Eternity'. The inclusive descriptions, 'workings of one mind ... blossoms upon one tree', glance back to the 'one surpassing life' imaged in the abstractions of geometry and the young poet's wreathing of his own imaginative life round the ash fused with ivy, 'One tree' in many senses, and appear to subsume thought into imagery, as Wordsworth has so carefully worked to do in the early part of the book. But Apocalypse and Eternity are opposed to one another, for one is an ending, a de-struction, the other is endlessness, permanence, timelessness. The great sentence reads two ways. The Apocalypse might be subsumed appositionally into the types and symbols of Eternity and the final line is an affirmation of resolution – the end of time becoming timelessness – 'Of first, and last, and midst, and without end'. Or Apocalypse and Eternity remain as irreconcil-able opposites within the landscape which offers, simultaneous but disjunct, an image of destruction and of permanence, and the final line breaks apart into a series of conjunctions, severed between time, 'First and last', and the impossible leap to Eternity, 'and without end'. Whether vainly or successfully 'and midst', appropriately in the 'midst' of this line, turns between the two. One can be in the midst of time, between the first and last, or one can be in a permanent state of 'midst', which must be Eternity.

The two syntaxes collapse into one another. The reciprocal universe of self and other collapses into a world of estranged and threatening objects, 'bewildered and forlorn' (which reduplicates 'bewildered and depressed' from the passage celebrating the connectedness of self and world in Book II) acting in disconnec-tion from themselves and the onlooker. The **reflexive,**

mind-construed universe increasingly thrusts towards dissolution, the identity of categories confused not fused, so that the
further the descent the greater the chaos and insanity. The
greater the chaos the more relationships become impossible.
They are immobilised. For all its violence paralysis is enacted by
this sentence. It moves towards inertia. Power turns against
itself and is blocked – 'winds thwarting winds'.

A landscape 'unfettered', clouds 'unfettered' from 'the *region
of the Heavens*', a space, the syntax allows, also unfettered from
the autonomous clouds, is the immediate impression of the
passage: signs or writings of the Apocalypse. Brook and road, to
begin with 'fellow-travellers', become dissociated as the 'giddy
prospect of the raving stream' moves independently from the
'drizzling crags that spake by the wayside', 'rocks that muttered
close upon our ears', threatening but uninterpretable: they
speak but not, it seems, to anyone (mountains and crags coming
close of course, are a recurrent threat in *The Prelude*). Torrents
shoot *from* 'the clear blue sky', out of it, or *away* from it as if
tearing themselves apart from it. At the same time as objects do
not appear to be acting on anything, their nature becomes
almost arbitarily fused with those of other categories. Woods
are 'decaying, never to be decayed', held in a permanent 'midst'
of death, but at the same time the 'immeasurable' *height* of
woods is decaying: space and trees are both in decay. With the
paradox, 'stationary blasts' of waterfalls, the collision of opposites makes neither word paramount, so that they are locked
in a state of opposition. 'Blasts', the qualities of the winds which
follow seem to be displaced on to waterfalls, just as the speaking
voice of torrent and streams (a common metaphor in *The
Prelude*) is displaced on to rocks and crags, and just as the
'prospect' we normally associate with a visual trajectory
upward and outward to rocks and crags is displaced downwards
on to the 'giddy prospect' of the 'raving stream'. And as the
passage proceeds the sense of the individual identity of a perceiver and a perceived world becomes lost. The 'sick *sight*'
and '*giddy* prospect' of the stream is also a possession of the
perceiver, the *poet's* sickness and giddiness coalescing with
the objects of perception and becoming one identity with them.

It is hard to believe that the massive inertia and intense
physical violence of this landscape can be so smoothly transformed into symbol, hard to believe they are *all* like workings of

'one mind'. The ambiguity of 'of' in the insistence upon symbol reawakens doubts about the source of power, 'characters *of* the great Apocalypse,/The types and symbols *of* Eternity'. The world inscribed by the Apocalypse could belong to it as its attribute or simply as its equivalent: the 'characters' could be a manifestation of it or a representation of it. The 'workings' of the 'one mind' could be God's activity or the activity of the onlooker's consciousness. And above all the abstracting and recombining of the symbol-making process *does* seem abstract, fixed and static, willed. It does not even match what it describes. For once Wordsworth's simile, the betraying 'like', does seem uncertain. 'Like' suggests equivalence, the attempt to match, and this fails. Unbound power breaks out of the image in chaos. Haunting this passage is the possibility that we can neither construe the universe as a world of self, objects and God nor as a world in which mind as God constitutes itself as object. There is no adequate image of relationship or of violence or control. Indeed, no account of human nature or nature and the relationship between them is possible.

The strange journey taken at the wong time is an analogue of the crossing of the Alps. There are recollections of Milton's hell – the mountains are seen by their 'darkness visible' (645) and the static, sick sea of Coleridge's '*Ancient Mariner*' – the 'dull red image of the moon' (636) on the water changes its shape but not its nature like a 'snake'. It is an uninterpretable landscape where everything is of the surface. If image-making collapses and idealist syntax is discredited, then you are left with a world of mere surface. The superficial bites of itching insects, the image of the moon 'bedded *on*' the water's surface, the travellers immobilised *on* the rock, express a world of superficial experience. Space and time are dislocated, the clock unintelligible, the noise of insects like those at noon. And yet there is comedy in this passage. And, always implacably surprising, the verse modulates to a summing up of the experience as the opposite of what it seems. The mind was *not* a 'mean pensioner/ On outward form' (667–8), simply, perhaps, because the poem has understood that mind can be. It knows itself. The description of the world of surface or 'outward form' itself constitutes and makes possible that creative act of awareness or *recognition*.

The inexplicable confidence here is akin to the great, confident celebration of imagination with its flagrant idealist optimism, another moment of *recognition*, which breaks into the poem before the crushing power of the descent. It refuses to recognise failure – 'to my soul I say – I recognise thy glory'. The syntax allows what is recognised to be the glory of 'my soul' which is identified with the imagination. And so the poet is self-consciously aware, with a reflex act of contemplation, of his own power. The invisible world of infinitude is ambiguously the world of God or of mind, released from and by the light of sense to the consciousness which projects, combines, conflates and synthesises experience because it is in a state of need and *desire*. The ardour of imagination needs to shape life by creating possibilities which give it meaning and value. Therefore the naïvely optimistic rush through France, the disappointed anticipation of Mont Blanc, the non-climax of crossing the Alps, are not to be undervalued because hopes were not realised. A 'soul-less image' need not usurp upon a 'living thought' (455), because it is precisely imagination's 'strength/Of usurpation' which creates living thought: The passage is a corrective in advance to the willed, static unity exacted from the descent, offering something 'ever more about to be', becoming instead of completeness. It is, of course, an intervention by the poet, who reads his poem retrospectively, with a significance it cannot know, and can only offer to him by having been written in the form it has taken up to this point.

And yet the usurping imagination comes 'Athwart' (529). 'I was lost as in a cloud.' The writer of the poem, a past self, or the young traveller, could be the subject of this sentence. Does the power of imagination occur in the past narrative or to the narrative of the present? 'Halted without a struggle to break through' (530): halted? obstructed? to break *through* into or *out of* the 'cloud' of consciousness or the ambiguous 'cloud' of some external power surrounding him? And why should one '*struggle*'? The extraordinary formulation here expresses the mystery of the power which comes 'Athwart', a mystery which has to be sustained if the power of mind and the power of destruction are not to come together and 'usurp'. 'I am lost,' Wordsworth says again after the ascent of Snowdon. The affinity between the power of imagination and the power experienced in the descent of the Alps, carefully maintained in its 'hiding place' in 1805, is made clearer in the 1850 *Prelude*. Just as the travellers experience the dissolution of the landscape when they enter the 'chasm' of Simplon, so imagination 'rose from the mind's *abyss*' (594) in the passage on imagination in the 1850 *Prelude*. The power of mind and the power of destruction (and correspondingly of idealism and revolution) come together here more explicitly, perhaps because Wordsworth had safely abandoned the dangerous claims of idealism by the time of writing this later version, a new poem, and could be clearer about the threatening convergence of imagination and destructive power.

In awe of his poem in the 1805 *Prelude*, Wordsworth writes as if the eye and progress of his poem is a mystery to him. Both the passage on imagination and the descent of the Alps are offered as mysterious, unassimilable involutes, holding the energies of destruction and creation within themselves, threat and triumph. The poem understands, 'recognises', its complexity without interpreting itself. True to the reflexive self-creative nature of this poem, the inexplicable passage on imagination offers the terms in which the literal details of the ascent of Snowdon are described. This is Wordsworth's last great attempt to reformulate an image which expresses the relationship of consciousness and world. The two passages are not equivalent but forms of one another. The flash of moonlight, the usurping mist 'upheaved', the chasm, the 'soul, the imagination of the whole': all these are literal occurrences which Book VI offers as metaphor in the passage on imagination. Image, indeed, creates the experience 'about to be'. The ascent of Snowdon is an attempt to redeem the negatives of the earlier passages connected with the Simplon Pass experience by reforming their elements. Yet, characteristic of *The Prelude*, the ascent asks the same questions. *The Prelude* is probably the most open of all Romantic poems, even as it claims decisions and affirmations.

The Prelude is a long search for adequate images of relationship which enable the mind to be lord and master while finally recognising the energy which comes so dangerously from the abyss. It is a search which is never really completed. In this sense it could be open to Marx's strictures on Hegel's idealism, perhaps. Everything is solved at the level of mind. Wordsworth can only go on repeating and recreating images of consciousness. On the other hand, the continual dialogue between the two syntaxes, reflexive and reciprocal, constituting the world as mind and challenging that assertion, disputing and refuting one another, enables Wordsworth to acknowledge the strengths of idealist language and its weaknesses. In this way the poem comes near to acknowledging Marx's claim that the self maintains its identity by being an object to something else, just as that other is an object to it. The turnings intricate between reflexive and reciprocal syntaxes make for an astonishing and complex dialogue.

It is interesting that the 1850 *Prelude* clarifies the ambiguities of most of the passages I have discussed, eliminating or muting the reflexive idealist possibilities. The coalescing syntax of the first paragraph, for instance, the description of the ash/ivy, the rapid river, are subtly rearranged so that things fused with one another in 1805 are pushed apart. The double concurrent syntax disappears, or appears fitfully and arbitrarily, without the continuous dialectical rigour of the 1805 *Prelude*. In 1850 the reflexive possibilities of imagination, 'lifting up itself', disappear, and Wordsworth inserts 'to my *conscious* soul I *now* can say ... I recognise thy glory'. The interpolation makes it possible to conceive of imagination as an irrational eruption of the unconscious which is dissociated from the poet's 'conscious' soul, not an organic attribute of self. In fact, imagination and power are mystified and made more inexplicable and more irrational by 1850 because they are excluded from the more 'rational' and directly theological account of the world offered there. The inconsistencies and contradictions are smoothed out, making it a superficially more orderly poem, but a poem which is less self-questioning. The 1805 poem points to complexities and contradictions and gives them meaningfulness and necessity by allowing difficulties to evolve fully out of the mystery of words. Holding as it does to a clearer universe of self and things, and moving towards a more overtly moral understanding of human nature, the 1850 *Prelude* is a fine and majestic poem, but another poem, not the 1805 revised. It is a Victorian poem, perhaps, but one which a Victorian could not have written. By 1850 its certainties could no longer be achieved.

NOTE

All references are to *The Prelude: A Parallel Text*, J. C. Maxwell (ed.), London, 1971.

Unless otherwise stated italicised words are my own.

Since Wordsworth's punctuation is largely the construction of editors I have been cautious about making punctuation of critical importance in my discussion of the syntax.

CHAPTER 3

Blake's Simplicity: Jerusalem, Chapter I

You shall not bring me down to believe such fitting and fitted. I know better ... does not this Fit, and is not Fitting most exquisitely too, but to what? – Not to Mind, but to the Vile Body only and to its Laws of Good and Evil and its Enmities against Mind.

Blake's furious and famous annotation to *The Excursion* expresses his rage against a universe seen in terms of mechanistic dualism and separation and so he attacked Wordsworth for colluding with dualism by describing the human mind as exquisitely fitted to the external world, the external world to the human mind. In *The Excursion* Wordsworth writes without the tentativeness, the sense of the mystery of his own poem, to be found in the 1805 *Prelude,* and perhaps the choice of the mechanistic word 'fitting' justifies Blake's fury. Blake's rage against 'fitting' as the principle of perception is categorical, and his account of mind is the boldest, the most extreme and, because absolute and systematic, the simplest, of any nineteenth-century poet. 'For all things exist in the human imagination' (Ch. 3, Pl. 69, 25). Nothing lies outside the self. The human mind and the universe do not exist inertly outside one another. The consistent present tense of this 'giant' poem, which seems to have been worked on over a space of nearly twenty years, strives to appropriate the *is*-ness of the verb to be, maintaining the presentness of pure undifferentiated being.

The distinction between subject and object is not exactly obliterated in Blake's vision: he has no need of this; the universe is simply and insistently constituted without dualism, *seen* without it. 'The tree which moves some to tears of joy is in the eyes of others only a green thing which stands in the way.' To see the vegetative world as something external, standing in the way, is not to see the world truly. It is to see things 'as deformity, and loveliness as a dry tree', as the monstrous Hand looks upon an alienated world (Ch. I, Pl. 9, 8). Things are not fitted together in Blake's poetry: they belong together without distinctions of category, just as Los sees past, present and future 'existing all at once'. There is narrative order in *Jerusalem*, but not a causal or temporal sequence to be derived from it. And so, too, a sigh, a smile, a tear, a hair, a particle of dust (Ch. 1, Pl. 13, 66) exist all at once in the same terms and as part of the same series, constituted without reference to their mental or physical categories. The tear, the precipitation of emotion, fuses both categories and participates in each. It is an 'intellectual thing', as Blake writes in Chapter 3, in a characteristically brilliant and stark conflation. Contraries can bleed without the mediation of explicit metaphorical signs, states behaving as if they are bodies. And it is possible to ask, which seems an arcane question even for Blake, whether Skofield is Bath or Canterbury (17, 59).

Los' question, arcane though it might seem, is simpler than it looks, and its unperturbed neglect of categories dramatises the procedure of the poem as a whole. Skofield, one of Blake's persecutors, is an ally of the three-headed Hand, (Blake's name for the brothers Hunt), and one of the sons of Albion. He has 'rooted' himself in Jerusalem, who properly belongs to Albion. He is propagating a corrupt and druidical morality of revenge and sacrifice, destroying the unity of Albion and Jerusalem which belong together because both Britain and Jerusalem are the 'primitive seat of patriarchal religion' and the wisdom of Abraham. Los will not allow him to assimilate or identify himself with the 'friends' of Albion, the Cathedral cities of England who have not lost the vision of Golgonooza and understand the identification of Albion and Palestine. The stark visual metonymy of the question condenses a typology in which Jewish and British legend are equivalents and an allegory in which places and persons are interchangeable. And yet to speak in terms of typologies and equivalents, of allegory, emblem, analogy, or even of geography and history, sequential time and space, or theories of mind, is to do violence to Blake's conception of imagination. It concedes to the epistemology of 'fitting' which he hated. It would mean the comparing and objecting which is the manifestation of the divided universe of Bacon, Locke and Newton.

Things are not seen as analogies or equivalents or images of one another but are compounded in a series of bold conflations and monistic amalgams. When Hand and Hyle root into Jerusalem, enrooting into 'every nation' and the sons of Albion are propagating 'over the whole earth', the narrative condenses legend, geography and the moral and imaginative terms by which we understand it into a multi-form amalgam. Los, to prevent the dereliction of Albion and Jerusalem by the twelve sons, attempts to reunite Albion with its Jewish heritage by identifying the counties of England, Scotland and Wales with the twelve tribes of Israel, placing them side by side in a formal inventory. Legend, geography, space, value, are conflated. The narrative refutes equivalence and correspondence, and so does Blake's language. The structure of his metaphor tends towards either synecdoche or metonymy, where the interchange of analogy and the movement between literal and figurative is not overt. In both figures you seize your part or your whole and declare that this *is*.

Such amalgamations mean that, though Blake himself writes of a 'system' in *Jerusalem*, and though indeed a system can be codified from it, the appearance of the poem is random and unsystematic. But it is not a kind of eschatological litter which requires indexing. Blake writes of his poem as a *vision* more frequently then he describes it as a system. The conflations are seen as entities, not mapped as correspondences, so that a reading of *Jerusalem* is a *seeing* of it. Hand, Hyle, the twelve sons of Albion and their dogma, coalesce grotesquely as 'a mighty polypus', a many-headed totality growing without any principle of order over the whole earth. The symmetry of Los' inventory of tribes and countries is a visualising of the living order he wants to maintain. This is clear when the inventory is seen in the original design of the poem. The symmetry and order of Plate 16 is set solidly in visual antithesis to the disorder which comes before it. 'But whatever is *visible* to the generated man/Is a creation of mercy and love from the Satanic void' (Pl. 13, 44–5). Blake utters this merciful understanding in parenthesis at the building of Golgonooza. The poem is organised as a seeing, and above all according to a principle of 'seeing' space. When the implications of this play with space are apparent the poem becomes the most highly ordered of structures, formed with the consistency and virtuosity of simplicity.

That Blake's seeing of his poem should happen with a seeming disregard for particularities and with a peculiar lack of reference to the familiar organisation of sense experience often accounts for the stark grotesqueness of his conflations. But this should not be surprising. Sensory experience should not, for Blake or for his readers, 'stand in the way' of perception. It is not a thing produced in response to a universe divided from mind. It has to be broken up, reorganised, seen anew, assimilated to new forms and different categories. To see is not to be enslaved by the literal, mimetic representation, but to compound new seeings. In this way Blake avoids the splitting apart of symbol and referent because his seeing *is*, a new experience. The arresting quality of his writing comes not from the abolition of the sensory but from the dislocation of normal expectations about it. Sensory experience is reconstituted, not done away with. Albion can walk in his own geography, a person and a place, but he can only do so when the paradox is pictured. In the same way states of mind can become spaces, the mythological history of Britain, biblical legend and rationalist philosophy can coalesce into persona. Los, his iron-shod feet 'on London stone', opens his furnaces to the spectre with whom he duels at the start of the chapter to reveal 'Babel and Shinar,/Across all Europe and Asia' (8, 23–4). It is necessary to see these as places mapped out, biblical and modern geographies immediately coexisting and superimposed on one another and stretching over London itself, so that the identification of Old Testament legend and modern Europe can be made.

It is with spaces and places that Blake's most dramatic visual conflations are made. To take some examples from the narrative which follows Albion's invocation at the beginning of the poem (the contents of Plate 5, to which I refer at several points in this chapter, are reproduced at the end of this chapter, pp. 111–12), and which actually contains the whole future of the poem within itself: just as Blake's hand 'trembles exceedingly upon the Rock of Ages' (5, 23), so 'Lincoln and Norwich stand trembling on the brink of Udan-Adan' (5, 10), the formless, passive lake of chaos, Entuthon Benython. The effect of these juxtapositions comes from their being seen as places (the lake) and solid things (the Rock) as well as being seen as abstractions, so that Blake's hand trembles on Rock and Eternity simultaneously, and the cities are ready to collapse into lake and chaos together. The sons of Los attack Golgonooza and 'revolve' upon the furnace of Los, hoping to destroy it (27) and, without temporal progression

'revolve into the furnaces' (31). The furnaces have multiplied
and pluralised without any mediating explanation. The furnaces
are built in Golgonooza, in Albion, and yet seem to encompass
both. Blake, 'in London's darkness', contemplating the infinitely
divided sons and daughters of Albion as golden looms and
furnaces of beryl (the male sons of Albion have elliptically taken
on the attributes of Los' furnace) is inside the things he contemplates – 'their rushing fires overwhelm my soul' (35). '*Their*
rushing fires': sons and daughters and Los' fires are fused as they
overwhelm the poet. Jerusalem, wandering 'upon the mountains' (48), the mountains of Gilead (40) or the mountains of
Albion (4) or both, towards the east where the furnaces are and
'Howling in pain' is, it seems, simultaneously included within
them. The sentence continues in a series of present participles
which make no distinction of temporal progression possible
because they conflate actions as simultaneity – 'redounding...
Out from the furnaces of Los' (49–50).

The expansion, conflation and contraction of space behaves
in the same way as the numerical versatility of the personages in
the poem who multiply, diverge, coalesce. The twelve aberrant
daughters of Albion, their names drawn from English myth-
ology, themselves the emanations or attributes of the sons of
Albion, whose names belong to the contemporary England of
Blake's jurors, 'unite' into Tirzah and Rahab. These have to be
'seen' as shifting, multiform figures and not in terms of a causal
sequence of transformations of identity. Similarly, when at the
end of the section, Los' tears 'fall/Incessant before the furnaces'
(66–7) because he has heard Jerusalem's 'lamentations in the
deeps afar' (66), he and Jerusalem are momentarily identified. In
'the deeps afar' locates or displaces both of them by including
them both. The spatial designation includes equally subject and
object – 'her lamentations in the deeps afar': 'Los heard ... in
the deeps afar'. The syntax accomplishes an inclusion of Los
within Jerusalem, Jerusalem within Los, just as the weeping Los,
whose 'tears fall/Incessant', exchanges attributes with Blake,
whose 'tears fall day and night'. But Blake, in London, seeing
and making his vision, is overwhelmed by the rushing fires of the
furnaces: Los, 'in the deeps afar', stands before the furnaces. The
parallelism is not there to keep the two descriptions apart, but to
enable the first to be included within the second, the poem's
maker to be included in what he has made. Los before his

furnaces encompasses the poet. In the same way the furnaces by which Los stands have included the spaces which included them.

The play with space in the section on Plate 5 is not arbitrary. The building of Golgonooza which is Los' answer to the decay of Albion suggests how space should be seen and read. Golgonooza is 'fourfold in every direction'; 'Each within other' (12, 48). Blake means that fourfoldedness contains fourfoldedness within fourfoldedness to infinity. East, West, South and North each including and reduplicating East, West, South and North within itself eternally enfolds each within the other, effectively obliterating mechanical duration and measurement. The visualisation of space in the poem, expanding by enfolding itself within itself, is a living rendering of this infinite expansion. This can be seen in the larger narrative organisation of the poem, in the working of Blake's syntax and in the structure of his metaphors.

The narrative structure is a reduplication of this enfolding. The narrative is not successive but simultaneous. 'Events' are like a palimpsest superimposed over one another. In fact, by the time the section on Plate 5 is completed, all the events in the first chapter have taken place. Blake prefigures the essential opposition of the poem – 'Of the building of Golgonooza, and of the terrors of Entuthon' (24), and defines the nature of the 'indefinite unmeasurable' night of Entuthon, 'Abstract philosophy warring in enmity against imagination' (57). Albion's sons and daughters have divided and are bending their fury 'to desolate Golgonooza', which is not described as being 'built' until later in the chapter (Plate 12). The destruction and building and rebuilding of the city are mutually existing states of being. If 'all things exist in the human imagination', they do not obey the dictates of temporal order or causal sequence. They are enfolded each within other, coexisting simultaneously. As the almost continuous present tense suggests, adding descriptions to one another and cumulatively enlarging but not arranging them sequentially in temporal succession, the experiences of the narrative are concurrent. The division of Los' spectre from him is described three times as if this is a continuous and recurrent process. 'But *still* the spectre divided' (6, 12), a division simultaneous with the division of his emanation (6, 3). The division of the spectre is recurred to yet again on Plate 17 (1) and not as a separate event but as part of the same 'event'. In the same way Jerusalem is timelessly 'wandering' in the void which is within Albion himself at many points in the poem (12, 18, 43). 'And Los beheld the mild emanation of Jerusalem, eastward bending/Her revolutions toward the starry wheels in maternal anguish' (14, 31–2).

Similarly, although at the end of the chapter Albion 'dies' and fled 'inward', the end of the chapter is enfolded within the beginning. But at the start of the poem Beulah's daughters 'hold the immortal form', the dead external form of Albion. And 'all within is opened into the deeps of Entuthon Benython' (5, 56). The 'centre' of Albion is already passing out into or giving access to chaos at the start of the chapter. There is a doubleness in 'opening into' which dissolves the syntax and the spaces it designates to formlessness as chaos seems to be something which is both entered into and invading at the same time. Albion is opening inwards in a shadowy negative reflection of the ever-expanding 'eternal worlds', the worlds of thought into which man's eyes can open 'inwards', which Blake describes with such triumph at the beginning of this section (5, 18–20).

To turn again to the beginning of the poem, and to Blake's celebration of imagination at the start of the chapter, is to see that its structure has that movement of expansion and ingesting of itself which is the principle of the poem. The structure of the language suggests how the imagination organises and includes within itself the world of non-being which, at the turning point of the chapter, Los fails to achieve in spite of his heroic anger – 'never, never shall thou be organised' (17, 41). Language constitutes the idea of mind in its organisation, but also, and particularly as the poem develops, it offers threats to the bold rejection of the world of subject and object. I shall move to these threats at a later stage in my discussion. For the moment, it is necessary to establish the expanding nature of the poem more fully.

> To open the eternal worlds, to open the immortal eyes
> Of man inwards into the worlds of thought – into Eternity
> Ever expanding in the bosom of God, the human imagination. (5, 18–20)

The infinitives 'To open ... to open' deny a subject/object relationship. The appositional series fuses the successive elements of the sentence together, expanding and identifying 'eternal worlds' with 'immortal eyes'. The line break holds them together as an entity momentarily before the new line asserts that these are the 'immortal eyes/Of *man*'. The 'immortal' eyes of man, already synonymous with 'eternal *worlds*', open 'inwards' into further '*worlds* of thought' which subsume the 'eternal worlds'. The worlds of thought which subsume the eternal worlds again appositionally became synonymous with 'Eternity', and 'Eternity' expands to include within itself both eternal worlds and worlds of thought. Eternity, 'ever-expanding in the bosom of God', is equated with the *human* imagination once more, which is also, the appositional syntax allows, equated with God. The human imagination, the syntax also allows, is also 'ever-expanding', and now includes itself and Eternity within itself. The effect is not of equation but of expansion as the elements of the language are enfolded each within other in a successive series of enlargements.

This ever-expanding, self-enfolding structure of language which expresses the nature of mind also inform the nature of metaphor.

> the false tongue
> Beneath Beulah, as a watery flame revolving every way,
> And as dark roots and stems, a forest of affliction, growing
> In seas of sorrow.

This is the false tongue of Tharmas, who inhabits the region of chaos. Tharmas, the vegetated tongue is already a giant synecdoche. The tongue, which has the horrible capacity to 'revolve', comprises a series of smaller synecdoches; brain, heart, bowels. It has, in fact, swallowed up those words for parts of the body which often signify the self. And in this consuming it has shifted its status from part to whole, from synecdoche to metonymy. The rhythm of Blake's metaphor is the splitting of synecdoche which strives to coalesce into metonymy which splits again, as Albion himself splits and coalesces, as persona, or geography. And just as the tongue subsumes these things so the structure of the metaphor subsumes its earlier terms until a second term engulfs the first, but, paradoxically, a second term which partakes of the first. The tongue is first 'as a watery flame', that is, behaving as, manifesting itself as; the 'as' moves away from simile, which would be to concede to the world of 'fitting'. It is 'watery' because it burns feebly and because in 'revolving every way' (a 'tongue' of flame licks in all directions) it *diffuses* itself.

The paradox of 'watery' also suggests that it subverts its own nature: it is not concentrated and intense (like the fires of Los) but belongs to a formless, shapeless element, the world of non-entity. The next line adds a second metaphor to the first as the pluralised tongues of flame become 'dark roots and stems', and a third metaphor to this as the dark roots and stems become 'a forest of affliction'. The forest of affliction is a metaphor of a metaphor, continuing and expanding the vocabulary of growth. The metaphor of roots and stems is subsumed in its entirety into the new one. Its elements do not correspond in an absolute parallel with the forest *of affliction* as the 'tongues' of 'roots and stems' correlate with 'tongues' of flame. Roots and stems are assimilated only into the first term, 'forest'. The forest of affliction is a radically different kind of metaphor, which misses out a mediating connection between vegetation and state of mind. 'Forest' and 'affliction' do not exchange qualities as the earlier metaphors do: we can only see what qualities of forest (its looming, oppressive aspect) are needed to illuminate affliction by deriving them from affliction itself and by thinking of affliction as a totality. Affliction is a new term which engulfs the earlier terms and abruptly assimilates them from biological into mental entities. But of course, it is affliction 'growing' as well as affliction alone which is the new term. Affliction does allow forest to confer some of its nature upon it by seizing and appropriating the idea of organic growth which is converted into the ever-expanding enlargement of a mental state. Affliction is itself in turn engulfed. Forests of affliction grow 'in seas of sorrow'. So nearly is 'sorrow' a synonym for affliction, that affliction grows in attributes of itself which turn out to include it. The formless, inchoate seas also take into themselves the 'watery' nature of the tongues of flame, include them and are included by them. Metaphor expands by enfolding itself within itself.

The autonomy of Blake's metaphor, refusing to be enslaved by rigorous correlations and expanding by including expansion within itself, is a fine model of an ontology in which everything exists in the human imagination. The poem's syntax is organised in the same way and though it is here in particular that one begins to wonder whether it is self-defeating there is no doubt about its virtuosity.

To turn again to the beginning of the poem and to Plate 5 which contains lines 1–68. Blake's sentences are often thought of as ramifying, casual imitations of the prolific repetitiveness of the Bible, and above all as monotonous and loose. Blake claimed otherwise: 'Every word and every letter is studied and put into its fit place'. (Plate 3, 43). His sentences proceed by addition and apposition without connectives or relatives, expanding themselves in a series of participles and participle phrases which repeatedly describe and redound upon the subject, growths from the subject. An astonishing versatility with verbs which take prepositions rather than being immediately followed by a direct object ensures a constant postponement of the object. Only three verbs in this passage are immediately followed by an object or else the language works with the verb 'to be' or infinitives. The effect of this is of a predicate indefinitely extending itself, never completing itself and never coming to rest. And so the sentences seem to be at once growing parthogenetically from the subject, and continuously moving outwards and expanding themselves. The syntax expresses a world which evolves without the existence of subject facing object, object facing subject, the world which redounds from and to the subject, all things existing in the human imagination.

Phrases or phrase clusters belong variously to several different words or phrases within the sentence without finally settling. These conflations of concord give the sentence a multifold enlargement. It grows in several directions at once. The poem evolves out of itself in no linear sense. Repetition continually returns upon itself and in doing so shifts and transforms relationships and configurations of description. It enables the poem to come into being in its prolific fullness by preparing for new relationships.

> The banks of the Thames are clouded, the ancient porches of Albion are
> Darkened; they are drawn through unbounded space, scattered upon
> The void in incoherent despair. Cambridge & Oxford & London
> Are driven among the starry wheels, rent away and dissipated,
> In chasms & Abysses of sorrow, enlarged without dimension, terrible.
> Albion's mountains run with blood.

'Are clouded ... are/Darkened ... are drawn ... scattered... Are driven ... rent away and dissipated.' Participles make all activities concurrent. Thames, Albion, Cambridge, Oxford, London are insistently acted upon by some indeterminate energy which does not find grammatical expression. 'Rent away' by what, and from what? In default of other relationships the actions return upon themselves. Clouded and darkened by cloudedness and darkness, drawn, scattered, by the volition and self-acting nature of drawn-ness, scatteredness. The agents of drawn and scattered are themselves. 'Drawn *through* unbounded space, scattered *upon*/The void ... driven *among* the starry wheels ... dissipated,/*In* chasms and abysses of sorrow'. These self-extending prepositions are extraordinary because they subvert the nature of prepositions by refusing to relate or come to rest. To be drawn *through* space without limit is to be drawn forever. 'Scattered upon' before the line break holds up 'uponness' indefinitely. It seems to come to rest in 'The void' in the next line but a substantive resting point is voided, as if the end of the line is a precipice which never ends, for the following line ensures that things are scattered upon nothing. The syntax allows that as well as being in a state of incoherent despair, these entities are scattered upon the void *in* incoherent despair, that is, the void, which is *within* incoherent despair itself. Void and despair become part of one another and of their subjects which become the terrible spaces of their own mental state, incoherent indeed.

'Incoherent despair' also relates to another part of the sentence: 'they are drawn ... in incoherent despair'. So the indeterminate energy acting as agent and the inner state of the subjects are identified. 'Incoherent despair' continually enlarges by enlarging different aspects of the sentence. It is truly incoherent because it is dissipating itself endlessly in space and mind. In the same way 'enlarged without dimension' describes equally the towns and the mysterious 'starry wheels' they are driven among, and these, alike are 'rent away and dissipated,/In chasms and abysses of sorrow'. Space shapes an unshapeable emotion, sorrow, which is truly 'without dimension'. Chasms, abysses and sorrow are like the entities of cities and the starry wheels 'enlarged without dimension'. Every component of the sentence is steadily enlarged and expanded with a multiple expansion. The exclamation, 'terrible', floating free at the end of the sentence includes the processes at work in the sentence itself. It *is* terrible because the structure of the language creates an ever enlarging formlessness. The endlessness of the process has a strange energy about it. The sentence manages to render that energy and to *organise* formlessness.

'Albion's mountains run with blood.' The poem moves inwards from dissipation in space to destruction on earth, which is the double of that dissipation, the cries of war 'Resounding' into the 'unbounded night' as Albion is drawn through 'unbounded space'. Albion, of course, personification and geography, contains the cries of war. As the entities expand and dissipate, other cities and places, Ely, Wales, Scotland, wither and shrink. This is another equal and opposite aspect of formlessness and death and it reduplicates the forms of the first five lines as passives act on themselves – 'small and withered and *darkened*' (Albion's portals are *darkened*). Places and actions are subsumed into the following sentence and without mediating transition the ancient biblical world enfolds Albion – Jerusalem is 'scattered abroad like a cloud of smoke through non-entity' (earlier, 'scattered upon/The void'). The conflated Albion/Britain/Jerusalem are incoherence, expanding, dissipating, shrinking, withering simultaneously. The mysterious, unlocated formlessness, the unexplained presences of the starry wheels, the unexplained actions and places, 'the brink of Udan-Adan', the 'warriors in the vale of Entuthon Benython', are gradually given content by the action of the sentences, their meaning as non-entity brought into being by the structure of the syntax. The nature of non-being is expanded once again in a shocking manifestation of the making of it, human sacrifice.

> Moab & Ammon ... Aram
> Receive her little ones for sacrifice and the delights of cruelty.

Dissipation is mental state and action. It has its issue in sacrificial murder. Significantly, 'her little ones' is the first direct object in the poem. The sacrifice is expanded once again as the sons of Albion wait to 'devour' the sleeping humanity of Albion.

The poem expands and subsumes itself in endless replication. But the word 'devour' here suggests the difficulties inherent in the structure of Blake's language: it could be described as ever-expanding or ever-subsuming, creative or devouring, enlarging or ingesting, engorging itself. The language of the poem has to construe what is creative and devouring, what is expansive and what is dissipating, within the same structures. It construes the ever-expanding world of human imagination and Entuthon enlarged without dimension out of the same elements.

'Contraries mutually exist,' Los says (17, 33), in his struggle with his spectre, expressing the struggle of this chapter. The language expresses at one and the same time the negative energy of destructive separation of experience into antitheses and negations (which 'exist not', according to Los) and the creative incorporation of negation as a contrary or opposition which belongs meaningfully to its counterpart. It has to do better than Los. 'While I write of the building of Golgonooza, and of the terrors of Entuthon,' Blake says (5, 24). Golgonooza and Entuthon are expressed as antitheses: Entuthon is 'fitted' or 'objected' (as Los puts it at the moment of his failure) to and against Golgonooza, compared and contrasted to it. At the same time it is expressed as a contradiction, which is to make it part of a reciprocal relationship. 'While I write of the building of Golgonooza... *and* [simultaneously] of Entuthon.' 'The building of', a gerund, a verbal noun, an action, is paralleled with 'the terrors of', indeterminately a mental state or something outside the self *inducing* terror. But the parallelism is not a true parallelism. The 'building of' Golgonooza incorporates Entuthon, for the syntax allows for another and expanded parallelism – 'while I write of the building of Golgonooza and of [the building of] the terrors'. As Golgonooza is built so the terrors are constructed, incorporated. The antithesis resolves itself into a contrary in which one extreme requires the other, constructing the other. Later in the description of the building of Golgonooza Blake says that Golgonooza 'contains' Ulro fourfold. It does not negate non-entity.

'Never, never shalt thou be organised/But as a distorted and reversed reflection in the darkness/And in the non-entity,' Los says to his spectre (17, 41–3). This is the moment of collapse and failure. He refuses to give creative embodiment and shape to non-being and in expressing it as a negation turns his back on it and thus partakes of negation. Creation and non-entity both become distorted reflections of the other. At Los' words the whole poem wheels or revolves upon itself and becomes a reversed reflection of the earlier part. The violation of a reversed reflection is typical of Blake's perfervidly systematic visualising. A mirror-image is already a reversed reflection, mirrors match images in true opposition, left to left, right to right, a counterpart which belongs meaningfully to its opposite as contraries do. A *reversed* reflection distorts this opposition either by reversing the reversal, or, and Blake meant this sickening and grotesque alternative, I think, by producing an image which *has its back to you*, a negation of the thing imaged. Appropriately the spectre divides from Los' back because Los has turned his back on him, refused to incorporate him. Los' emanation, Enitharmon, turning her back on him, divides from his bosom. Los is an enslaved replication of Hand, who sends Hyle and Coban forth 'from his bosom' (18, 42).

An image with its back to you is truly external. It is another visualising of the 'objecting' which occurs when the spectre is negated. With a brilliant spatial conceptualising of the Lockean thinker first noticed by Northrop Frye (*Fearful Symmetry*), the barren world of subject and object is conceived as a total 'outside'. 'There is an outside spread without and an outside spread within' (18, 2). The self, reduced to an '*outline* of identity', conceives the external world as negation, separate from him, outside and 'without' (deprived is the secondary meaning which follows): but his own 'within' is also conceived of as cut off, divided from the external world. It is an 'outside' to that 'outside'. The identity is cut off from itself, 'outside' itself, as the reversed reflection is outside what it reflects, 'rent away and dissipated', as the first section of the poem describes chaos or non-being. And both conceptions of outside lead mutually to chaos because they exist in dead externality to one another, without the possibility of growth or relationship.

Hence the deadness which defeats Los and Albion by hardening into rocky 'outsides' of imprisoning inorganic matter, locking in and locking out: both 'in' and 'out' are 'outside'. The rigidity is another paradoxical form of arbitrary formlessness. So by the end of the poem Albion's 'affections' are all 'without-side: all his sons – Hand, Hyle and Coban...' (19, 16–17). Appropriately, the dead spaces of Albion ingest Los, for what is outside can both engorge and dissipate the things outside it – 'And Los was roofed in from eternity in Albion's cliffs' (19, 33), roofed in and roofed out: 'and withoutside all/Appeared a rocky form' (35). Albion now enfolds Los as the terrors of Bacon and Newton enfold Blake like vast serpents (15, 11–13), and the relationship between them is reversed. Earlier in the poem Albion 'sat in eternal death/Among the furnaces of Los', encompassed by him. The proper contrary of 'outside' is not inside, for in that antithesis each stands over and against the other. That is to concede to the world seen as subject and object. The true

contrary of outside is not to construe boundaries between self
and world at all. Earlier in the poem, when Los is still struggling
for mastery, Los' sons and daughters 'encircle' on 'both sides/
The starry wheels of Albion's sons' (12, 17–18), appearing
'within' and 'without' the furnaces and within and without the
starry wheels. They are effectively annihilating division by belonging simultaneously and mutually to both inside and outside,
incorporating both, creating the spaces they live in. In the same
way God is 'within and without'; he is even in the depths of hell
(12, 15) because hell is something he has made and its depth
belongs mutually to the heights of human experience.

For Albion in the final lament at the end of the chapter God is
a negation outside, split off from human experience, a reversed
image of Los' God who is within and without. 'God in the
dreary void/Dwells from eternity, wide separated from the
human soul' (23, 29–30). He dwells *apart* from eternity, the
human soul, and *eternally* separated from it. Albion has
murdered God in murdering contraries, which is why they bleed.
He is the static reflection of the spectre who can 'separate a law
of sin'. The engraving which contains the division of Los' spectre
is neatly scored into separate sections. Blake carries the principle
of division and negation systematically throughout second part
of the chapter. Division is a monstrous birth, a negative reflection of creative expansion and unity. It is also murder, for
splitting contradicts wholeness (and as we have seen from Plate
5, it *issues* in murder). Splitting is the barren complement of
'fitting'. The dominating figures of the poem are synecdoche and
metonymy, the part for the whole, the whole for the part. The
names of people and places or people/places which so thickly
populate the poem, Hand, Hyle, Jerusalem, Enitharmon, Vala,
Babel, Ninevah, Asshur, Aram, Cambridge, Ely, London, Bath,
Albion himself, are synecdochic splits from a larger whole which
defines them. But just as easily they become giant metonymies,
whole which define parts. And it is possible for this to happen
because both figures are complementary and interchangeable:
both imply splitting, the existence of autonomous and independent entities existing in a continguity which can just as easily
split as converge. They can be 'outsides', and outside one
another. Los sees man as 'a little grovelling root, outside of
himself' (17, 32). Life itself is outside for the spectre. 'Life lives
on my consuming', a human sacrifice which is also self-murder.

'*My* consuming', is equally a consuming of myself and a consuming by life of myself. Splitting is also a dissipation, the
logical conclusion of 'fitting'. Los' sons significantly acknowledge the division of Albion's sons: they 'stand round him [Los]
cutting the fibres from 'Albion's hills,/That Albion's sons may
roll apart over the nations' (15, 23–4).

Formally the poem dissipates, from dialogue to choric lament
and solitary reverie, both reverse reflections of dialogue.
Dialogue enacts contraries as Los and his spectre furiously challenge one another. After Los fails, the energising anger of
dispute is succeeded by lament. Albion's encounter with the
daughters of Beulah, echoes but reverses the encounter
between Los and his spectre, because it is carried on in disasso-
ciation from them. He and they lament independently of one
another, failing to answer each other, in incoherent despair.
Earlier in the poem Los attempts to 'organise' non-entity, to give
a 'body' to falsehood by smelting and incorporating it within the
shaping fire of his furnaces. Hence his 'halls' contain 'every
sorrow and distress', the emotions and actions which dissipate
the latter part of the poem. The dialogue between Los and his
spectre is a dialogue of contraries, between energy and non-
being, as each in his turn calls forth the affirmation of the other,
each defining the other. It is possible for Los to say that he
knows 'far worse' (7, 51) than anything the spectre can tell him
because at this stage he 'contains' the Spectre as a contrary.
Jerusalem and Vala sing to Albion in the same terms of despair
and shamed sexuality as the Spectre expresses to Los. But there
is no dialogue, merely assent. When Los fails to organise
negation the poem dissipates in a monstrous negative parody of
his activity, engorging his creativity with the propagative
organic power of prolific growth. Hand sends his allies over the
world as Los calls his sons and daughters to aid him. He forges
prison bars as Los forges his furnace. Non-being is inverse
creation and when Los can no longer include it it is propagative.

It would be right to ask whether the wheeling round of the
poem upon itself in reverse reflection does not force Blake
merely to represent the triumph of non-being in a way which
means that he is caught linguistically in Entuthon, in a language
of dissipation rather than expansion. The structure of fission
and fusion, splitting and amalgamation, which is at work in the
language of *Jerusalem* perhaps contains these things as con-

traries but, like the double syntax of *The Prelude*, it is always liable to fall into onesidedness and to collapse. And the threat of onesidedness is more extreme for Blake than for Wordsworth. For Wordsworth the opposition is between a world constituted by mind and a world of subject and object. For Blake the opposition is between a world constituted by mind and nothing.

Blake's answer would be that non-entity is organised through language. Language is central to his vision, and perhaps more important to him than to any other Romantic poet, because it can do what Los cannot do. He does not express that distrust of words which is to be found in both Wordsworth and Shelley in spite of their celebrations of language. The building of Golgonooza, arranged as a block on the same page against the description of Entuthon in his engraving is a living example of the mastery of the language of dissipation by a language of inclusion. Entuthon 'conglomerates' but cannot create; it is everlasting but has no form. It grows but cannot develop. It is the 'incoherent' double of the supreme artefact, Golgonooza. The same terms belong to each.

The gates of Golgonooza partake of the same elements to be found in chaos – clay and stone, the land of earthquakes, ice, the land of snows. They incorporate the wheels of Albion's sons, 'the land of snares and traps and wheels and pit-falls and dire mills.' In describing Golgonooza Blake puts phrases and nouns together like blocks without copula, as if to render the absolute substantiveness of its state, preferring to put epithets after the nouns with the same curt, unconnected, laconic listing and, if possible, to turn epithets into nouns.

And that toward Beulah four – gold, silver, brass, & iron.
And that toward Eden four, formed of gold, silver, brass, & iron.
The smith, a golden gate, has four lions, terrible, living;
That toward generation four, of iron carved wondrous;
That toward Ulro four, clay-baked, laborious workmanship;
That toward Eden four, immortal gold, silver, brass & iron. (12, 66: 13, 1–5)

These gates are made, 'formed' by art and labour. They master and contain the elements of the universe, even the hostile elements – '*formed of* gold', '*of* iron *carved* wondrous'. Where 'of' is used in the description of chaos it does not mean made of but possessed by, belonging to, and the 'of' adjunct has reversed its function, denoting control of the elements in one case,

control *by* the elements in another. The land *of* darkness, of
snows, of earthquakes, of snares. The Golgonooza passage is
structured as carefully ordered symmetry – 'And that toward
... And that toward ... 'four ... four.' There is a logical necessity to the forms taken by the gates. The structuring of the chaos
passage is a terrifying successive series of *connected* phrases
which multiply prolifically but which never escape from the
categories they begin with. The listing here is arbitrary and incoherent. The successive items have no meaningful progression or
order, neither defined against one another nor related to one
another. Repetition is random. It is a landscape of dispersal.
Since each item has no existence but in itself it is a landscape of
pure matter. Correspondingly words here become pure matter.
If fire, snow, sand, have no meaning but in themselves they are
meaningless, and so 'the voids, the solids' (13, 50) are equivalents and collapse into one another.

> The rocks of solid fire, the ice valleys, the plains
> Of burning sand, the rivers, cataract & lakes of fire,
> The islands of the fiery lakes, the trees of malice, revenge,
> And black anxiety, & the cities of the salamandrine men.
> (But whatever is visible to the generated man
> Is a creation of mercy & love from the Satanic void.)
> The land of darkness, flames but no light & no repose;
> The land of snows, of trembling, & of iron hail incessant,
> The land of earthquakes & the land of woven labyrinths. (13, 40–8)

Blake's interpolated parenthesis here is important: in spite of its
terrors this landscape *is* a *creation* of mercy because it has been
made 'visible'. It can be incorporated as the contrary of Golgonooza. It is as if each description necessarily lives on the other,
contraries of creation and dissolution. The forming of one
requires the dissolution of the other to be formed. Fire is the
means by which the 'wrought' metals of Golgonooza can be
smelted. Entuthon, surrounding Golgonooza 'on all sides' (54),
is the contrary of the moat of fire which surrounds the centre of
the city (13, 25).

Blake's is an intensely analytic language, offering seeing and
structure simultaneously, and a rigorous conceptualising of the
visual. Nevertheless, there are moments in the poem when it
seems to be locked into a mimetic language which reproduces
non-entity rather than mastering it. (This may be why the prophetic 'gate of the tongue, the western gate' is closed to the sons

and daughters of Los: Blake's rigour would never allow him to turn his back on the possibility.) It would be difficult to say, to return yet again briefly to Plate 5, whether the repetition in that section shapes or is shaped by formlessness.

One word, the word 'revolve', expresses the inherent problems of Blake's language. Blake is fond of the 're' prefix which suggests endless repetition. 'Resound' (7); 'redounding' (49, 51); 'Revolve' (27, 31, 53); 'revolved' (46); 'revolutions' (61). In the insistent repetition of forms of revolve and cognate words, and in the configurations in which these occur, the language creates the endless revolution, the meaningless Newtonian motion which spins upon itself, turning, but without changing in a closed cycle. 'Skofield, Kox, Kotope and Bowen revolve most mightily upon/The furnaces of Los ... They revolve into the furnaces ... and are driven forth.' The section expands upon its beginning – 'Cambridge & Oxford & London/ *Are driven* among the starry wheels'. They revolve upon themselves, self-moving, and 'are driven'. Indeed, in the next occurrence of revolve the sons of Albion are silently conflated with the starry wheels themselves – 'The starry wheels revolved heavily over the furnaces', and with this repetition it is as if the action has gone full circle, turned back upon itself without progression. Sinisterly, and unusually, the verb is in the past, as if the action is endlessly trapped in its own past revolutions. And again, the words look back to the earlier lines: 'The starry wheels revolved.../Drawing Jerusalem' (46–7): 'they [Thames, Albion] are drawn through unbounded space'. In this new revolution of the poem the starry wheels are given the power of 'drawing', like the power of a magnet which does not change in order to exert its power. With the reintroduction of Jerusalem the poem revolves again back to 'And Jerusalem is scattered abroad like a cloud of smoke through non-entity'. And though this statement is revolved upon, repeated and expanded in different forms, the language does not advance but simply redounds upon itself.

> The starry wheels revolved heavily over the furnaces,
> Drawing Jerusalem in anguish of maternal love
> Eastward, a pillar of a cloud with Vala upon the mountains,
> Howling in pain, redounding from the arms of Beulah's daughters,
> Out from the furnaces of Los above the head of Los,
> A pillar of smoke writhing afar into non-entity, redounding

Till the cloud reaches afar, outstretched among the starry wheels
Which revolve heavily in the mighty void above the furnaces. (46–53)

And there Jerusalem wanders with Vala upon the mountains,
Attracted by the revolutions of those wheels, the cloud of smoke
Immense. And Jerusalem & Vala weeping in the cloud
Wander away into the chaotic void, lamenting with her shadow
Among the daughters of Albion, among the starry wheels,
Lamenting for her children, for the sons & daughters of Albion. (60–5)

The repetition occurs with the agents of action reversed:
'*Drawing* Jerusalem ... Jerusalem ... *attracted* by the revolutions of those wheels'. But 'the cloud of smoke/Immense' has
now been 'attracted' to the identity of the starry wheels, whereas
in the first passage it was an attribute or metaphor for the being
of Jerusalem herself. The free, dissipated syntax of these
passages dissipates and conflates the identity of Jerusalem and
the starry wheels as the being of both partakes ambiguously of
the nature of a 'pillar of a cloud ... A pillar of smoke ... the
cloud of smoke/Immense'. Subject and object, parent and
children, (for the starry wheels have earlier been conflated with
the sons of Albion), merge into one another. Plurals shift unaccountably to singulars. 'And Jerusalem and Vala weeping ...
Wander ... lamenting with *her* shadow ... lamenting for *her*
children.' Vala disappears from the syntax, or else 'they' and
'her' become one, for since Jerusalem is inextricably a part of her
shadow it is possible to talk of them both as plural and singular.
Jerusalem's identity is scattered. She is 'upon the mountains',
'outstretched among the starry wheels' and weeping *in* the cloud
which is herself, her sons, the starry wheels. She is truly 'outstretched': since her own identity, her sons and daughters and
the starry wheels are simultaneously fused and separated from
one another. And so Jerusalem seeks her children without discovering the objects of her search which are inextricably part of
herself, 'writhing', 'redounding', reflexively with her. The last
sentence ends on a series of unresolved, 'outstretched' participles.

Formlessness or *formed* formlessness? Enlarging language or
words which have 'outstretched' themselves? Conflations which
include or dissipate? Repetition which recoils reflexively upon
itself or which disperses? Blake's language is vulnerable.
Nothing could more expose itself to redundancy or seem superficially more naïve than his choice of a sentence structure which is

a simple accretive series and which allows both of an infinite en-largement and an infinite fragmentation. To concede to a naïve Blake would be to concede to that split world of 'objecting' alter-natives which he refused. It is the simplicity which deliberately risks the naïve, and we do not have to express his simplicity as an alternative between success and failure. The stark amalgams and metonymic visualising of his images is done with a primitive directness and disregard for categories and yet is fiercely con-ceptual; hence their enigmatic intellectual power. The recreation of space in the poem, liberated by the act of seeing from the con-straints of the physical, is sensory and analytic. The analytic nature of his language and its understanding of contraries must be respected before its vulnerability is recognised.

The risks Blake's language takes are part of its virtuosity. Its structure renders the ever-enlarging movement of the human im-agination and yet, like Los, it knows 'far worse than this'. It knows the threat of formlessness. 'I am alive and all things live in me.' Los returns to furious affirmation at the end of *Jerusalem* as the Spectre and Enitharmon resume a dialogue with him. It is as if an excruciating act of energy and will has to be undertaken in order to see negations as living contraries, to make all things exist in the human imagination, to force nothing to stand in the way, nothing to be 'outside' the ever-expanding human mind. The violence and passion of assertion partakes of terror. Blake's remorseless dismissal of a subject/object universe liberates him from the sense of pressure of one on the other which all Roman-tics feel, and makes him the only pure idealist among the nineteenth-century poets. But it opens up a threatening possibility – chaos, formlessness, nothing – or worse, that chaos expressed as object and reasserting dualism all over again, may be waiting 'outside' to invade the energies of creative life with all the powerful totality of the imagination which refuses them. Perhaps they can only be warded off by an act of will rather than organised. It is characteristic of Blake's sanity that he did not let his language turn its back on that possibility and exclude it, for that would be to concede to negation. He allowed his language to express a simple, starkly intransigent account of mind along with the possibility of its overthrow. The language rarely expresses an achieved inclusion of disorder as contrary but it expresses the struggle to incorporate it. With extraordinary faithfulness to the idea of contraries the poem acknowledges that its vision can only be there because of the threat to it.

Appendix to Chapter 3, Jerusalem, Chapter I, plate 5.

The banks of the Thames are clouded, the ancient porches of Albion are
Darkened; they are drawn through unbounded space, scattered upon
The void in incoherent despair. Cambridge & Oxford & London
Are driven among the starry wheels, rent away and dissipated,
In chasms & abysses of sorrow, enlarged without dimension, terrible.
Albion's mountains run with blood, the cries of war & of tumult
Resound into the unbounded night, every human perfection
Of mountain & river & city, are small & withered & darkened.
Cam is a little stream, Ely is almost swallowed up,
Lincoln & Norwich stand trembling on the brink of Udan-Adan,
Wales and Scotland shrink themselves to the west and to the north,
Mourning for fear of the warriors in the vale of Entuthon Benython.
Jerusalem is scattered abroad like a cloud of smoke through non-entity:
Moab & Ammon & Amalek & Canaan & Egypt & Aram
Receive her little ones for sacrifices and the delights of cruelty.

Trembling I sit day and night; my friends are astonished at me.
Yet they forgive my wanderings, I rest not from my great task –
To open the eternal worlds, to open the immortal eyes
Of man inwards into the worlds of thought – into Eternity
Ever-expanding in the bosom of God, the human imagination.
O Saviour, pour upon me thy spirit of meekness & love;
Annihilate the selfhood in me, be thou all my life.
Guide thou my hand which trembles exceedingly upon the Rock of Ages,
While I write of the building of Golgonooza, & of the terrors of Entuthon;
Of Hand & Hyle & Coban, of Gwantok, Peachey, Brereton, Slayd & Huttn;
Of the terrible sons & daughters of Albion and their generations.
Skofield, Kox, Kotope and Bowen revolve most mightily upon
The furnace of Los, before the eastern gate bending their fury.
They war to destroy the furnaces, to desolate Golgonooza,
And to devour the sleeping humanity of Albion in rage & hunger.
They revolve into the furnaces southward & are driven forth northward,
Divided into male and female forms time after time.
From these twelve all the families of England spread abroad.

The male is a furnace of beryl; the female is a golden loom.
I behold them, and their rushing fires overwhelm my soul
In London's darkness, and my tears fall day and night
Upon the emanations of Albion's sons, the daughters of Albion,
Names anciently remembered but now contemned as fiction,
Although in every bosom they control our vegetative powers.

These are united into Tirzah and her sisters, on Mount Gilead:
Cambel & Gwendolen & Conwenna & Cordella & Ignoge.
And these united into Rahab in the Covering Cherub on Euphrates:

Gwineverra & Gwinefred, & Gonorill & Sabrina beautiful,
Estrild, Mehetabel & Ragan, lovely daughters of Albion;
They are the beautiful emanations of the twelve sons of Albion.

The starry wheels revolved heavily over the furnaces,
Drawing Jerusalem in anguish of maternal love
Eastward, a pillar of a cloud with Vala upon the mountains,
Howling in pain, redounding from the arms of Beulah's daughters,
Out from the furnaces of Los above the head of Los,
A pillar of smoke writhing afar into non-entity, redounding
Till the cloud reaches afar, outstretched among the starry wheels
Which revolve heavily in the mighty void above the furnaces.

O what avail the loves & tears of Beulah's lovely daughters?
They hold the immortal form in gentle hands & tender tears;
But all within is opened into the deeps of Entuthon Benython,
A dark and unknown night, indefinite, unmeasurable, without end –
Abstract philosophy warring in enmity against imagination
(Which is the Divine Body of the Lord Jesus, blessed for ever).
And there Jerusalem wanders with Vala upon the mountains,
Attracted by the revolutions of those wheels, the cloud of smoke
Immense. And Jerusalem & Vala weeping in the cloud
Wander away into the chaotic void, lamenting with her shadow
Among the daughters of Albion, among the starry wheels,
Lamenting for her children, for the sons & daughters of Albion.

Los heard her lamentations in the deeps afar. His fears fall
Incessant before the furnaces, and his emanation divided in pain,
Eastward toward the starry wheels. But westward, a black horror...

CHAPTER 4

Shelley's Perplexity:
Prometheus Unbound

He gave man speech and speech created thought.

II, iv, 72

Language is a perpetual Orphic Song,
Which rules with Daedal harmony a throng
Of thoughts and forms, which else senseless and shapeless were.

IV, 415–17

Shelley liked to construct his poems as processions, passing rapidly across the field of vision; figures appear and vanish in quick succession whether in the fleeing procession of *The Triumph of Life*, the ceremonial cortège of qualities in *Adonais*, or the remorseless but curiously limber dead march of *The Masque of Anarchy*. Though *Prometheus Unbound* is a lyrical *drama*, as much about drama as it is a formal dramatic structure, the figures in it, spirits, furies, phantasms, driven and driving impetuously on rushing winds, currents, sounds, arrive and depart, are superseded by other figures, in an on-going movement of change, and alteration. Words, too, behave as if they are passing by in procession. Language quickly reaches its vanishing point, drinking the wind of its own speed. The rapid energy and volatile mobility of the verbal life, the evanescent, glittering iridescence of the language, makes words flow into one another. The poetry is a linguistic equivalent of the everlasting universe of things which 'rolls' through the mind in 'Mont Blanc'. Supersession is its principle. The verse sets up a flux of sound into superseding sound: configurations of vowels and consonants in one group of words dissolve into those which follow them, and these maintain trace elements of previous sounds in delicate mutations and conflations: 'By the odour-breathing sleep/Of the faint night flowers, and the waves/At the fountain-lighted caves' (II, i, 182–4). The coalescences of syllable and sound-value here make new words into traces of former nouns ('faint' and 'flowers' converge in 'fountain'; 'night' is carried into 'lighted'). A syllable from the middle of one line will 'rhyme' with the end word of the line above. The effect of this flux and coalescence is simultaneously of obliteration and preservation. The print of one syllable remains on the next even as it vanishes. It is as if the glow of the notorious fading coal in Shelley's *Defence of Poetry* is revived as it fades. The language is negated as swiftly as it is recreated and recreated yet again as swiftly as it is negated. The halo effect of Shelley's words means that we cannot give priority of emphasis negatively to the disappearance of sound or positively to its revival, for the language oscillates between obliteration and renewal. Shelley liked to use words which suggest oscillation, quiver, tremble. Even when the weightlessness of his language is most insistent the words quiver between moving beyond themselves, creating new materials out of their sounds, and becoming a vaporising trail of prints and traces, fading in the wake of superseding sounds. This fluency is as far from the weight and pressure exerted by the substantive, geological formations of Wordsworth's language as it could be. Fluidity and light are its appropriate metaphors.

The quiver or tremble between fading and becoming, between negative and positive accounts of the same phenomena, is at work throughout *Prometheus Unbound*. It is there in the two accounts of language, each suggesting a different account of mind and cognition, which head this chapter. 'Speech created thought.' Speech brings thought into being. But in the second quotation though it is antecedent to language, pre-existing until it is shaped and ruled by it. However, the word 'rules' proposes a difficulty of deciding upon priorities. The thoughts and forms might well be the residue of earlier forms of language. Which is prior? Thought or language? I shall return to the problem of language. Meanwhile, the two quotations are a paradigm of the oscillation of relationships which occurs throughout the poem.

There is a visual flicker or oscillation in Shelley's poetry which enacts cognitive problems through perceptual processes. As things appear and disappear, are obliterated and preserved, the language persuades one to ask which elements in experience are prior to which. The question of priorities leads to the question of dependence, and the perceptual movements in particular question whether there is a relationship of prior dependence between mind and things in the world or things in the world and mind. Shelley maintains a flickering present tense. Not the willed, static presentness of Hopkins' poetry, stilled by the energy with which the poet keeps it there, or the timeless presentness of Blake, but a repeated renewal of presentness as one present tense succeeds another – 'the darker lake/Reflects it: now it wanes: it gleams again' (II, i, 21). With every present the world takes fresh form, 'gleams' into being. At the same time the emphasis is as strongly on waning. Akin to this is Shelley's way of using words with the widest, most unspecific semantic range possible so that they fade at the edges – shape, shade, shadow, form, spirit – only just rescued by perception into form before they vanish from the senses again. Prometheus talks of 'shapeless sights'. Properly, what is without shape cannot have form and cannot be seen. But by being constituted as a sight, seen by means of its very lack of form, it just enters into the range of perception, acquiring new definition, new form. Things constantly attain new forms in Shelley's poetry, and just as constantly dissolve forms, transmuted by an act of abstraction from sensory experience and substantive physical particularity into the forms and attributes which belong to things. The act of abstraction depends vitally on sensuous life, or perhaps sensuous life depends on the act of abstraction. Shelley's poetry does not reject sensory experience in favour of an imprecise and mystical vagueness. His language offers an intensification of it in an idealised and transmuted form achieved by a systematic dematerialising of the sensory into the *structure*, not the 'feel', of immediate sensory experience. It is a refinement which brings the subtlest areas, the vanishing points of perception into being. 'And far on high the keen sky-cleaving mountains/From icy spires of sun-like radiance fling/The dawn' (II, iii, 28–30). The syntax of Asia's speech allows that these are 'icy spires ... of radiance'; that is, they do not merely give out radiance like the sun but their nature is actually constituted out of radiance and becomes the quality of shiningness itself fused inseparably with it. Here, perhaps, is one of the 'forms more real' of the poet, because it is here more truthful to the nature of mountains in the dawn than a seemingly rational account of solid dawn-lit crags. But it would be equally possible to say that these 'real' forms represent an 'unreal' abstraction of mind. Congruent with this is the landscape of Asia's previous sentence, 'forests', 'twilight-lawns', 'stream-illumèd caves', 'And wind-enchanted shapes of wandering mist', where the syntax allows either that the literal world is actually composed of wandering mist (and so that world dissolves into substancelessness) or that it is the 'shapes *of* mist' because the landscape is the mist's creature, formed and created by its qualities.

The agent of this flux and coalescence, of course, is Shelley's syntax. In its fluid making and remaking of relationships and categories, dissolving and fusing forms and structures, it is more open than the syntax of any other nineteenth-century poet. It quivers between fusing and giving one identity to things, obliterating priority and dependence, and keeping things separate and distinct.

> The point of one white star is quivering still
> Deep in the orange light of widening morn
> Beyond the purple mountains: through a chasm
> Of wind-divided mist the darker lake
> Reflects it: now it wanes: it gleams again
> As the waves fade, and as the burning threads
> Of woven cloud unravel in pale air.
> 'Tis lost: and through yon peaks of cloud-like snow
> The roseate sunlight quivers: (II, i, 17–25)

The mutual 'quivering' of the single star and the roseate dawn which echoes it are appropriate for the quivering of relationships between one thing and another here throughout the passage. The syntax makes things tremble and merge into one another refining qualities into one another and yet asserts differences. The word 'still' quivers between meaning 'yet' or 'stilly'. Spatial relationships are dissipated as 'Beyond' serves the widening morn and the quivering star and two dimensions of 'beyond' exist, particularly as the star *penetrates*, 'deep in' the orange light which is paradoxically *diffusing* in the 'widening morn' as if new dimensions are in the process of being created. The line break 'through a chasm/Of wind-divided mist' transmutes physical chasm into a metaphorical chasm, so that mountains and mist mutually partake of one another's substance and substancelessness. The mysterious comparative which comes from nowhere, 'the darker lake' suggests that the real lake glimpsed through the mist is not only darker than the sky but that it is another lake darker than another lake, the lake of the sky, and there is another exchange of qualities. 'Now it wanes; it gleams again'; 'it' quivers indefinitely between being the star in the sky or the star in the lake or the waves of the lake itself waning and gleaming, oscillating in sympathy with the sky, as they certainly do with 'fade'. Another reciprocating exchange of qualities takes place as the mountain peaks are expressed as 'cloud-like snow', and mountains and mist take on one another's being again. The effect of the language here is to dissolve priority and dependence by achieving a perfect reciprocity of identity, exchange and difference. Things merge into one another's being and maintain their being.

One of the consummate examples of dissolution and preservation is in Act III, following the descent of Jupiter and his divided world. The subaqueous world of blue Proteus and his humid nymphs, a serene translucent double of the human world above it (III, ii, 18–34), is gradually fused by the syntax with that human world. The water world sees ships from below as if led by their shadows, echoing in the heaven-reflecting sea the real heaven, in which the moon is drawn along the sea-like sunset by the evening star, 'Tracking their path no more by blood and groans,/And desolation, and the mingled voice/Of slavery and command; but by the light/Of wave-reflected flowers, and floating odours,/And music soft, and mild, free, gentle voices,/And sweetest music, such as spirits love'. 'Tracking' draws Proteus and mortals together, for it serves both; so both mortals and nymphs, above or beneath the ocean, might become aware of the light of 'wave-reflected flowers' and 'floating odours': the light of wave-reflected flowers might shine upwards into the air or downwards into the water as flowers gaze into the waves, and give forth the light which is given back to them in the perpetual interchange of reflection. Odours can float in air or in water, or both. The experience of mortals and immortals merges and blends and the relationships established by the syntax, fusing the two worlds in harmony and identity, achieve the reciprocity from which blood and groans, slavery and command, must necessarily be absent. This interdependent world, however, belongs to one of the moments of triumph in the poem. Very often the halo-effect of Shelley's language and its evanescent, shifting relationships create difficulties. It raises by its form the question of relationship itself, of priority and dependence.

It is necessary to look further at the problem of relationship before going on to consider how the language and form of *Prometheus Unbound* adumbrates this perplexity. Shelley celebrates an almost rhapsodic belief in the creative possibilities of mind and language at the same time as he sees both as 'feeble'. In the famous fading coal passage, language is subservient to thought and can never capture it. 'The mind in creation is as a fading coal, which some invisible influence, like an inconstant wind, awakens to transitory brightness. When composition begins, inspiration is already on the decline, and the most glorious poetry that has ever been communicated to the world is probably a feeble shadow of the original conceptions of the poet' (*Defence of Poetry*, published in 1821, within two years of Shelley's work on *Prometheus*). This is congruent with the beginning of 'Mont Blanc' which seems to be saying that mind is a 'feeble' brook in comparison with the massive energies of the universe of things. Mind 'cannot create, it can only perceive' (*On Life*). True to the Enlightenment spirit of this statement, Shelley's language is always expressing the escape of the receding universe from the reach of consciousness and language. The uncreativeness of mind is reiterated. It is subservient to the materials of perception. What is perceived is the basis of its being and mind has no experience except of itself and its perceptions. 'Nothing exists but as it is perceived' (*On Life*).[1] There are times when a pessimism about the capacity of language to construct the world appears in Shelley's poetry. 'But a voice/Is wanting, the deep truth is imageless,' Demogorgan says (II, iv, 115–16. At the beginning of the poem Earth cannot communicate with Prometheus, Panthea and Asia hold a wordless converse (II, i, 108–10) as if the only way to communicate is to transcend language.

And yet the poem makes the ground of pessimism provide the reason for celebration. Affirmation comes out of the wreck of hope and creates the thing it contemplates. Demogorgan's 'want' means both is 'deprived of' and '*wishes* for', creative desire. If mind cannot create, it needs the world of things. The mind requires the universe of things in order to experience its own being and its relationship to that world. And the world of things needs mind in order to come into being through it and to have a relationship with it. Hence the infinitely propagative power of 'the human mind's imaginings' in 'Mont Blanc' which is a consequence of relationship and not a contradiction of the mind's dependence on sense. It could be seen as a corroboration of it. What can be achieved is a unity of reciprocity and interchange, an ecstatic oneness which annihilates the dualism of subject and object and their subservience one to another in the fusion of self and other in which each is created in and by each. Hence it is quite in order for Shelley to say that the signs '*I, you, they*' are arbitrary marks, constructions of language employed to indicate an opposition where none exists, and at the same time to conceive of *relationship* between the self and 'surrounding universe': 'Those who are subject to the state called reverie, feel as if their nature were dissolved into the surrounding universe, or as if the surrounding universe were absorbed into their being. They are conscious of no distinction'.[2] But they *are* conscious of relationship. And this is a mutually reflexive continuous recreation of one another by self and world through identity and exchange of being. So it is theoretically just possible for Shelley to resolve the contradiction of the simultaneous feebleness and creativity of mind and language by constructing a world which has relationships, but without priorities, a world where mind and language are each dependent, but without being secondary to one another. And it is possible to say that speech creates thought while being dependent upon it.

These contradictions are precariously resolved in Shelley's metaphors, which suggest a resolution and the difficulties of that resolution. In the Preface to *Prometheus Unbound* he wrote that his imagery was 'drawn from the operations of the human mind'. He meant imagery in a wider sense than that of metaphor, but his use of metaphor does illustrate the propagative possibilities of the activity which is constrained by external materials. These are materials which it cannot create but only perceive, yet they can be recreated and recombined internally almost indefinitely until they virtually become new categories. Asia's description of the coming of spring (her first speech in Act II) replicates the two terms, spring and emotion, and substitutes each for the other in a series of exchanges which multiply the materials of the metaphor and reproduce them in new forms. The effect is of repetition and recombination of materials to infinity. For all the difficulties inherent in Shelley's use of repetition, which I shall discuss, it is true to the beginning of *The Defence*, which claims that mind, acting on thought, its materials, colours them with its own light and composes from them, as from elements, other thoughts. I have already shown in Chapter 1 how one of Shelley's metaphors exchanges the qualities of the literal and figurative term in such a way as to refuse priority to either term. To begin with the rarefied intensity in which spring is taken up into a non-corporeal world of emotion in Asia's first speech in Act II: 'Yes, like a spirit, like a thought ... O Spring!' A succession of mental things or feelings precedes in a rush, the discovery of the likeness, 'Spring', which is delayed for six lines creating the suspense which waits upon it. So we discover spring through the emotions it creates or the emotions it metaphorically becomes.

> From all the blasts of heaven thou hast descended:
> Yes, like a spirit, like a thought, which makes
> Unwonted tears throng to the horny eyes,
> And beatings haunt the desolated heart,
> Which should have learnt repose: thou hast descended
> Cradles in tempests; thou dost wake, O Spring!
> O child of many winds! As suddenly
> Thou comest as the memory of a dream,
> Which now is sad because it hath been sweet;
> Like genius, or like joy which riseth up
> As from the earth, clothing with golden clouds
> The desert of our life. (II, i, 1–12)

'Like a spirit' one comparison vanishes into the next – 'like a thought' – and mental experience and the affective, physical expression it creates – tears, palpitations cause and effect – are expressed as if they are forms of emotion, spirit, thought. But these affective states move fluidly between the two terms of the metaphor. The syntax allows for it to be spring 'which makes/ Unwonted tears' or that it might be 'spirit' or 'thought' which themselves are *like* spring, which do so. By belonging to both sides of the metaphor these lines undermine the separateness of the terms. Just as 'Spring' is refined into a mental state by being like spirit or thought mental states themselves are refined. 'As suddenly/Thou comest as the memory of a dream.' Not a dream, but the memory of a dream, one stage away from the experience itself. The memory adds another layer of emotion and perception to the dream, another transmutation takes place with 'Which now is sad because it hath been sweet'. 'It' is ambiguous: was it a sweet dream or perhaps a sweet memory of a dream which preceded this memory, which is sad because it mourns the loss of the earlier sweetness? The effect of such refinements is of an acute, quivering nervous sensibility, stretched as far as it can be in reproducing and recompounding feeling and spring. Once again this comparison is rapidly superseded and the passage continues with 'Like genius or like joy' and comes full circle by re-appropriating the property of spring to make a *new* metaphor for joy– 'which riseth up/As from the earth, clothing with golden clouds/The desert of our life'. Joy is an exhalation, air and water, as if the irrigating tears of the first metaphor have become part of the atmosphere, while the desolated heart has expanded to 'the desert of our life'. This fusion of the object of comparison with another metaphor takes it further and further away from its being as an event and transforms it into the experience it evokes, but, of course, this *is* the *experience* of spring. Shelley's metaphors are like ever-widening circles, holding themselves within themselves, the two terms continually expanding to contain one another. And yet the secondariness of the activity is also there. The replications of the metaphor are reproductions as spring recedes as an event.

Consider another metaphor – this time of reproduction itself – which later, in Act II, gets into greater difficulties.

> Apollo
> Is held in heaven by wonder; and the light
> Which fills this vapour, as the aërial hue
> Of fountain-gazing roses fills the water,
> Flows from thy mighty sister. (II, v, 10–14)

Here is another model of reciprocity and relationship using with sensuous delicacy the structural form of reflection as its basis. Gazing roses (gazing implies rapt contemplation of the other) suffuse water with their colour: air and water paradoxically unite as an 'aërial hue' is diffused in water and the fountain gives back the image of the roses to themselves; gives it back, indeed, with the additional glow of colour spread through the water which you cannot find in air, and thus gives it back suffused with the qualities of water.

It is a finely succinct metaphor for the creative interchange of being in which no side of the relationship has dominance over the other, roses or fountain. It might be described in the best sense of 'perplexed' as each thing is intervolved with the other. But the image of reflection also asks for the more usual meaning of perplexity as puzzlement to be uppermost. It constitutes relationships *and obliterates* them. The raptly gazing rose is absorbed in an extension of itself. It is gazing at its own image. The fountain serves the rose, objects are subservient to mind: on the other hand, the rose depends upon the use of the fountain to enlarge its image of itself, and so mind is subservient to objects. Because it is locked into a contemplation of itself the gaze is locked into itself and out of the world. It is secondary. Reflection appropriates what it reflects but at the same time reflection is excluded from or subservient to it. The analogy of reflection, like its cognate analogy, the echo, is a suspect one from the start. Reflections and echoes suggest fertile, propagative self-creation and at the same time suggest ever weaker forms of the same sound or image – they fade and die away. They are dependent for their life upon their source. Echoes and reflection are to their source as servant to master, slave to tyrant (the 'beautiful idealisms' of *Prometheus* do not prevent us from seeing that the poem is about enslavement). The unequal relationships encouraged by reflection and echo reinstate the unequal dualism of subject and object all over again. Shelley's account of triumphant reciprocity constantly quivers into the possibility of onesidedness and is in danger of collapsing into the opposite components which Shelley strives to transcend, attempting to fuse together thoughts and words, form and substance, subject and object, master and slave. Either the self is forced into an absorbed contemplation of the self in its own image, asserting its dominance but putting forth replications of itself which are static and not generative or it is captive to the tyrannical pressure of things from outside, uncreatively reproducing *them*. This takes to an extreme Wordsworth's sense that two ways of constituting the world lurk in language, but for Shelley each possibility separately is unacceptable. The structure of relationship falls apart in each case.

The form of *Prometheus Unbound* comes into being because it creates a series of paradigms of relationship and its 'work' is almost ceaselessly to offer models which will be protected against a collapse into ungenerative, static opposites or into unequal dualism. Interestingly, and characteristic of Shelley, the poem is built up through a complex interrelation of repetition and doubling of itself. The form of the poem sets up the problem of repetition and reproduction. Like the Magus Zoroaster the poem meets its own image in different forms and grows by contemplating these. Shelley allows the poem's form, reflection, echo, to question itself and ask whether static replication and dependence rather than a propagative self-creation and interaction is the dominant model of relationship. It begins with a ritual act of repetition, the restatement of Prometheus' curse against Jupiter. The action of the poem is over almost as soon as it is begun, and is in any case a psychological act – 'for I hate no more' (1, 57).

The whole of the first Act turns on the significance of the repeated curse, and the rest of the poem turns on a multiple repetition of that significance and of the significance of repetition itself. Although 'no memory be/Of what is hate, let them not lose it now!' (1, 71–2). The memory of *hate* must not be lost. Prometheus is seeking to revitalise the hatred of his curse through repetition in a magnificent testimony to the power of language. The reiterated, ritual incantation of his curse must not lose its power in 'thrice three hundred thousand years', even though a memory of his curse exists no longer. Significantly, the curse is transmitted through the reduplicating power of echoes. The Earth, however, interprets the 'power' of repetition pessimistically, assuming that it will concede to Jupiter and simply reproduce the universal disruption of its original. The first part of the poem is a dialogue between an affirmative and negative, fear-haunted account of repetition. For Prometheus repetition is a relearning of himself and his relationship to Jupiter. He meets his own image in a creative self-externalisation which to him is generative, like the spring which 'struggles to increase' at the end of the act. It is fitting that the *Phantasm* of Jupiter should speak the curse, an 'empty voice' (1, 249) informed by 'no thought', for the curse is a shadowing forth of the mind of Prometheus which achieves new being and dominance through repetition. The Phantasm of Jupiter belongs to the images of that secondary world which is 'underneath the grave' (197), a shadowy, inverted reduplication of this world, coextensive with life and consciousness (*not*, like eternity, beginning where life ends). It is a place where thoughts, events and images of events exist together (195–207).

Earth sees this world as a dim, nether reflection of the upper

world of being, estranged from it, as if thought and living consciousness, image-making and being, ideas and the forms of
conscious life and action are cut off from one another and
necessarily alienated. But these upper and nether worlds are
restored to one another through the repetition of the curse. In
Act III, which was originally the last Act of the poem, flanking
the visit to Demogorgon's cave in Act II, the structural principle
is an antithetical repetition or counterpart of the first Act.
Jupiter descends in contrapuntal relationship to the liberated
Prometheus, a negative double of his one-time victim. Thetis is
thawed into a dew with poison, repeating in negative terms the
vaporising of love as it dissolves the being of Asia, Panthea and
Ione. The blowing of the conch parallels the utterance of the
curse. The unified, fused worlds of sea and earth, air and water,
where halcyons gaze at their own images and in which Proteus,
humid nymphs and mortals live interchangeably, suggest the
transparency of one to another, of upper and lower, inner and
outer. These forms restate the estranged, double world of action
and thought, being and memory, conceived by Earth as dim and
alienated, in terms of crystalline interchange and reciprocity.
The divisive dualism of the Furies and Spirits, who are doubles
of one another in negative and positive forms in the first Act,
locked in antithesis, is replaced by accounts of unity and wholeness. The repetition of the curse has restored a totality because
the recognition of the potency and energy of hatred gives one
power over it. Hatred is recognised in all its force and received
into the consciousness as it *is* (Shelley never talks about the abolition of hatred) in order for Prometheus to be released from its
subjugation. In unity with itself the world of Act III offers
images of liberation and harmonious interchange. Set against
the Furies and Spirits is the unifying propagative power of intellectual beauty. A form of the fountain which 'struggles to
increase' at the end of Act I is freely playing in the cave of Act III.
Language and speech are fully realised activities of communion
rather than the struggling potential verbalisation and silent
interchange of the first Act, in which Earth and Prometheus
speak without understanding, without *exchanging* one
another's words, and Asia and Panthea intuit each other's
language.

One might say that the poem has brought its language into
being and created its thought through repetition and doubling

by this stage in its life, fusing shape and sense, forms and thoughts. Repetition uses repetition as its materials, externalising and constituting itself through a reflexive process of doubling and pairing. The repetition of the curse releases the possibility of reduplicating and enlarging its significance by the very fact that it can be seen as an externalised form. The first and third Acts are in binary opposition to one another, developing out of pairing, echo, reflection, and using the Act of reduplication to create negative and positive mirrorings of one another. These antithetical mirrorings redefine the model of reflection as relationship (a model they both create and are created by) from one of reflection as subjugation to one of reflection as reciprocity. They redefine their own materials both formed by and liberated from them. It is not surprising that the central event of Act III is birth, or rather rebirth, as it repeats the myth of the birth of Venus, using language of a limpid, hard clarity unlike anything else in the poem, antithetically pairing it with the cruel myth of the crucifixion in the first Act.

The shifting or unbinding of the model of relationship as reflection from subjugation to reciprocity is clearly to be seen in the relation between the Furies and the Spirits in Act I and the relation between these and the great account of creativity in Act III. But – and this is the power of *Prometheus Unbound* – it is too clear, too easy. The opposition between the first and third Acts depends on an inversion which is won too easily, and which avoids the difficulties of a structure of repetition and reflection as a creative principle. The poem recognises this by creating the hiatus of Act II, the ritual catechism of Demogorgon, and offering another model of relationship even though it is one which also has its difficulties. Act II is left as a cluster of unanswered questions. Shelley also recognised the problems of the poem when he added the extraordinary visionary frolic of Act IV which restates the questions of Act II. Ultimately, the poem considers the permanent possibility of Prometheus' statement, 'Pain, pain ever, for ever', which locks up in its structure the principle of endless repetition.

To return to the attempt to redefine the model of reflection from Act I to Act III. The Furies and Spirits are doubles or echoes of one another, and through both Shelley explores the possibilities of the paradigm of reflection. They are doubles of the curse of Prometheus, an amplification of the 'image' he meets in it, because they evolve out of his recognition that 'ill deeds' and 'good' are 'infinite'. For good and evil are alike *creative* of themselves, and depend for their being on the human imagination, for which the paradigm of reflection is used. The 'image' met by Prometheus is made objective to itself in their appearance. The Furies, 'ministers' of pain and fear as Mercury is, coming as he does to persuade Prometheus to submit, in particular testify to the human power to imagine. A minister is both an agent and a giver, an instrument and an attender upon need. The doubleness of the word brings out the way in which pain and fear are both agents of the imagination and substantive facts, using and used by the human mind. Unbelief and moral fear survive in the consciousness as an intense imaginative experience, a reality propagative of further imaginings even when their actual cause has departed: 'terror survives/The ravin it has gorged' (518–19). Unsated terror lives on after its prey is consumed, searching for an object, and since its prey is terror itself it recreates itself as its object. The homonymic possibilities of ravine and gorge here, the deep physical gap or fissure which has been cleft, and the exchange of possibilities in the idea of a gorge or gap gorged, lend support to the primary meaning of substantive self-acting ruin in the activity of terror.

In each human heart terror survives
The ravin it has gorged: the loftiest fear
All that they would disdain to think were true...
The good want power, but to weep barren tears,
The powerful goodness want: worse need for them.
The wise want love; and those who love want wisdom. (1, 618–20: 625–7)

The poem rises to a rhetoric of hard, severe abstraction here, in an intransigent recognition that Prometheus' change does not change the world. Playing on the idea of 'want' as both lack and need in a series of reversals the passage asserts that to 'want' is a capacity of the imagination, a kind of inversion of creativity, and goes on *creating* 'want'. 'The good *want* power... The powerful goodness *want*.' The structure of the language expresses an infinite regress of impotent lack and incompletion as subjects lack objects to enable them to act, objects lack subjects to bring them into being. What might seem at first an unassimilated passage of moral categories is a living account of moral failure made by an inverted creativity which creates emptinesses. (Yeats, echoing this passage in 'The Second Coming', does not fully absorb the structural necessities of the language here, and Shelley's words become abstract in the borrowing.)

The Furies and Spirits erupt into the poem in a series of metrically complex strophes of great virtuosity, emerging out of a world of carnage and bloodshed which are both the cause and the consequence of the idealised psychological structures they represent. Both depend on the propagative principle of reflection, both are assimilated to forms of erotic feeling and sexuality. The Spirits 'feed' on 'aerial kisses' of thought; the Furies describe themselves as 'lovers'. They share one another's vocabulary – 'aerial', 'shape', 'form'.

> The beauty of delight makes lovers glad,
> Gazing on one another: so are we.
> As from the rose which the pale priestess kneels
> To gather for her festal crown of flowers
> The aëreal crimson falls, flushing her cheek,
> So from our victim's destined agony
> The shade which is our form invests us round,
> Else we are shapeless as our mother Night. (Second Fury, 1, 465–72)

> Nor seeks nor finds he mortal blisses,
> But feeds on the aëreal kisses
> Of shapes that haunt thought's wildernesses.
> He will watch from dawn to gloom
> The lake-reflected sun illume
> The yellow bees in the ivy-bloom,
> Nor heed nor see, what things they be;
> But from these create he can
> Forms more real than living man,
> Nurslings of immortality! (Fourth Spirit, 740–50)

The Furies appropriate the passions of sexuality and religion to offer the mutually self-reflecting gaze of lovers and the transference of colour from see-er to seen and back as a paradigm of their activity. These are experiences where imagination is at its most intense and the intensity actually corroborates and creates the self-enclosed world of reflection. The victim's 'aëreal' thought (his terrors and fears) gives meaning and potency to and actually brings into being, 'form', the nature of the persecutor. 'Else we are shapeless.' The mutual self-creation of subject and object is perpetual enabling the tormentor to give further terror as the victim invests him with further terror yet. 'The aëreal crimson falls, flushing': the convergence of falls, flushing in the

line suggests the reciprocity of the process. The aërial crimson
falls from rose, from flushing cheek alike; the flushing cheek is
both a reflection and an organic blush which falls reciprocally
back to the rose as 'aëreal' things create physical presences. The
shade of the blush, of rose, of cheek, which 'invests' the formless
with form in this orgiastic creativity is as much a 'nursling' of
immortality as the Spirits' forms. And in the Spirits' words the
paradigm of creation out of self, of reflection made out of reflection is exactly the same. The sun is 'lake-reflected', literally
compounded by its image. Reflection of sun into lake refracts
against and illuminates 'the yellow bees in the ivy bloom' as if
the creative transformation of light returns to a world ready to
be transformed by it. In this sense it does not matter 'what *things*
they be', whether lake, light, bees, ivy, for all are forms of
thought or sensation because all experiences, physical and
mental, are transmuted by mind. Hence 'shapes', reflections of
forms or forms themselves, 'haunt' thought's *wildernesses*,
spaces of mind barren of immediate sensation or *'mortal
blisses'*: and yet, paradoxically, mind 'feeds' on the things of
mind, restructuring and transforming perceptual experience.
This is a strange world, warm and frigid, rich (yellow bees, sun,
ivy) and yet empty, barren, and yet propagative of 'nurslings',
feeding and fed on itself. This passage emphasises the restructuring nature of reflection but at the same time, and more than the
Furies, it stresses the waning aspect of reflection. The light of the
sun is at several removes from its source. The refined sterility of
the 'wildernesses' of thought overmasters this limpid, sure transparent diction.

   The account of creativity in Act III (iii, 30–63), attempts to
break out of the negative implications of reflection and echo. It
is best described by its most incisive commentator, I. A.
Richards:[3] 'This mind arising from 'the embrace of beauty' is no
separate individual mind spellbound in adoration of its own
products... It is an ultimately inclusive whole achieving in this
way its own self-realisation.'

> And hither come, sped on the charmèd winds,
> Which meet from all the points of heaven, as bees
> From every flower aëreal Enna feeds,
> At their known island-homes in Himera,
> The echoes of the human world, which tell
> Of the low voice of love, almost unheard,

And dove-eyed pity's murmured pain, and music,
Itself the echo of the heart, and all
That tempers or improves man's life, now free;
And lovely apparitions, – dim at first,
Then radiant, as the mind, arising bright
From the embrace of beauty (whence the forms
Of which these are the phantoms) casts on them
The gathered rays which are reality –
Shall visit us, the progeny immortal
Of Painting, Sculpture, and rapt Poesy,
And arts, though unimagined, yet to be.
The wandering voices and the shadows these
Of all that man becomes, the mediators
Of that best worship love, by him and us
Given and returned; swift shapes and sounds, which grow
More fair and soft as man grows wise and kind,
And veil by veil, evil and error fall:
Such virtue has the cave and place around. (III, iii, 40–63)

The intervolved syntax here organises the statement in such a way that the activity of mind 'arising bright/From the embrace of beauty' is described in a parenthesis which 'embraces' a parenthesis '(whence the forms/Of which these are the phantoms)', and these parentheses are themselves embraced by phrase clusters describing what man is and what he will become. The embrace of beauty is no static thing (as Richards says, this is Intellectual Beauty, the pure essence of creative knowledge). The lovely apparitions which come ambiguously from the human world which sends to the cave its echoes and its 'music' – 'itself the echo of the heart', another parenthesis – and from the cave of beauty itself are in any case the shadows or phantoms of the forms created by beauty. So they are simultaneously phantoms and incandescent realities deriving both attributes from the same source, beauty. Source and derivations from it are inseparable. The mind, in union with beauty, is itself indivisible from it, and, like the sun's rays concentrated through a burning glass, casts on both phantoms and forms 'the gathered rays which are reality'. Distinctions of category dissolve: feeling and forms of feeling, experience and its embodiment. Everything is involved with everything else; beginnings and endings, phantoms and forms, (shape and sense, as Shelley has it earlier) creators and creations, subject and object, negate distinctions in the act of making them. An embrace is an inclusion of each in each, a separation and a fusion, and the syntax declares this. Echoes and apparitions, simultaneously the shadows and the realities of beauty, are also the *progeny* of the arts. So these, too, become inseparable from beauty. The fluent, unitary sentence expresses the echoes and shadows of the human world as things of the present but simultaneously projections cast on to futurity. Projections are the 'mediators' of love, which is a movement beyond the present to the other, and the other, correspondingly, becomes reciprocally aware of the need to go beyond itself in an effort to grasp the meaning of this projection. This is 'want' defined creatively. Subjects find and create objects. Objects find and create subjects as they become identified. Shelley is describing the process of imaginative making, the creation of unknown possibility out of human thought.

The poem liberates itself from the closed world of reflection and echo here by acting out the transforming energy of the embrace. But it is at a cost. The syntax is so fluent, of such pouring ambiguousness and dissolution, that whatever its virtuosity the old charge of the obliteration of relationship cannot be forgotten. The poem takes a risk here and perhaps it is able to take a risk because before it, in Act II, another and different model of relationship has evolved which solves some of the problems of the paradigm of reflection. It does not conflict so much as runs parallel to it. This model is both supremely simple and paradoxical. It is intrinsic to the very nature of dramatic form itself – dialogue, or rather, question and answer. At the centre of the original poem is Asia's ritual interrogation of Demogorgon, a stark model of dramatic interchange. In it the central questions of the poem are given form: 'Who made terror, madness, crime, remorse?' (11, iv, 19); 'Who is the master of the slave?' (114) It is the first point in the poem at which dialogue becomes really possible. As I have said, the interchange between Prometheus and Earth in Act I takes place without language, and there are no answers to the violent questions of Prometheus – 'I ask the earth, have not the mountains felt?' It is as if he exists in a world without an object. The converse of Asia, Panthea and Ione is wordless: 'Your words are as the air – I feel them not.' The journey to Demogorgon's cave, following echo inwards to its source, reverses the movement of the curse which sends out echoes, reduplicating its image in a cycle of repetition. Language comes into being in the act of interrogation, a kind of daemonic catechism. But paradoxically the form of the dialogue is a turning back of every interrogation on the asker, and what is discovered is arrived at because the formulation of the question dictates the formulation of the reply which reflects back the question. Demogorgon, 'a mighty darkness', 'Ungazed upon and shapeless; neither limb/Nor form, nor outline' (11, iv, 5–6) is like the Furies, given form only by Asia's questions, which are an interrogation of formlessness, perhaps nothing. But being given form by the questions, he gives *them* form, returning them upon themselves, externalising them and enabling a recognition which is the growing point of all thought. Demogorgon can only repeat, simply, tautologically, 'He reigns,' in answer to Asia's questions. 'All spirits are enslaved which serve things evil,' he replies to her question 'Is he [Jupiter] too a slave?' (110–11). 'I spoke but as ye speak.' 'So much I asked before,' Asia says, 'and my heart gave/The response thou hast given' (121–2). But the self here is not living in the hollow reverberation of its own echoes however much this pattern of dialogue might seem to repeat the paradigm of echo and reflection. The very structure of question and answer precludes the closed circle of repetition because dialogue is dialectic. The mind knows and possesses what it knows only by repossessing that knowledge. The act of reformulation – '*He reigns*', 'All spirits are enslaved', is the discovery of knowledge through a reshaping which enables further questions to emerge. It is not simply the earlier knowledge in a new form but the reforming is a new structure, a new experience. 'All spirits are enslaved' introduces the vital new description, 'which *serve*'. To serve, to be a minister, to be active or passive agent? This is how, in Shelley's own words in *A Defence*, knowledge grows. Mind acting on thoughts composes 'other thoughts'. Each contains within itself 'the principle of its own integrity', because thought is not an arbitrary principle of addition, but a new content grows out of preceding forms of thought and is genetically determined by it. Furthermore, the naming which goes on here could not take place without the mutuality of self and other returning one another's statement in objective form. The paradigm of dialogue and dialectic breaks the relationship of domination. This is how we deal with our Furies, by *mutual* interrogation. Prometheus' first speech is caught in a syntax of domination and opposition which precludes the dramatic structure of mutuality. The pronouns oppose 'Thou and I', thou and me, thy and mine remorselessly as one fights the subjugation of the other.

> *Prometheus.* Monarch of Gods and Daemons, and all Spirits
> But One, who throng those bright and rolling worlds
> Which Thou and I alone of living things
> Behold with sleepless eyes! regard this Earth
> Made multitudinous with thy slaves, whom thou
> Requitest for knee-worship, prayer, and praise,
> And toil, and hecatombs of broken hearts,
> With fear and self-contempt and barren hope.
> Whilst me, who am thy foe, eyeless in hate,
> Hast thou made reign and triumph, to thy scorn,
> O'er mine own misery and thy vain revenge? (1, 1–11)

And so, in reasserting *drama* as the centre of the Demogorgon catechism the poem justifies its own structure and liberates the possibility of its growth, releasing new modes of relationship. Characteristically, though, it does not *seem* to do this. Demogorgon asserts that an ultimate truth is unknowable. 'But a voice/Is wanting, the deep truth is imageless.' Shelley is very fond of the negative '-less' suffix, where perception is made possible only by being defined as what it is not, or cannot do. Demogorgon seems to be conceding to a notion of numinous transcendent essence, an ever-hidden source, unseen, unknown. He seems to concede to an unreachable beyond, and with it to a Romantic nihilism about language, which vaporises, turns into the mist and foam of its vanishing point, destroying itself in the effort to reach beyond. And yet there is a counterpart to this account of things, Asia's 'and speech created thought', which precedes Demogorgon's statement, and is not in fact incompatible with it. The mind can only know what language can image. But language and relationship emerge at the point of negation. The deep truth is imageless. It is at this point that a voice is lacking, but at which language is *needed*. The word 'want' moves from its designation as deprivation to a more positive designation of *need*. Imagelessness calls images into being if only by being defined as such. The not, the -less, is an *is* not. 'Poetry enlarges the circumference of the imagination,' Shelley wrote in *A Defence*, 'by replenishing it with thoughts of ever new delight which have the power of attracting and assimilating to their own nature all other thoughts, and which form *new* [my italics] intervals and interstices, whose voice for ever craves fresh food.'[4] The ambiguity of 'wanting' as both negation and affirmation, lacking and *needing*, shifts the definition of want offered by the Furies – 'the good *want* power' – in a positive direction, and points to the possibilities inherent in Demogorgon's pessimistic statement. The act of negation is a creative structuring of the world. The definition of lack simultaneously creates and discovers need. By seeing want, indivisibly lack and need, as *not*, as other, what is not known, the void and interstice is brought into being and into relationship with the self. To acknowledge that experience is 'imageless', is a way not of closing but of liberating areas of experience for definition and discovery. The act of verbalising gives form to imagelessness and creates the possibility of further form which in turn depends on the opening up of new spaces. Demogorgon occupies a realm of negation, where perceptual experience is dissipated in dew blanching, breezes dying, light scattering. It is just such 'thought's wildernesses' that the poet opens up, on the edge of perception. In her final song Asia moves amid a 'paradise' of 'wildernesses' and 'wildernesses calm and green'.

The act of negation, of course, is a self-creation in Hegel's sense because it defines the subject against the not incorporating it as part of being. But the labour of the negative here is also a differentiation, an interval which is inalienably other. And so the wilderness both creates and negates being. Want creates need, need creates want and lack. If the shapeless, limbless Demogorgon is to be described as anything (Necessity? the life force? the deep truth? the unknowable source?) he is the moment of coming into being, the moment of definition which is other to the self and both primal and recurrent, the coming into being of negation, the moment of want which needs a voice to create thought and relationship by constituting that void *as* void. Interestingly, behind both the *Defence* and *Prometheus* is an atavistic account of primal lack in terms of food and sexuality – 'craves fresh food', 'aëreal kisses'. It is as if language arises from an analogous deprivation and gives structure to it.

To create the not is to create thought. With spectacular consistency the Demogorgon scene evolves the song of the Voice in Air, the voice which is wanting, the voice from the air, the voice coming out of nothing and made out of nothing. It answers the pure, wordless sound of the nightingale in Demogorgon's realm, which is perpetually dying and recreated, inexhaustible but repetitive, only expressive of itself, sung (like the Nightingale poet in the *Defence*) to 'cheer its own solitude', a sound without a language. The opposition of pure sound is not only silence but language or meaning, just as the antithesis of Demogorgon's shapelessness is a double opposition which is both form and emptiness. Converse, dialogue, emerges through the interaction of all three 'converse' elements. The language seeks to express the converse. This is why the proper mode of discourse in the song of the Voice in Air, celebrating the mystery of Asia's being, is paradox. The *cold* air is *fire, dim* shapes are clad with *brightness*. Paradox depends upon opposition and negation. It says that something is and is not simultaneously. It is the embodiment of that flicker, quiver or tremble which is the principle of Shelley's language. Its being is oscillation.

> Life of Life! thy lips enkindle
>   With their love the breath between them;
> And thy smiles before they dwindle
>   Make the cold air fire; then screen them
> In those looks, where whoso gazes
> Faints, entangled in their mazes.
>
> Child of Light! thy limbs are burning
>   Through the vest which seems to hide them;
> As the radiant lines of morning
>   Through the clouds ere they divide them;
> And this atmosphere divinest
> Shrouds thee wheresoe'er thou shinest.
>
> Fair are others; none beholds thee,
>   But thy voice sounds low and tender
> Like the fairest, for it folds thee
>   From the sight, that liquid splendour,
> And all feel, yet see thee never,
> As I feel now, lost for ever!
>
> Lamp of Earth! where'er thou movest
>   Its dim shapes are clad with brightness,
> And the souls of whom thou lovest
>   Walk upon the winds with lightness,
> Till they fail, as I am failing,
> Dizzy, lost, yet unbewailing!

This is a transposition of the traditional language of spiritual extremity into philosophical terms and achieves that peculiar fusion of rationality and ecstasy which is characteristic of *Prometheus Unbound*. The structure of paradox enables negation, and affirmation, creation and denial, to be experienced simultaneously – 'make the cold air fire': cold air is, is not cold air: cold air is, is not fire: fire is, is not fire: fire is, is not cold air. It is not simply that the impossible transgression of sensation from cold to heat ignites the 'is not' into an 'is', converting negative into positive, cold into heat (and, it follows, cold air unseen into heat felt and *visible* fire); one sensation succeeding another. Paradox will not allow such supersession because it does not depend on the substitution of one quality for another. The substitutions continually construct and deconstruct themselves. The new meaning it insists upon is a new category evolving out of a new relationship between *is* and *is not* which are continually changing places, 'is not' defining 'is', 'is' defining 'is not', 'is not' becoming 'is', 'is' becoming 'is not' – visible air, invisible fire, burning cold, cold heat. The language flickers, quivers endlessly between negation and assertion and this quivering oscillation discovers new definitions. It is not merely a paradigm of the activity which forms intervals and interstices whose void forever craves fresh food, but it *is* that activity, constituting meaning in and through its structure. Paradox is language moving to the edge of itself, where new definition just hovers into being through the assertion of negation. It is language discovering the void in the double sense of finding and exploring it, reaching out to possess the spaces it opens almost to the point of attenuation. With each successive statement of paradox and with that characteristically physical quality, a sensuous knowledge of non-being which is itself paradoxical, the voice faints, loses itself, fails – 'Faints ... lost forever ... till they fail as I am failing,/Dizzy, lost, yet unbewailing!' Sounds melt down into one another through the stanza as rhymes soften and fail with the dissolution of line endings. The grammar faints: 'then screen them/In those looks', 'hide them', 'divide them'. The persistent ambiguity of 'their', 'them' is 'entangled in *their* mazes'. 'Their', 'them' either serves two subjects at once, failing the differentiation between separate entities, or returns upon the subject as its own object: 'thy lips enkindle/With *their* love the breath between *them* [lips]': 'then screen *them* [lips, smiles]/In *those* looks [smiles], where whoso gazes/Faints, entangled in *their* mazes' (the mazes of the smile, the onlooker's own amazement). But with each sinking or failure of relationship, with each entry into annihilation, paradox re-emerges in a new form as a means of constructing experience, coming into being out of nothing, as it were, but with a structure made possible by that condition.

Paradox is a living example of the transformation of categories and the creation of new ones. What it construes here, with
characteristic daring and virtuosity, is that experience of 'is' and
'is not' which is the condition of the expansion of language and
knowledge. Asia is unknowable, imageless, concealed and yet
revealed. With a dazzling rearrangement and reversal of paradoxical statement in negative and positive terms, each of which
grows out of antecedent forms (the dazzle is in the words –
enkindle, fire, burning, radiant, shinest, brightness), the paradoxical structure asserts that to construe a not seen is to shape a
seen, that to construe a seen is to define a not seen. 'Screen
them', 'hide them', 'shrouds thee', 'folds thee', 'clad with brightness'. The poem risks mystical language and the metaphor of the
veil and barrier to knowledge (with its cognate implication that
language is the inadequate dress of thought), and yet enables
these to contradict themselves. 'Then screen them/In those
looks, where whoso *gazes*.' To screen is to constitute a presence
as well as to hide it: there could be no screen without something
behind it. Reciprocally, a presence brings into being a screen.
And so a visible screen brings the possibility of 'looks' and
'gazes' into being. Screen generates its opposite, seen is not, is.
Those looks, the syntax allows, are the screen, and also what is
screened, 'them', the smiles which are consequently, simultaneously, consecutively, reflexively, screening themselves.
Appropriately, as smiles are present and absent, given transient
form in physical features without being physical features themselves, and giving form to physical features and indeed requiring
them for its existence. A smile is neither the body nor the disem-
bodied, but it might be called the 'Life of Life' in the strict sense
that it both animates and is animated by the physical, a presence
which cannot come into being without the physical, cannot be
subtracted from it and yet mysteriously does not belong to it, is
not *of* it. What the paradoxes have done is to give new content to
the paradox of 'Life'. The first paradox moves towards creating
a being for 'imageless' 'Life'. The poem gives itself the right to
call Asia 'Child of Light' in the next stanza. She is made of light,
generated by it, but also the progeny of knowing, born out of
what is known, as the next stanza is born out of the paradoxes of
the first.

It is the negative side of the known, not known, revealed, concealed paradox which is uppermost in the second stanza. Screen, seen, 'shrouds', 'shinest': the contradictory words become closely allied in sound. Shrouding is dependent upon shining for its activity. The not seen creates the seen and yet is intuited through it, known by what conceals it. 'Thy limbs are burning/ *Through* the vest which seems to hide thee.' 'Seems' here, appropriately, asks the perceptual question arising from the ambiguity of 'through'; burning behind and shining through, burning by means of, burning up, penetrating through, but in all cases the nature of covering vesture and limbs is interdependent, the one coming into being as known through the other 'As the radiant lines of morning/*Through* the clouds ere they divide them': the ambiguous syntax here allows a similar reciprocal interdependence of being to radiant sunrise and concealing clouds. Either clouds divide, *expose* radiance, or radiance divides, penetrates, clouds. 'Them' is radiance and cloud indivisibly. We cannot see a voice or the source of a voice, so the third stanza proposes; and yet being is folded in sound like a shroud. It can be sensed. Again, and paradoxically, absence is intuited as present and therefore presence from the sourceless song. Again, precence is negatively intuited from positive absence in a fluid grammar: 'for *it* folds *thee*/From the sight, that liquid splendour'. The song, 'it', is liquid splendour and so is 'thee', the being of Asia, and so is 'sight' which designates both self and seen, liquid splendour created by and creating splendour. Being is *flowing* radiance, or beauty as splendour, is taken back to its primal sense as lustre. The source and its derivation are fused as the not seen creates, not the seen, but the known. And the lyric proceeds to its final paradox – 'Its dim shapes are clad with brightness'. The concealing element is light itself as screen and shroud reverse their sense of obliterating physical barrier. Dimness is created by brightness. The deep truth is imageless and known, but, the paradox of the paradox, each condition enables, creates the other and this in itself is being. It is also language, as speech creates thought and is indivisible from it.

The poem fulfils itself here, one would have thought, creating and denying negation as the principle of growth and allowing speech to create thought by fusing shape and sense, form and meaning. Perhaps the new confidence in the use of reflection as a paradigm of relationship which is returned to in Act III, and the emphasis on its restructuring and creative possibilities, is born of the discovery of the possibilities of dialogue and creative negation in Act II. Indeed, the 'interval' of Act II would enable one to see the insistent pairing doubling and antithesis of ideas of reflection in Acts I and III as an attempt to create not a simple opposition but a paradox out of the contradictions of reflection itself. It is, and is not an enclosed self-creation of object by the subject. The poem solves some of its problems in Act II, proposing the finding of an object in the very fact of its negation and the fact of lacunae by turning want into need, the need which creates a new object and new knowledge. However, the rigour of this lyric, and of the whole poem, is unremitting. They carry their own criticisms along with them. Since the finding of the object depends on the losing of it, on lacunae, a reading of Act II does not entirely resist an account of it as that condition in which mind constructs itself as other, not the thing but thought. 'Faints', 'lost forever', 'failing', 'Dizzy': these words do not withstand the familiar attack on idealism. The negation created as other, the hungry void and interval craving for being, can be defined, as Marx defined it, as that void from which reality is continually disappearing, reaching its vanishing-point where the distinction between subject and object dissolves into thought's wildernesses. The gazer entangled in the amazement of the 'mazes' of what it sees, 'those looks' is also entangled in 'their' or his *own* mazes, and through the ambiguity of the syntax 'those looks' are his own seeing and the seen without distinction. In the same way the 'sight' is the 'see-ers' sight and the sight he sees, as the fluent syntax of 'that liquid splendour' moves indeterminately between 'it' as voice, 'thee' as Asia and 'sight' as perceiver and perceived.

The last line of Act III, 'Pinnacled dim in the intense inane', unintentionally corroborates these doubts, and, despite its certainties, the triumphant assertion of freedom is less confident than it might seem. Nor yet exempt, though 'ruling them like slaves,/From chance, and death, and mutability' (iii, iv, 200–20): men rule the slaves of chance and death, but, the syntax allows, exposing the complexities of power and freedom, they also rule them as slaves rule. If the poem had ended at Act III it would have left too many things closed and too many things open. The rapturous coda of the fourth Act is a necessity. Neither Act II nor Act III entirely free themselves into a universe of reciprocity, despite the play of energy, of motion and flight, of rush and speed, of beings drawn and driven, impelling and impelled, active and passive, fleeing and pursuing, first and last. The models of relationship evolved raise doubts as the paradigm of reflection reasserts itself, either suggesting the subjugation of secondary forms as the self encloses the object in a reduplication of itself or creating a state where relationships are obliterated altogether in undifferentiated exchange of qualities. The coda of Act IV does not leave aside the perplexities of the poem. Instead it releases itself into the energies of freedom and delight by another act of repetition – the interpenetration and flow of light, wind, water, the leap of energy through and into being and being, the synaesthesic fusion of like and unlike. Act IV repeats the images of the earlier poem, recirculating them to act out the energies of circulation and movement. It is constructed out of dialogue and dance, echo and reflection but gives primacy to none of these paradigms of relationship, simply including them all. Included, too, but redefined by the released energies of delight and compassion, are the implications of subjugation and dissolution which so threatened the earlier acts. They are not forgotten. The poem includes and acknowledges its perplexities within itself. It can do this because it is a celebration of *Hope* rather than an achieved triumph. Hope, creating 'From its own wreck the thing it contemplates' is another and more affirmative definition of want. Meanwhile, reminding itself of the recurrent pattern of dependence and subjugation, the moon, circling in dizzy maenad-like movement round the earth, dependent on it for light, repeats the structure of the Furies' relation to Prometheus in Act I, though not its form.

> Drinking from thy sense and sight
> Beauty, majesty, and might,
> As a lover or a chameleon,
> Grows like what it looks upon. (481–4)

As the moon dissolves in the light of the sun, Earth answers, 'And the weak day weeps/That it should be so', mourning its own and the moon's dependence on the sun. The mourning here, amid the celebrations of Act IV, sounds the great perplexity of this poem, which cannot obliterate the pattern of dependence and subjugation. Nor, correspondingly perhaps, can it entirely acknowledge that language 'rules' and creates thought.

NOTES

1 'On Life', *Shelley's Prose*, David Lee Clark (ed.), Albuquerque, 1954, p. 174.
2 Ibid.
3 *Beyond*, New York, London, 1973, 199.
4 *A Defence of Poetry*, *Shelley's Prose*, p. 283.

CHAPTER 5

Browning,
The Fracture of Subject and Object:
Sordello, Book III

> The common sort, the crowd,
> Exist, perceive; with Being are endowed,
> However slight, distinct from what they See,
> However bounded; Happiness must be,
> To feed the first by gleanings from the last,
> Attain its qualities, and slow or fast
> Become what they behold; such peace-in-strife,
> By transmutation, is the Use of Life,
> The Alien turning Native to the soul
> Or body – which instructs me. (111, 159–68)

'Who *will*, may hear Sordello's story told ... Only believe me. You believe?' So Book I of *Sordello* begins. *Sordello* is written as if it is willed into existence as a demonstration of the creative act of bringing history into being. The act of will – *who* will – is made by both poet and reader, who also brings the poem into being. The language behaves as if the poem is always in the making, just at the point of being brought into being, always becoming, maintained by fiats and acts of mental and physical bravado which deliberately draw attention to the *display* of making fiction 'Appears/Verona'(1): 'One more day, one Eve – appears Verona!' (111). Verona comes into sight – as *seen* and Verona *seems*, the ambiguity of 'appears' asserts. 'Will' is Browning's word for the imagination, and this willed and wilful poem includes its own self-conscious virtuosity as its subject. It displays the energies which turn the 'Alien' mass of inchoate historical material which is Sordello's story 'Native' to the poet's being in order to challenge that activity and its claims to discover history as living process. The choice of the word 'Alien' to signify the object (a prophetic act) denotes a conception of it as unreachably apart from the subject. The passage about the transformations of perception quoted above, one of Sordello's meditations in Book III, is one to which I shall return. The poet ('motley on back and pointing pole in hand') exposes his fiat as 'trick', conjuring, performance. 'Lo, the past is hurled/In twain: up-thrust, out-staggering on the world,/Subsiding into shape, a darkness rears/Its outline, kindles at the core, appears/Verona' (1, 73–7). The lines subside into shape. A darkness 'rears', momentarily undifferentiated shape. The line-break plays a perceptual trick as the historic present subverts succession into instantaneousness. Verona coalesces into being as a concretion of sensory experience. (The Body 'instructs me', confirms the sensuous otherness of the world the self labours upon, Sordello later meditates, in the passage I have quoted as epigraph.) 'Up-thrust', 'out-staggering' from the poet's energy, Verona 'appears' as if out of some physical upheaval more potent than the earthquake which throws up Alberic's 'huge skeleton', a model of the inert life of the past, at the end of the poem. And so Browning reverses the fading coal of verbal life, the passing out of being, which he found in Shelley's poetry, and persuades language to ignite, to kindle at the core, and create the materials and the structure of perception in front of you – 'a darkness rears/Its outline'. The conscious act of construction enforced by the break persuades one to come hard up against the nature of cognition as a process which 'Attains' or 'Becomes' 'what it beholds', as my epigraph describes, by going through the work of discovering and making shape emerge. The beginning of Book III parodies Sordello's Romantic assumption that he can rinse his identity clean in 'Nature's strict embrace' by returning to Goito, the place of his early life. Culture, not Nature, is the Alien thing that 'becomes' the Native being in *Sordello*. The dangerous edge of idealist thinking is more exposed when the claims of history are substituted for Coleridge's claims for Nature – and in our life alone does History live. There is something wanton, a kind of dare, about the choice of the Guelf-Ghibelline struggles of medieval Italy before Dante as the material of the poem. The poem dares itself and the reader to enquire into the status of the act of imaginative reconstruction. A second generation Romantic poem, published in 1840, nearly twenty years after *Prometheus*, *Sordello* is a self-aware analysis of its epistemology.

From the beginning a strategy of rhetoric establishes that the making of the poem depends as much on the reader's 'will' as the poet's – '*Who* will' – and asks questions implicitly about the status of interpretation. The reader enables the poem's fiction to come into being and constructs it himself. *Sordello* is a multiple poem, constructed by poet and reader.

> And the font took them: let our laurels lie!
> Braid moonfern now with mystic trifoly.

So Book III begins. It is necessary to grope twenty lines back into Book II to discover that the font is Goito's font, the source of Sordello's early creative life, begun in solipsist isolation in his childhood as an orphan. 'Them' refers to Sordello's troubadour favours, won in the poetic contests which have dissatisfied and ravaged him. '*Our* laurels lie' – Sordello's, reader's, poet's – and these are replaced by healing herbs, moonfern, trifoly. The multiple syntax here registers that the poem is in possession of three different historical times, Sordello's time, the poet's, writing in the nineteenth century, the reader at any time after that. 'Braid moonfern': the reader, the poet, braid or weave the poem into being, and the being of the poem is a triple process, a 'mystic' trifoly or three-leaved clover, because Sordello's 'story' is mediated by the poet, the poet's mediations by the reader. That is why it is simultaneously and unashamedly about the predicament of Romantic, idealist poetry and the struggles of a medieval troubadour. By the same token it is a modern poem, a twentieth-century poem. The effrontery of the imperatives and rhetorical questions insist upon the reader's activity as creator of the poem. 'Enough. Now turn –/Over the eastern cypresses: discern!/Is any beacon set a-glimmer?' (III, 295–7). It is a directive without a content. The question is unanswered. What is important is that the perceptual structure of the search for an object sharpens an awareness of the problematical nature of discerning and of the act of constructing an object. All this declares that the poem is not a story or a linear narrative at all. There is a real sense in which the poem *is* a trick or sleight of hand. It is and is about the act and process of mediation itself. It lives out its epistemology, experiencing the contradictions of the unstable process of discerning, becoming what you behold, which is continually falling into onesidedness.

There is another moment of effrontery towards the end of Book III when Browning emerges from his poem, in the middle of an unfinished metaphor for creation, into his own history, into contemporary Venice, out of medieval Verona. I deal with this in detail later. At present it is enough to show that the break is a model of interpretation or mediation. The poet breaks with his fiction and re-establishes the poem as commentary on the poem and as his own historical situation – 'put aside –/Entrance thy Synod' (609–10). The syntax allows the Synod, corporate debate or commentary (again, it is the poet's and the reader's debate – *thy* Synod) to describe the poem he has left and his own interpolation alike. And it is a justifiable description of poem and poet. Book III is a series of debates and commentaries, Sordello with himself, Palma with Sordello, Taurello Salinguerra with Palma. At the point of the poet's entry into the poem the climactic moment of decision which Sordello has just reached, when he is persuaded by Palma to take a leading part in the Ghibelline faction, dissolves into or is displaced by commentary. The poem begins with this moment in Book I and returns to it at the centre of the six books in Book III, but the centre is displaced by Browning's intervention into or departure from his poem, which is an exit and an entrance alike. *Sordello* is a poem without a centre. It is not an event six hundred years ago because ''Tis six hundred years and more/*Since* an event' (1, 77–8), and must be the construction of an event. So if history is the experience of construing, always in the present tense, always a becoming, this is what the poem will be, a series of displacements, of makings and remakings, interruptions and transitions.

The poem is constructed as a becoming, constantly interrupted by voices interposing and breaking off the narrative – the voices of the poet, of participants in the events: indeed it cannot be called a 'narrative' in the conventional sense of the word. The 'dishevelled ghost' of the prostitute breaks in upon the poet's meditations in contemporary Venice. 'Naddo *interposing* leant/ Over the lost bard's shoulder' (111, 222–3). Naddo, preposterous theorist of poetry and political go-between, appears over Sordello's shoulder, the poem's shoulder, breaking in on his self-analysis to call him back from exile to Salinguerra's Ghibelline military activity. Naddo's interpolation is not a detached commentary on events in the poem, displacing the 'real' narrative: it is the poem. Not 'about' experience, it *is* experience. The rush of inchoate information on the latest Guelf-Ghibelline strife is precisely inchoate because it is rendered as the consciousness of Naddo experiencing events – interpretation, not narration. The facts of the situation are so internalised, so casually assumed, that family connections, causal and temporal relationships, remain ungiven. The significance of the immense flow of details is hidden beneath the surface of the news: He neither names – 'The father of our Patroness [Ecelin and Palma, Ghibellines] ... Parts between Ecelin and Alberic [divides his inheritance between his sons]' nor clarifies the order of events: 'the Count and Palma plighted troth/A week since at Verona [Count Richard Boniface, Guelf, making a union between Ghibellines and Guelfs] ... 'Ere Richard storms Ferrara.' (Richard intends to attack Taurello Salinguerra, the Ghibelline military leader who is isolated at Ferrara by Ecelin's withdrawal from the conflict into a monastery.) Naddo's account of events is mediated by his evaluation of them in terms of exciting anecdotal gossip – Ecelin 'Has played Taurello an astounding trick' – and sanctimonious morality – 'Inaugurate a new and better rule'. His commentary shapes itself in the continuous present, a historic and an *actual* present tense, evolving by remembering and projecting; such analysis means that the past is always unfinished, always becoming, and paradoxically always moving beyond itself into futurity because interpretation itself is a becoming, a bringing of possibility into being.

The core of history is illusory. 'Only, do finish something' (731) the poet breaks in upon his own meditations. 'Presumptuous ... interrupts one' (833). The constant displacements of this Synod galvanise the poem into becoming. Experience is its construing – Naddo interposing – and possibly this ought to imply that experience is constituted purely by mind. The poem continually seeks to avoid and as continually reintroduces this proposal. Among the innumerable models for creativity proposed and abandoned with prolific ease in this poem, the one most constantly under attack, and at which the hectoring, self-chiding, mock-heroic-grotesque manner of *Sordello* intensifies, is the idealist notion of the world as the creation of the self's subjective life. There is a confident knowingness about the fallacies of Romantic accounts of creation. The first allusion in the poem is to Don Quixote seeing an army in the cloud of dust made by sheep in a valley.

Book III ends with a facetiously blasphemous inverted

analogue to the Quixote episode – St. John seeing the shadow of his own statue and pastoral cross as the Devil with his prong, a Feuerbachian fable. Just before the Venice commentary the poem satirises a metaphor for creation: art is not *'transcendental* platan', the mystic tree of fire, made by a mage to amuse a queen (wizardry, magical, Faustian violation always clings to Browning's metaphors for creation). The autonomous thing of pure mind, *sui generis,* and incandescent, is self-creating and self-consuming, turns to nothing – 'Bloom-flinders ... and leaf-dust'. A poet is neither prophet (striking the rock 'awkwardly enough' (826) in imitation of Moses) nor God, entering and leaving his intact creation at will – 'as a god may glide/Out of the world he fills, and leave it mute/For myriad ages as we men compute,/Returning into it without a break/O' the consciousness!' So Browning parodies his own exit/entrance into his poem, for the exit/entrance mediates the poem, so that poet and poem stand inevitably in a new relationship to each other. A 'break/O' the consciousness' – characteristically the line-break enforces this – is part of the being of the poem.

The god analogy is subverted by being made formally an interruption, actually constituting the 'break' of consciousness which establishes the poet in Venice. The dispersed, centreless syntax at this crucial point lives the significance of the break.

>   he decrepit, stark,
> Dozes; her uncontrolled delight may mark
> Apart –
>   Yet not so, surely never so
> Only, as good my soul were suffered go
> *O'er the lagune:* forth fare thee, put aside –
> Entrance thy synod, as a god may glide...
> Returning into it without a break
> O' the consciousness! They sleep, and I awake
> *O'er the lagune*, being at Venice. (605–10; 613–15)

The structure of these lines offers an account of consciousness quite different from the 'transcendental platan'. This is just the point at which the poem severs itself from historical Verona, and appropriately ends on the word 'Apart' as the poem comes apart. 'he decrepit, stark,/Dozes; her uncontrolled delight may mark/Apart – ''Yet not so, surely never so/Only' The transcendental platan, apart in another sense as autonomous entity of mind, generating a world of life which we may 'mark/Apart' is subjected to scepticism – 'not so'. '*He* ... dozes ... *her* ... delight ... Apart –.' He and her, the mage and the queen in the metaphor for creation of pure mind, or he and her, the dozing Sordello and the delighted Palma who belong to a resumption of the 'narrative' which is to be severed almost immediately and made to stand also in metaphorical relationship to the mage and queen. Or 'he' the poet, who stands as mage to his poem. The pronouns conflate narrative, metaphor, creator, indivisibly, and yet these could not be conflated without the 'rhymes' which introduce the mage analogy. Rhyme holds together and separates – 'my rhymes – that spring, dispread,/Dispart, disperse' (593–4). Rhyme enables the conflated things to be seen simultaneously as differentiated elements because rhyme words simultaneously fuse and distinguish sounds. Another sense of 'Apart' is then generated. Being can 'become' 'what it beholds' only by beholding what it becomes, only by preserving the relation of subject and object as 'distinct' and 'Alien' (to use the language of Sordello's meditations on being) in the process of re-lationship, a 'break/O' the consciousness'. The transcendental platan is 'not so', cannot exist *only,* solely, or alone; but with that ellipsis which makes the break and the conflation depen-dent on one another, 'only' is attracted backwards and forwards to different parts of the sentence. It denies the partial onesided-ness of the transcendental account of creation and also supports 'as good my soul' – Only, as good my soul were suffered go'. Not so, not transcendental *except* in so far as my *soul* is allowed to go over the lagune. The mundane lagune can be crossed in spirit and becomes a possession of the mind. But it could not be so unless the lagune is understood as that concrete, substantive other, possessing the independent being of external things on which the self labours. The pun 'good my soul', spirit and, jocu-larly, the physical self, acknowledges the literal, physical negotiation of the lagune. The imagination is only transcenden-tal in the sense that being is an act of perception, volition and projection. 'And I awake,/O'er the lagune, *being* at Venice'. 'O'er the lagune' has shifted its sense and relationship with rep-etition, preserving its form but changing its meaning. The rhymes on the god which have disparted the first occurrence of the phrase from the second have established a 'break/O' the con-sciousness', a temporal break, so that the simple prepositional meaning of over, across, has become verbal in the second phrase, conflating the *action* of having crossed and the *projection* of crossing with the action of *overlooking* and retrospection in a new present. The achieved moment supersedes the projected moment in a lightning contraction because between the first 'O'er' and the second 'O'er the lagune' the poet has performed the act of crossing, not in mind but in body. 'O'er the lagune, *being* at Venice': to wake to consciousness, 'I ... *being*' at Venice, is also to acknowledge 'I ... O'er the lagune, being'. Being is not a pure state of consciousness standing over and against the world or a condition which duplicates the self as object. It is 'I ... being ... O'er ... at'. Being is relationship in transition, the constantly changing relationship of self to world, world to self, in projection and in action. The space of the mundane lagune is a metaphor for the notion of transition. Being is 'over' or 'o'er', across, having crossed, overlooking, experienced both as continuity and break. But it is always o'er, across, *something*. The core of being as essential, stable self, like the core of history, is illusory, but the world of objects is not banished.

It is now time to look more closely at the long epistemological meditation which takes place at Goito. The relevance of Sordello's meditations on the 'Alien' world to the Venice interlude become clearer. 'To feed the first by gleanings from the last': the reciprocal relation of subject and object preserved by 'transmutation' is the 'Use of life'.

> The common sort, the crowd,
> Exist, perceive; with Being are endowed,
> However slight, distinct from what they See,
> However bounded: Happiness must be,
> To feed the first by gleanings from the last,
> Attain its qualities, and slow or fast
> Become what they behold; such peace-in-strife,
> By transmutation, is the Use of Life,
> The Alien turning Native to the soul
> Or body – which instructs me.

Being, the first, is fed, constituted by the lagune, the object, the last. The 'first' and 'last' are interchangeable words, displacing one another. They can mean primary and secondary, earlier and *latest:* the last becomes first, the first last. The same words allow a subject-object relationship or an object-subject relationship. 'Gleanings' shifts from noun to verb. The lagune then becomes constituted by being; the object offers 'gleanings' to the subject, the subject makes 'gleanings' from the object. The language of Sordello's meditations is reversible. 'Attain its qualities ... Become what *they* behold': 'its', 'they' assert the mutuality of subject and object by referring interchangeably to each. 'Its', 'they', allow the ceaseless creation and reversing of subject and object in the act of transmutation. 'The Alien *turning*': turning is reversibly active and passive. The 'Alien' is acting and being acted on by the subject. The language moves in two directions, simultaneously separating and eliding subject and object. Life lives us, we live life. The one becomes the other in a process of constant interchange and reversibility. Subject and object are in a state of constant transition, on the way to being their opposites. The passage retrieves a substantive world for the subject without making each 'Alien' to the other.

The emergence into Venice is expressed with a happy sense of ease as if the poet is suddenly released into a world of objects and human activity, peasants, prostitutes, people at work – 'That Bassanese/Busied, among her smoking fruit-boats' (681– 2). Sordello's speech on 'turning' appears to release the poem from an account of the universe as self-duplication which haunts it. It secures 'distinct' the real sensuous world as Marx described it for the subject. The subject does not wholly constitute the world as a category of mind since the world constitutes him. However, in locating being as the subject's transitional act of mediation in the Venice passage the poem retrieves for itself once again the primacy of the subject's consciousness, and reintroduces idealist problems in another form. So much so that at times *Sordello* seems engaged in a physical struggle to take language back to the sensory in order to maintain the world 'in flesh'. Sordello wishes to 'Include a world, in flesh', to make a world which is a part of the physical being, but which is simultaneously 'in flesh', substantive, other. His meditations on the 'Alien' and 'Native' world which conclude his exile in Goito appear to reach a point which enables him to go forward, but this is only apparent. Certainly, his meditations return upon and revalue the earlier parasitic 'palmer worm' phase at Goito in Book I. The 'inert', 'clogged', volitionless world there, for all its marvellously pullulating generative physical life is described with idealist hubris. The universe is a thing of the 'simplest combination' (1, 543) in comparison with mind's 'complexest essence' (1, 546), 'a mere twin/With a distinctest consciousness within' (1, 525–6). The syntax refuses to distinguish between Sordello's creative existence and the world's, and makes him virtually responsible for it – a 'footfall there/Suffices to upturn to the warm air/Half-germinating spices' (1, 471–3). This hubris encounters a corrective in Book III, but the Venice passage offers another reading of being as transition which is less reassuring than the confident resolution of the Alien/Native meditation.

> Venice seems a type
> Of Life – '*twixt* blue and blue extends, a stripe,
> As Life, the somewhat, hangs '*twixt* nought and nought. (723–5)

Transition, turning, ''twixt', is the 'type' of Life. The repetition of ''twixt' lives transition, and yet, like so much of Browning's parallelism, the same form acquires another content in a lightning mediation of new relationships. The changing nature of ''twixt' embodies the restructuring that goes on in the process of transition. If being is a hanging ''twixt', a mediation, the substantive relationship between subject and object can be either maintained and abolished, preserved or negated. It is preserved in the sense that being is a movement between the two, dissolved in the sense that the movement ''twixt' involves a constant exchange of qualities which are in any case subsumed into the *process*, 'the somewhat' of becoming. So that subject and object could equally well be nought and nought, paradoxically dissolved in the act of mediation. The shifting syntax here, the eliding appositional dash refusing to clarify the status of relationships, allows a double reading. One reading puts the emphasis on the terminal points of subject and object, the other on the state of transition itself. A 'type/Of Life – 'twixt blue and blue extends, a stripe'. 'Life' is the totality, the stripe which includes blue and blue in the movement between them: or 'a stripe,/*As* Life, the somewhat, *hangs* ''twixt', and the repeated ''twixt' is redefined as the state between, excluded by, and excluding nought and nought. The state between easily becomes a state of transition in which consciousness is experienced as a state of displacement, outside, nullified by and nullifying the world of subject/object relations. That is why the language of the poem is unstable, structuring and dispersing relationships simultaneously. It is not simply that subject and object displace one another, continually granting each other the primacy of acting and being acted upon, as in Sordello's 'Alien, Native' speech: transition simply becomes a gap, a state of emptiness. There are two syntaxes here, yet there are not, as for Wordsworth, alternative syntaxes; they force one another further and further apart.

Both in the Alien, Native speech, and in the Venice commentary a third activity is at work in the fractured sentences constructed out of ambiguous appositional dashes and parentheses. The appositional construction, like some kind of loosened verbal floe, attaches amorphously between what precedes and what follows it. The parentheses are both gap and bridge, held outside the sentence and uniting the parts they separate. The principle of transition and displacement governs each, and in both the break and the elision achieve the same function: both 'dispart' and both merge relationships, both create a syntax without a centre. For transition has no centre. It is becoming. Rhyme, which makes elements of different words 'become' one another, but which is both a closure and a separation, is a paradigm of the disparting process in *Sordello*.

Sordello forces a construing of its language, and sharpens the necessity present in all dealings with words. They come into being with the reader's activity. The reader wills the poem into being, allows and creates it, by constructing the relationships of the sentences as if they were in another language. The 'Alien' and idiosyncratic vocabulary is another way of bringing the reader's activity about, forcing him to feel out new semantic areas which may overlap with a word's 'translation', but never quite match it. Translation never achieves a fixed and stable solution to meaning, but it invests the activity of mediation with significance by asserting the brute otherness of the thing to be translated: its terms, your terms, modifying one another. It is the paradigm of 'turning' but it is also a paradigm for disparting. It forces an awareness not of the results but of the process of construing relationships, the constant, unstable adjustments between multiple possibilities which cannot be fixed but which can be construed as ambiguous. The structure of mediation is laid bare in translation. The construing is its own meaning.

Sordello's meditations at Goito, which form a prologue to Book III, are acts of construction ''twixt', memories or projections which attempt to be bridges but which phantasmally dissolve in a movement between nought and nought. His memory of love actually has the effect of making the past vanish.

> Not any strollings now at even-close
> Down the field-path, Sordello! by thorn-rows
> Alive with lamp-flies, swimming spots of fire
> And dew, outlining the black cypress' spire
> She waits you at, Elys, who heard you first
> Woo her, the snow-month through, but ere she durst
> Answer 't was April. Linden-flower-time-long
> Her eyes were on the ground; 'tis July, strong
> Now; and because white dust-clouds overwhelm
> The woodside, here or by the village elm
> That holds the moon, she meets you, somewhat pale,
> But letting you lift up her coarse flax veil
> And whisper (the damp little hand in yours)
> Of love, heart's love, your heart's love that endures
> Till death. Tush! (103–17)

It has to be seen how easily the syntax, which makes the act of construction paramount and lives the idea of meaning as transition, can lend itself to a notion of experience as displacement. The memory of Elys, one of those fragments of lyric feeling thrown up with a kind of violent poignance and yet cynicism into Sordello's strenuous introspections constructs itself as a becoming, continually displacing the status of 'now'. The 'now' of his present turns into the 'now' of the past and paradoxically into a new present as the past is discovered afresh. 'Not any strollings now at even-close/Down the field path, Sordello': the verbless sentence deprives any hypothetical future 'even-close' of possible existence, but a new verbless series carries the 'now' into a past coextensive with the present as a succession of sensory experiences unfold ambiguously, as an actual visual experience, or associative memory, or projections into the *future*. What we get is a new 'now', generated in front of us, moving ahead, as the sentence paradoxically moves into the past. 'Strollings ... Down the field path ... by thorn rows'. Each sensory moment brings another into being: 'by thorn rows,/Alive with lamp-flies', lamp-flies, 'swimming spots of fire and dew', spots, 'outlining the black cypress' spire'. Then the sentence discovers an impediment, '*she* waits you at, Elys, who heard you first woo her'. It changes its structure, stumbles up against a verb and on an ambiguous form. 'She waits you at' attaches to cypress as a contracted relative clause, the black spire at which she waits you. But it is as if the sentence has discovered its real subject and

a new object: *she* ... by thorn rows ... waits at *you*. Elys waits
for Sordello, now an object to himself, 'you'. 'She waits you at'
lives in a suspended, open present, the present of the past, the
present of the present, the present of the hypothetical future.
'Now' has moved both back from and beyond the now of the
present. 'You' is a multiple identity, a conflation of 'you's': you,
Sordello, now, the not you in the past, the not you of the future,
or indeed could even be any you, any typical lover who is not
Sordello. 'She waits you at' both waits apart from the sentence
as a displaced, postponed unassimilable element and at the same
time supersedes 'strollings' as the core phrase. For Elys lurks as a
concealed subject fused with the passionate experience of even-
close, interposing at any of the successive descriptive phrases.
'She waits you', by thorn rows, alive, swimming, outlining. And
'you', too, 'you', Sordello as lover, 'you' the reader as lover, par-
ticipate in that experience. She waits you, you, 'by thorn-rows',
you, 'alive'. 'She waits you at, Elys', both at the centre and displaced, questions by its form whether the past is ever pure and
intact, and inevitably whether our 'now' is fixed, stable. ''Tis
July, Strong/*Now* and ... she meets you'. This 'now' denotes a
new past and a new present, but it has modulated into a different
experience. The recreation of memory is a transformation of it,
shaped here by Sordello's subsequent scepticism and distrust of
the naïveties of sexual love. The parentheses are redefined by the
ironic hyperboles which follow, and become patronising and
diminishing rather than tender – '(the damp little hand in
yours)'. The parentheses belong to a 'now' of the past and a new
'now' of the present, roughly interpolated by another and scepti-
cal you. It undermines the lyric of sexual feeling and abrasively
ironises the protestation of permanence which is already precluded at the start – 'No more strollings *now*'. '*Your* heart's love
that endures/Till death. Tush!': '*Your*' may mean variously
ours, mine, yours but not mine, according to which of the 'nows'
it is attached. The village elm vainly 'holds' – embraces and
arrests – the moon. Experience is a construction ''twixt'. It is
hard to know whether or not the celebration of Elys, conceived
with such a passionate understanding of a lover's sense of
totality, resists the construction ''twixt'. It seems to be both
created and undermined by it.

The problems of seeing being as mediation, as a movement

''twixt' enable us to place the contradiction of Sordello's experience at Goito and during his attempt to take political action in
the Guelf-Ghibelline conflict. At the conclusion of his meditations on the 'Alien' and 'Native' duality of experience, which
ends the prologue of meditations at the start of Book III Sordello
makes the fatal onesided idealist shift which is potentially but
not necessarily present in his analysis. 'My will/Owns all
already' (176). Everything takes place within the self. Life is a
continuous act of construction which abolishes the substantive
otherness of the concrete world because it is construed as an
aspect of the self. The contradictions of this position are already
embedded in the syntax of the poem. To include all within the
self may just as easily be expressed as an *ex*clusion. The fragile
equipoise of the Alien/Native passage is dissolved. Being
becomes an experience of displacement, movement between
nought and nought, and this leads Sordello to a desperate
attempt to reintroduce the object he has abolished and to constitute that as 'life' and not the relation between it and the self. If
life is a continuous act of construction, then where is *living*?
Sordello displaces 'life' from his experience and vainly attempts
to reunite himself with it. Life is always outside him, he outside
life. 'Living' is a constantly deferred activity. Sordello never can
'begin to Be' (172). A sense of severance, dryness, and a greedy
desire for fullness is the immediate symptom of this failure 'to
Be'. Immediately after the Elys passage, interestingly, Sordello
attempts to appropriate or 'acquire' as he puts it the unreachable
voluptuary orgies of the Emperor Friedrich in a frustrated and
unsatisfied rage for the sensual. The Elys passage modulates
abruptly into the account of Friedrich.

> Till death. Tush! No mad mixing with the rout
> Of haggard ribalds wandering about
> The hot torchlit wine-scented island-house
> Where Friedrich holds his wickedest carouse,
> Parading, – to the gay Palermitans,
> Soft Messinese, dusk Saracenic clans
> Nuocera holds, – those tall grave dazzling Norse,
> High-cheeked, lank-haired, toothed whiter than the morse,
> Queens of the caves of jet stalactites,
> He sent his barks to fetch through icy seas,
> The blind night seas without a saving star,
> And here in snowy birdskin robes they are,

Sordello! – here, mollitious alcoves gilt
Superb as Byzant domes that devils built! (117–30)

His sense of being deprived of a world to act on or with has
political significance as well as being an epistemological and
psychological fact for him. If consciousness is experienced as a
continual construing, continual becoming, placing itself outside
'life', choice or action is meaningless, because all activity
becomes a series of consequenceless improvisations of the ego.
The decision to make men 'act' (582) which justifies his following of the fussing Naddo to Verona and glorious (or
vainglorious) participation in Palma's schemes (Palma is
throughout his idealised object) is not the constructive move it
seems to be. It reinstates another separation and establishes and
confirms a split between will, imagination, and action. The
sense of life, the violent galvanising of activity, is substituted for
living. The need to have men 'themselves *made* act' is a need to
have his own being and potency confirmed by the process and
not a real political ideal. Hence his failure at the end of the poem
to choose between Guelf humanitarianism and reactionary Ghibelline when he is contemptuously offered the Ghibelline
leadership by Salinguerra, his newly discovered father.

Sordello is an orphan at the start of the poem, as well as
making himself one metaphorically. Browning attempts to show
that his dilemma and its contradictions emerges through real
and substantive conditions. And since the mode of the poem's
narrative, commentary, intervention, experience as construing,
is Sordello's mode, since the poem's syntax is Sordello's syntax,
it follows that the poem assumes these problems as its own. The
edgy uncertainties and even edgier certainties of Browning's
Venice intervention are no meta-commentary standing over and
against the poem, but simply re-explore the implications of
Sordello's 'story' in another context and reintroduce its
problems, with an added awareness posed by the implications of
writing the poem itself. If history and Sordello's story are mere
postulates of the consciousness, how does the poem begin to
'be'? Its being is a constantly deferred activity. The complexity
of the poem arises because its account of idealism emerges
through affirmation and critique simultaneously. The form and
language have to work for and against themselves. The poem
lives through and lives *through* its contradictions. One position
rescued undermines another, which rescues another and under-

mines it. A continuous peripeteia is at work in the processes of language, shifting statements as they are made.

To return to the prologue of meditation which occupies the first two hundred lines of Book III, the fractured syntax of Sordello's analyses during his period of withdrawal from Mantua to Goito moves with his attempts both to exclude and reincorporate the object he has dissolved. Repeatedly the sentences set up structures which leave elements of themselves out of account or else establish two mutually exclusive structures which leave each other out of account and fail to mediate one another. The double grammar imperceptibly at work in *The Prelude* moves to extremity in this poem.

> The last face glances through the eglantines,
> The last voice murmurs, 'twixt the blossomed vines,
> Of Men, of that machine supplied by thought
> To compass self-perception with, he sought
> By forcing half himself – an insane pulse
> Of a god's blood, on clay it could convulse,
> Never transmute – on human sights and sounds,
> To watch the other half with; (23–30)

'The last face glances … The last voice murmurs, 'twixt the blossomed vines,/Of Men'. These are images of the figures of the Mantuan period, which Sordello regards as 'factitious humours' 'grown' over the self. They are banished in the cause of achieving pure being stripped of self-consciousness, stripped of the past, history. As if to establish the fallacy of this – Browning calls it 'imbecility' – the images of memory delicately recombine with the substantive growth of eglantine and vine in Goito. No factitious growth, and as much a part of the identity as the memory he assumes he can excise. The voices call up Sordello's problem of relationship. The voices speak 'Of Men, of that machine supplied by thought/To compass self-perception with, he sought'. There are mutually exclusive constructions here: of men *and* of that machine, or of Men *as* that machine: of men supplied *with* thought to compass their own self-perception or men *created* by the thought of the thinker, Sordello, to effect his own reflexive self-perception. 'Men' act autonomously apart from the thinker's thought or else they are included in it. The sentence ends up as two self-enclosed tautologous constructions as the loose unattached 'with' (*with* what? Browning's syntax is full of unattached prepositions) circles back to two possible nouns each creating a kind of grammatical closed circuit. 'Of Men ... To compass self-perception with [that machine, Men]': 'by thought/To compass self-perception with [that machine, thought]'. Thought supplies some mechanism to include itself in itself, an attempt to include self-perception as an object of consciousness, but this construction excludes 'Men': 'Men', likewise, the opposite construction claims, excludes the thought of the thinking subject. The subject/object relation is further severed as the sentence continues: 'he sought', either 'Men' or 'self-perception', 'he sought,/'By forcing half himself ... on human sights and sounds,/To watch the other half with'. Again, the free-floating 'with' circles back to two possibilities. 'By forcing half himself ... To watch the other half with [half himself]': or 'By forcing half himself/To watch the other half with [human sights and sounds]'.

Pure consciousness is watching pure consciousness, or it is responding to the sensory evidence of human sights and sounds (becoming them, both supplying them in thought and conceiving them as substantive thinking beings, as other) to confirm its sense of relationship with the world, the other half. The split sentence can be expressed as an irrevocable fracture between monistic idealism and dualism. They are two 'halves', but cannot make a whole. Each emphasises the limits of the other. Thought and men, mind and world, thinking and experience, are pushed further and further apart. The ambiguity of 'supplied by thought' offers a precarious resolution of the two positions. 'Men', as independent and substantive thinking beings are nevertheless 'supplied by thought', created in and for the consciousness out of the evidence of sensory life which becomes a category of mind. The ferocious corrective parentheses support this by refusing the Romantic prerogative of creation as the operation of pure mind on a dead universe and describing it as 'insane', bringing the pulse of God's blood and the clay of the universe together with a physical shock. An 'insane pulse/Of a God's blood, on clay it could convulse,/Never transmute'. Sordello can only convulse or galvanise an object into being because he conceives it as inert and dead until he invests it with his own life, like a God. He cannot 'transmute' the universe outside him creatively because he cannot conceive it as living and capable of change and interaction with him. (Sordello continually reneges on the resolution of the Alien/Native meditation.) Ironically, the fierce parenthesis is a structural fracture, splitting 'half himself' from 'the other half' of its syntax by intervening, creating the onesidedness it aims to redeem. The physical ordering of those sentences, forcing the conceptual and epistemological struggle they are about, 'become' the fracture they express. The effort of construing and mediating the variants of their forms becomes their meaning.

And so Sordello fractures pure being and living further apart.

> No! youth once gone is gone:
> Deeds, let escape, are never to be done.
> Leaf-fall and grass-spring for the year; for us –
> Oh forfeit I unalterably thus
> My chance? *Not two lives wait me, this to spend,*
> *Learning save that?* Nature has time, may mend
> Mistake...
>   – I
> Must perish once and perish utterly. (93–9: 101–2)

The severance of the line-break, distinguishing the impossible 'two lives', this and that, both denies and confirms the impossibility of 'two lives'. This life for the prodigal energies of living, that life saved for and saving itself in 'Learning', contemplation and pure thought? This is one way to construe the cryptic statement. The line-break reinforces the sealing off of one activity from the other: 'Learning save that' – learning everything save for or except the spending of life. Again, however, the arrangement of the words is ambiguous and the same words produce another exclusive construction: 'this to spend/*Learning*' – the spending of life is integrally fused with the learning of it, and in this way the interdependent spending/learning process discovers through its activity all 'save that' two lives 'wait me' and denies the split it asserts. As a corollary, a last possibility of the syntax, 'Learning' can 'save' or rescue 'that', the life of action, for itself by understanding it, since deeds and the consciousness of acting them proceed concurrently. But no construction takes precedence over the other and all possible construings are dominated by the suspect verb *wait* me. Life is conceived by Sordello as waiting for him, apart from him, just as Elys 'waits' him in the following passage. 'Life' is like unspent sexuality.

For the potential split between learning and living moves to an avid reaching out in imagination to the sensuous and to passion in the Elys memory and to the blind sensuality of the Emperor

Friedrich, distrusted but desired – 'The hot torchlit wine-scented island house/Where Friedrich holds his wickedest carouse'. This episode is again almost resolved and almost undermined by the collapsing syntax of another analogy for experience, 'the life I waited' (142) now conceived as both ladder and platform. Sexuality, defined as the very centre of 'life' is experienced as hunger, life deferred in the projecting of it, something in wait, but also something perpetually waited for.

> What are ye
> But roundels of a ladder which appeared
> Awhile the very platform it was reared
> To lift me on? (142–5)

Experience and thought, consciousness and living, interchangeable ladder and platform in this drama of consciousness, supersede one another in a syntax of displacement. '*It* was reared', either ladder or platform, is on the precipice of a line-end and the precariousness is not resolved by the following line because 'to lift me on' reads doubly – to lift me *onwards* (into space), to lift me *on* (a foundation). Experience is either a restless series of projections from nought to nought or it is a fixed foundation for activity according to whether the ladder or the platform is paramount as the thing 'reared'. Either you have to project in order to experience or you have to experience in order to project. The physical arrangement of the lines, 'it was reared/ To lift me', suggest the interdependent activity of rearing and lifting – you have to lift in order to lift. An alternative discovery of the sentence is that projection enables and *becomes* experience, and that experience enables projection. This is all we can 'rest' upon, but the other suggestion of the fractured syntax, that projection and experience never meet, also coexists with this discovery.

The movement of over-charged erotic feeling in the Friedrich episode, in which the sensuous hunger for life becomes the materials of life, lives through the precarious resolution of the ladder/platform analogy. The acquiring of Friedrich's life in longing – 'Norse ... Queens of the caves of jet stalactites ... mollitious alcoves gilt' – becomes an acquisition not of that sensuous life itself but of an understanding of its sensuous reality and Sordello's own longing. It is a double 'self-revealment,' of his own nature, and Friedrich's objective nature, only to be achieved through longing. What is revealed is that sexuality, life itself, perhaps, is lived as a consuming condition of desire. Sensualist, aesthete and poet live through leaps into futurity. Friedrich's ships in the 'blind' night, monstrously ransacking the world for new erotic specimens, the blind architect, Dandolo, another cultural and aesthetic ransacker who took Byzantine art to Venice (where Browning emerges – typical of the palimpsest of *Sordello*) and lived in the 'promised life' (see 119–39) of touching, not seeing, his spoils there, are alike. They live through projection, becoming.

That projection might *be* life, becoming, and not the reaching out to elusive life beyond it is both understood and rejected by Sordello and possibly at times by the poem itself. He always conceives of himself as a 'pure' identity, outside life, free and unattached to history or circumstance. It is difficult to know whether this is the cause or effect of his assumption that life 'waits' him. The notion of pure identity is decisively satirised at the start of Book III. If being is transition then it is in time and through time and in and through concrete circumstances. It is no abstract process. *Sordello* is the most sensuous as well as the most theoretical of poems in order to allow the experience of becoming *as* experience, as sensuous being rather than abstract consciousness standing over and against 'life'. The savage epistemological comedy which initiates Book III asserts this, and yet its metaphor pulls in another direction as Sordello slips free of history, and it of him.

> Nature's strict embrace,
> Putting aside the past, shall soon efface
> Its print as well – factitious humours grown
> Over the true – loves, hatreds not his own –
> And turn him pure as some forgotten vest
> Woven of painted byssus, silkiest
> Tufting the Tyrrhene whelk's pearl-sheeted lip,
> Left welter where a trireme let it slip
> I' the sea, and vexed a satrap; so the stain
> O' the world forsakes Sordello, with its pain,
> Its pleasure: how the tinct loosening escapes,
> Cloud after cloud! (7–18)

Sordello divests himself of his social and cultural identity as if it were a dye like the ceremonial Tyrrhean purple of the ancient world. But the 'forgotten vest' of identity – by an elliptical metaphorical leap the language turns against itself – is 'Woven of painted byssus, silkiest/Tufting the Tyrrhene whelk's pearl-sheeted lip'. It is woven out of the mollusc's primary biological life, not of a substance merely extracted from it. It is indissolubly fused with the creature's total, sensory, organic being. So it is a 'culture' in the proper sense and insists that culture in the wider sense and identity are fused. Browning's metaphor always tries to represent experience as primary, sensory and perceptual processes because these dramatise the necessity by which being mediates and becomes the other, 'in flesh'. In 'silkiest/Tufting', 'Tufting' shifts delicately from noun to verb as the sentence is completed – 'the Tyrrhene whelk's pearl-sheeted lip'. 'Silkiest' becomes both part of the *activity* of 'Tufting', absorbed into its life, and also stands alone as pure attribute, pure superlative quality – the 'silkiest'. The shifts make 'silkiest' and 'Tufting' perform several sensuous functions simultaneously, drawing attention to what sensuous nature and what sensuous experience of it are. The isolation of minute parts of a minute organism, each possessing their own tactile and visual metaphors – paint, silk, pearl – invests the biological being of a mollusc with extraordinary complexity and prolific fullness and activity. The immediate life of the minute organism sharply ironises the confusions of the other metaphors in this prodigally playful sentence. Nature will 'turn him pure' (purity itself is almost like a dye, the satirical expression has it) like some 'forgotten vest' let slip by a trireme which vexed a potentate by failing to deliver his robe. The fanciful story of this metaphor, in which a galley from a generalised Graeco-Roman past vexes an eastern potentate, conjures up a generalised 'history' (in a happy conflation of vocabularies) with causes and consequences of its own, which sails on independent of Sordello's being. The syntax behaves as if it has forgotten Sordello's relationship to the metaphor and moves on without him. Yet it is Sordello who has let slip, forgotten, his identity. The 'trireme' is history and himself whatever the wilful satiric needs of the metaphor convey. And yet the very 'disparting' of the metaphor, placing Sordello in two places, as forgotten vest and trireme suggest the divisibility the metaphor seeks to ironise. History and self are indivisible and yet dissociated. The complex organic mollusc can, after all, be divided into its parts and attributes, silkiest, tufting.

Sordello's solution is to divide himself from himself in a vain attempt to identify himself with 'life'. He joins Palma and begins a political life. 'Will, he bade abdicate' (573). In a struggling, fragmented sentence which reintroduces 'Will' resistantly whenever it is negated, Sordello abandons self-consciousness, suppresses imagination and turns to the self-pleasing 'rapturous/ Exclaim at the crowd's cry' (563–4) – it is *his* rapture at the crowd's support of him, not theirs.

> He vivifies, assimilates. For thus
> I bring Sordello to the rapturous
> Exclaim at the crowd's cry, because one round
> Of life was quite accomplished; and he found
> Not only that a soul, whate'er its might,
> Is insufficient to its own delight,
> Both in corporeal organs and in skill
> By means of such to body forth its Will –
> And, after, insufficient to apprise
> Men of that Will, oblige them recognize
> The Hid by the Revealed – but that, – the last
> Not lightest of the struggles overpast, –
> Will, he bade abdicate, which would not void
> The throne, might sit there, suffer he enjoyed Mankind. (561–74)

Sordello as leader of men, convinced by the exhaustive persuasion of Palma in Verona, is subjected to mock-heroic assault. He is ironically invested with God-head by the lamp flame which flutters over him – 'Like the alighted planet Pollux wore' – and the sentence describing his aims peters out into an account of Brennus assaulting the capitol (586–91), defeated in the moment of triumph by the trivial absurdity of the noise of awakened geese. And 'I awake, being at Venice'. "Tis Venice and 'tis Life.' Like one of the awakened populace the poet awakes and begins his commentary.

Musing 'on a ruined palace step/At Venice' (676–7) the poet considers the arbitrariness of both resuming and breaking off his poem. The aggression, the wayward changes of direction and aberrant elliptical transitions are particularly emphatic here. The captured Hercules slew his slayers at the point of being sacrificed by them – a parable against the reader wishing to capture the Venice commentary as authoritative statement. The Venice interlude (615–1020) is a paradigm of the nature of commentary and is as vulnerable as any of the interposings which have gone on in the poem. It defers the poem and is the poem. And yet its status as both gap and bridge protects it. The exit which is also an entrance which is also an exit, establishes the relationship of any interpreter to the materials for interpretation – of any maker to what he makes. For though, in a wanton and prodigal act of Will he brings the poem into being, the poem also brings him into being. The commentary is Venice and Life, but also Venice and poem. Poem and maker stand in reciprocal relation to one another, each alien, each 'turning' native to one another. Appropriate to the musing on a 'palace step', the commentary is both ladder and platform to the first three books just as they are ladder and platform to it. Commentary becomes experience and that experience enables commentary. But it also possesses the instability inherent in the notion of transmission as transition. The Venice commentary is both bridge and parenthesis, a binding and a disparting. It is protected from displacement because it is always becoming, vulnerable to it because it is never finished. It is threatened with contentless abstraction, falling outside the materials it works upon and by its nature it is incomplete. Hence the frustration of its mood. Sordello's Mantuan competitor, Eglamor, achieves the complete poem which is a perfect, and sterile, matching of song and singer, poem and poet's ideas (615–22). Turning expressive thinking on its head, which conceives the poem as incomplete because it is a mere fragment of the poet's life – 'his lay was but an episode/In the bard's life' (629–30) – Sordello lives with 'a passion and a knowledge far/Transcending these (627–8), his own songs. But this disjunction is correspondingly a possession of the song itself, which generates a knowledge and a passion it cannot encompass and ideas unknown to it. The true maker trying to make sense of his poem will by definition never do so. (Sordello is always potentially a good poet in spite of the ravages of his genius.) He will never 'finish' his poem in this sense. 'Only, do finish something' (731) – a sudden interjection of the commentary – marks the frustration of the unfinished, and yet celebrates it with bravado. To 'finish' is the reader's prerogative. The Venice commentary, careless, arrogant, uncertain, is a fierce challenge to the poet and the reader – 'Why should I break off: not sit/Longer upon my step, exhaust the fit/England gave birth to?' (677–9).

The incompleteness of the commentary guarantees that no authoritative absolutes can be derived from it. The maker cannot 'Figure as Metaphysic Poet' (829), a grotesque figure, like Moses 'awkwardly enough' (826) smiting the rock to bring forth water for an arid culture. 'Presumptuous!' interrupts one. 'You, not I, ... magnify/Such office' (833–5), the poet answers. The Moses blasphemy, it is true, both outrageously magnifies the poet's function and negates it. And at the same time as it refuses the poet's conventional functions, the commentary seeks to make claims for the 'office' of poet. It satirises the construction of absolute schemes of good and evil, refusing a moral function for poetry. 'The complicated scheme to make amends' for evil (802) is an arrogant assumption of moral superiority by men who 'think all men stupider than they' (800). To seek for a centre, 'a kernel of strange wheelwork' (844) in the dead machine (the analogy is deliberately mechanistic) is to look for an illusory secret among its mysterious teeth, valves, springs. 'And, while you turn upon your heel,/Pray that I be not busy slitting steel/Or shredding brass ... Under a cluster of fresh stars' (857–60).

The desolation of the mechanistic analogy – man and a dead machine in a universe of cold stars – is used both in contempt and in despair of an ultimate account of things. The 'kernel' or centre of the machine is nowhere but in its *workings*.

> we watch construct,
> In short, an engine: with a finished one,
> What it can do, is all, – nought how 'tis done. (840–2)

We 'watch construct ... an engine.' The multiple possibilities of this laconic 'construction' beautifully represents the relations of the poet, the 'alien' world, the reader. The 'engine' may be the self, or an object. The verb 'construct' points towards the subject or the object. It may be an infinitive, a participle or a contracted future tense, active or passive. Or it may be a noun. We watch as subjects *to construct*, we watch to construct an object, or we may *be* a construct, as object. The commentary can defend its 'defection' (930) from moral and metaphysical absolutes and action because the poet is one of the 'Makers-see' (929), which implies making people see and a making of seeing, the perceptual process. 'Men of action' (920) – the jocular irony does not dispense with them – keep the 'Makers-see on the alert' (929). The 'real' activity of the poet is to 'Impart the gift of seeing to the rest' (868), the transformation of consciousness. Art cannot

reform society, or alter lots, or make any moral comment on the
peasant girls and prostitutes kept 'in corners out of sight' (735)
on which the commentary meditates at its beginning. But it can –
and this is what the description aims to do – bring their energies
and natures into being. See and make see.

> Sordello's story? Nay, that Paduan girl
> Splashes with barer legs where a live whirl
> In the dead black Giudecca proves sea-weed
> Drifting has sucked down three, four, all indeed
> Save one pale-red striped, pale-blue turbaned post
> For gondolas.
>   You sad dishevelled ghost
> That pluck at me and point, are you advised
> I breathe.' (691–8)

To make see is, and is the prerequisite of, new thought. This is
the 'office of ourselves' (864). 'Office' precisely combines the
idea of function and action – the function and action of ourselves. 'Ourselves', reflexively includes poet, the alien world, the
reader, within itself, and asserts the interdependence of see-er
and seen, each 'turning' the consciousness of the other. 'Clothe
in poetic vest/These doings at Verona' (250). Naddo's superficial interpretation of the poet's function, much earlier in the
poem, is unnecessary. ''Tis of the mood itself I speak, what
tinge/Determines it, else colourless' (909–10). We are back with
the ineradicable dye of history with which the poem begins in
Book III. The analysis of moods and states of consciousness, the
phenomenology of the experiencing suffering subject as it is
created by his world is the 'office of ourselves'. These moods and
states of consciousness are not extra-historical, but determined
by particular conditions, the dye of circumstance. Plara's lyric to
Zanze (873–5), another of the lyrics which erupt unaccountably
from the poem (Plara is casually mentioned as one of Sordello's
troubadour competitors in Book II) does not stand by itself.
Plara's lyric is the incantation which keeps him sane while he is
'prisoned in the Piombi' (876) for (it is hinted) either religious or
political reasons. And his potential insanity includes in itself the
objective conditions of his life, his youth in a 'grim town' (883)
dominated by the Cathedral. Even his capacity to write only
unreal, pastoral poetry is not simply a reaction against his environment, but a fracture which belongs to his potential
madness and this and the madness can only be placed in the

totality of the conditions in which he lives. Similarly the Venice commentary does not exist in isolation but includes in itself the phenomenology of its mood. 'I *being* ... O'er the lagune, *at* Venice'; meditating and including in itself the conditions of its experience, it arises from a contemplation of peasants, the beggar or prostitute, 'care-bit erased,/Broken up' (747–8), who plucks at his sleeve. It includes in itself the historical conditions of nineteenth-century Italy which pluck importunately at the visitor's sleeve, just as the meditations on the poet's office include in themselves their cultural cause. It is as if Browning is attempting here to give Victorian expressive theory a historical base.

The phenomenology of a mood includes its own objects and causality. The mood of the experiencing subject is constructed by and constructs these. And so the interdependence of subject and object ensures the continuity and the renewal of the poem. A poet in the nineteenth century, writing of an event 'six hundred years since', or even an event seven hundred years since in the twentieth century, will be constructed by and construct the poem, mediating it through a culture and a subjectivity of which it is unaware. The new culture and subjectivity certainly recreates a new poem but in turn it is created, shaped by the very alienness of the poem. This is the tenuous resolution here. It is, as I shall suggest, a very optimistic solution.

Necessarily, Sordello haunts the commentary, looking over its shoulder – 'God ... selects our yoke,/Sordello, as your poetship may find!' (781–3). The 'yoke' is the binding act of mediation, the act of making-see in particular conditions, which Sordello misunderstands. ''Tis Venice, and 'tis Life', the commentary affirms, over-confidently denying the exclusion of 'Life' implied in its metaphor, for it reintroduces Sordello's fragmentation in spite of its efforts. There is an incipient, casuistical slide from the transformation of consciousness to the instrumental changing of society (distinctions difficult to keep apart in any case). For all its unashamed, self-chiding irony at its own expense, the idea of making men *act* (Sordello's solution) intervenes, and the commentary is full of an aggressive irritability about its failure to *affect* things. 'When at some future no-time a brave band/Sees, *using* what it sees, then shake my hand/In heaven, my brother!' (926–8). Browning's irony is unstable, directed against an instrumental view of poetry and the impotence of the brave

band. The commentary's hostility to *practical* political involve-
ment and to 'men of action' who 'engage/With [another
prophetic word], do not gaze at ... The work o' the world'
(922–4), comes about because activity is incapable of insight
into its own nature, which is only understood by the poet who
'watches construct' his activity. But this is to re-establish a
fracture by disassociating the poet from his environment yet
again. The familiar frustrations of displacement reappear. He
exists in a condition which is unable to act on the 'alien' consciousness because his capacity to see depends on detachment
and on depriving what is seen of an answering awareness. His
detachment brings about an effort of making see which exhausts
itself in its own activity, fulfilling itself simply in the act of so
doing and expending its energies on itself. Sordello's experience,
in which subject and object do coexist but disown one another,
reappears in the commentary in an extreme form – 'makers-see',
'the rest' (a dismissive formulation). The social and political
world takes on the contradictions of the epistemology. And
when the world of objects – which should constitute him and
enable his mediation – falls away, the corollary of Sordello's experience reappears – a world split apart from him, or a world
which is a reflection of the subject's life – St. John seeing his own
shadow as the devil.

'And you shall hear Sordello's story told', the last line of Book
III; Sordello's story may not be history, his story, but the
narrator's, and the narrator's may be commentary rather than
story at that. A positive and a negative account of history exists
simultaneously in the poem. On the one hand, it may be like the
materials for translation, maintaining its own substantiveness
while creating the possibilities you see in it – in Naddo's gossip,
in the august typologies with which Salinguerra persuades
Palma to assist the Ghibelline cause, or in the typology of the
Romantic poet found by Browning. Salinguerra confidently uses
the past as authoritative 'model' (his own word) by which the
present is shaped. The setting up of the Romano family has its
analogue in the actions of Adelaide of Susa (439–62), the
Trevisan and Italian history in biblical history. The Venice commentary seizes with assurance upon the Moses story as
analogue, a living example of the fiction which does not know
its future significance. It unashamedly projects a modern subjectivity upon the biblical story because it creates the possibility for

a modern interpretation – a parched, impoverished, culture, unaware of its own lacks – 'A hungry sun above us, sands that bung/Our throats' (819–20). With a challengingly self-conscious bravado it appropriates items of biblical narrative which could not 'know' their modern application and conflates them outrageously for a satirical purpose to make an assault on a trivialising culture – 'And you, 'twixt tales of Potiphar's mishap,/And sonnets on the earliest ass that spoke' (822–3). Those details could not 'know' their modern application.

Typology, model, analogue, archetype, however, have a way of becoming extended 'stories' or autonomous, self-enclosed fictions. The abstract typology as metaphor or example is the complement of the metaphor which returns to the immediacy of cognitive process in the rendering of substantive sensory detail. Between them they are a paradigm of the healing and fracturing of subject and object which is at work in the poem. The metaphor which seeks to become the sensory process it describes (tufting, pearl-sheeted lip) claims that experience is not *like* but *is* experience. The abandonment of the idea of similitude reduces it to nothing other than what it is. In giving us the cognitive 'presence' of the mollusc the words have actually abandoned the cognitive tools by which they can be interpreted, likeness, similitude, referent. The typological metaphor also abandons 'like'. It splits apart from the material it represents and loses the idea of similitude in the process of becoming self-referential, a map of itself. The poet-sailor's history which, told in the present, is the present, generates an independent narrative, at the start of the Venice commentary (652–68), progressively departing from the material of comparison. It is the same with a later analogy: 'Mother Venus' kiss-creased nipples pant/Back into pristine pulpiness' (V. 44). Art may return back to and from the life it works upon in Sordello's 'Archetype' of the complex growth of Roman civilisation in which dreaming enables shaping, shaping enables dreaming. But again, the 'story' of Rome begins to take precedence over its referent. History may merely be 'a pact/And protest against chaos' (V. 555–6) as Sordello argues to Salinguerra, a myth of order which is imposed on it. In that case history falls paradoxically outside experience, outside the models it should belong to, inaccessible, a core that cannot be acted upon. The split between subject and object is reintroduced into Sordello's story in the subsequent three books. 'Life' is always eluding the empty consciousness. He experiences an alien world which resists interpretation, choice and action, and a corresponding sense of impotence and confusion. The nightmare of history is not that he is trapped into it but trapped out of it. The Guelf-Ghibelline conflict continues with a brute, intractable violence as if it is autonomous. A boy cut in half, a gangrenous face, a man living as a limbless trunk, another perpetually weeping. These sights convince Sordello of his impotence and at the same time of the powerlessness of the sufferers to act upon the forces which destroy them. All participants *in* the conflict are defined as being *outside* it because they are powerless to interpret it or affect it.

> The rabble's woes,
> Ludicrous in their patience as they chose
> To sit about their town and quietly
> Be slaughtered, – the poor reckless soldiery,
> With their ignoble rhymes on Richard, how
> 'Polt-foot,' sang they, 'was in a pitfall now,'
> Cheering each other from the engine-mounts, –
> That crippled spawling idiot who recounts
> How, lopped of limbs, he lay, stupid as stone,
> Till the pains crept from out him one by one,
> And wriggles round the archers on his head
> To earn a morsel of their chestnut bread, –
> And Cino, always in the self-same place
> Weeping; beside that other wretch's case,
> Eyepits to ear, one gangrene since he plied
> The engine in his coat of raw sheep's hide
> A double watch in the noon sun; and see
> Lucchino, beauty, with the favours free,
> Trim hacqueton, spruce beard and scented hair,
> Campaigning it for the first time – cut there
> In two already. (V. 261–81).

'Who would has heard Sordello's story told.' What has been 'told' is an innumerable series of models for telling the story. What has been 'told' is a desperation and effrontery which treads the dangerous edge between mediation as a construing out of and as an imposition on history, between becoming as a constant movement between subject and object and a self-enclosed activity. History is a model for the poem, the poem is a model for history. *Sordello* takes its contradictions to extremity and allows them to include itself. The restive construing of models is the meaning of the poem, and is simultaneously a justification and denial of it. 'I heard the Old Canon say/He saw with his own eyes.' Alberic's 'huge skeleton' (VI. 790–3), erupting into the present, at the end of the poem, challenges the relation of history to poem, poem to reader. But the model of inert and lifeless framework is displaced by the narrator's naïve and casual non-sequitur. 'He added, June's/The month for carding off our first cocoons/The silk-worm's fabricate' (793–6). The silk worm's fabricate – the living, continously spun thread of history and poem, carded off, 'turned' round itself, but also turned by the reader round his own spool, his own present. The alien turning native. We talk of the 'thread' of discourse. The organic filament is ready to be woven into a new form, a form that neither history nor poem can know about but which is still a continuous part of them. The disjunction of the non-sequitur, however, the structural figure of *Sordello*, casts doubt on the precedence of skeleton or silk-worm, dead object or living object, passive or active subject. 'Double news,/Nor he nor I could tell the worthier. Choose!' (795–6) Poem and reader are turned back into the inexhaustible 'story' as the reader is asked to 'Choose'.

The desperate bravado of *Sordello*, which encounters nihilism and withdraws from it into an analysis of the conditions of nihilism, resiliently refusing either comfort or pessimism, is a turning point in Romantic poetry. It is the first poem to link epistemology and politics overtly (though that is incipient in all the poems considered here): the first to offer a critique of idealism overtly and to embody this criticism in the structure of its language and organisation. It very nearly turns idealism on its head, as Marx did, but refuses to. Too much would be lost. Instead it struggles with the implications of idealism even at the cost of the seizure of language and the dispersal of relationship which continually threatens it. The obvious relevance of Marx's 1840 criticisms of Hegel to this poem of 1840 cannot be lost. It has not been made explicit because it is not the intention of this study to use Hegel and Marx as an explication or gloss of Romantic poetry but rather to show their writings as belonging to the same complex of problems: 'A world begins and *ends* there, [i.e. in the mind]' and though, for a fleeting moment, the constructs of the consciousness have the 'role' (rather than the 'reality') of independent, real beings, this is only 'momentary'. 'The sun is an *object* for the plant ... just as the plant is an object for the sun.'[1] This is said with a certainty *Sordello* lacks. Browning's riven poem, with an oddly hubristic confidence, withstands certainties.

NOTE

1 Karl Marx, *Early Writings,* London, 1974, 388–9. See Chapter 1.

CHAPTER 6

Tennyson,
The Collapse of Object and Subject:
In Memoriam

'Lawn Tennyson, gentleman poet'; Tennyson's persistent self-deprecating account of his art as play might be reason enough for endorsing the twice-told joke of Stephen Daedelus and for regarding *In Memoriam* as a delicate, anguished epistemological game. 'And hence, indeed, she sports with words' (XLVIII): 'Or love but play'd with gracious lies': 'A contradiction on the tongue' (CXXV): grief which will 'with symbols play' (LXXXV). His habitual use of the word 'fancy' for imagination, which carries the more restricted, eighteenth-century limitation of meaning and even suggests the idle fancy, a game with poetic artefact, is congruent with the hesitancy which makes him describe the poem as play. But the extraordinarily sophisticated (and daring) version of Catullus, 'O Sorrow, will thou live with me?' (LIX), in which sorrow and sexual play are allied – 'I'll have leave at times to play/As with the creature of my love', the understanding of the blind man's minute gesture – 'He plays with threads' (LXVI) – as a movement of displaced anxiety, should indicate Tennyson's alertness to the complexities of play. So often in the poem a defensively meticulous technical perfectionism carrying an exposed, openly naked poignancy, continues ingenuously with the cadences of pathos, as if oblivious of the irony and contradictions it is dealing with. The gratuitousness of play grants the poem its freedom to be art, and certainly to be artful: it grants it a freedom to experiment, not to 'close grave doubts' but to liberate possibilities unknown to it except in play. Yet a profounder necessity is at work in the need to play. Play *is* a necessity. The poem has to sport with words in order to enable itself to continue, to bring itself *into* play. The sport is willed to rescue language from collapse by enabling it to continue as a game. 'I do but sing because I *must*.' I *must* implies that song is involuntary and imposed as a duty at one and the same time, willed and unwilled. Involuntary song liberates feeling, '*loosens* from the lip' (XLVIII) the pressure of paralysing emotion. The poem is partly, but only partly, about the psychology of expressive language, about the process of naming a 'something', 'clouds' of 'nameless sorrow' (IV) which can only be named with difficulty. It is a highly studied study of bereavement. 'And with no language but a cry.' Regression to the inarticulate cry is inevitable when words are not adequate to express emotion. There may be no words to use. In that case the continuance of language can perhaps be enabled by a sport which brings it into play, by inventing it as a game.

There is a fundamental anxiety in *In Memoriam* about the dissolution of language altogether. The breakdown of language is collateral with the obliteration of the regulative 'Type' in the external world. 'So careful of the type? But no ... a dream,/A discord' (LVI). Discord; the consequence of the collapse of relationships is the absence of agreement and correspondence, the absence of syntax. Nature depends merely on the 'dream' of each solipsist subject for its organisation; nature is 'A hollow echo of my own (III) – a hollow echo of my *own* hollow echoes. 'For words, like Nature, half-reveal/And half-conceal the Soul within' (V). The governing analogy between words and Nature is half-concealed in this first poem on language, offered as an aside and interposed almost unnoticed, before the account of the failure of language which occupies it. Half-concealed, perhaps, because nature necessarily breaks down as an analogy. Nature is estranged from language, providing no analogies for it and no connections with it except in so far as it is *like* words, which, the poem shows, are external forms, refusing the vital change of meaning, the soul within, which renews the life of language, because they cannot sustain analogy and relationship. They are 'like Nature', empty of self-renewing life, a discord. If there is a 'soul within' language and Nature it is incompletely realised, half concealed, half revealed. The *world* cannot guarantee the structure of language. Relationships are either arbitrary or break down, and it is the same in language. The resilience and intelligence of *In Memoriam* lies in its willingness to confront, however reluctantly, the derangement of idealist language with play, to 'frame' words, to invent them, perhaps even, as the secondary possibilities of 'frame' come into play, with some duplicity. The sport with words enables the poem to keep in existence and ultimately to reconstruct both itself and the 'use' of measured language.

The extremity of idealist language in *In Memoriam* is accompanied by a corresponding intensification of artifice. The poem tries to 'fix itself to form' (XXXIII) like the simple faith of the woman in the Lazarus sequence. The fastidious, carefully compacted units of pairing and parallelism, word with word, phrase with phrase, line and line, the 'stepping stones' (1) by which the poems are built up, express the need to make a form in which matching, concord, correspondence, analogy, are possible. The masking circumlocution of poetic diction, artful personification, insist upon the poem as minutely self-conscious verbal artefact, insist that something can be *made*, even if it is the almost unapproachable patina of surface perfection. But the coexistence of an ambiguous syntax with the formal pattern frequently disrupts the poem from within so that the formal organisation of the poem comes to exist independently of its meanings in a self-enclosed separation and autonomy which severs it from the correspondences it tries to make. 'I scarce could brook the strain and stir': the hiatus after this pairing allows the wild conflation of self and world, psychological strain and the stir of the storm in section XV. Because the stanza breaks after 'strain and stir' the condition can belong to the poet as much to the storm. The archaism, 'brook', enables the language not to be sure whether the poet *allows* or suffers upheaval, just as the meticulously parallel verbs are not sure whether they are active or passive, acting or acted upon – cracked, curled, huddled, dash'd. 'And but for fancies ... And but for fear it is not so.' Parallelism veers apart into contradiction. The poet would disintegrate into the storm unless his fancy insists upon the calm progress of the boat carrying Hallam's body. But because the words 'it is not so' in this deranged syntax relate immediately to the storm the repetition intended to intensify this fancy – 'And but for fear' – reads as a fear of calm, and also wills the strain and stir of the storm upon the dead man, forcing him into an identity with it. The poet would disintegrate except (but) for his fear that it is *not* calm, and but for fear that the 'wild unrest' is *not* so, fear that the strain and stir does *not* belong to the ship. The construction, 'for fear', carries with it the meaning of expectation, even hope. If the ship *were* calm and the dead man not sharing in the storm's and the poet's strain and stir, then disintegration would follow. The readings of the parallelism are athwart one another, like the movement of the ship placed in strangely obstructive relation to the sea which carries it, '*Athwart* a plane of molten glass'. Either way the poet and the syntax go mad, making no distinction between self and objects. Undifferentiated, internal unrest and external cloud drag 'a labouring breast', and the syntax, the cloud, the poet, 'topples' to disintegration with an unclosed phrase which is not organically part of the sentence – 'A looming bastion fringed with fire'. Poet and storm become inseparable.

> To-night the winds begin to rise
>   And roar from yonder dropping day:
>   The last red leaf is whirl'd away,
> The rooks are blown about the skies;
>
> The forest cracked, the waters curled,
>   The cattle huddled on the lea;
>   And wildly dashed on tower and tree
> The sunbeam strikes along the world:
>
> And but for fancies, which aver
>   That all thy motions gently pass
>   Athwart a plane of molten glass,
> I scarce could brook the strain and stir
>
> That makes the barren branches loud;
>   And but for fear it is not so,
>   The wild unrest that lives in woe
> Would dote and pore on yonder cloud
>
> That rises upward always higher,
>   And onward drags a labouring breast,
>   And topples round the dreary west,
> A looming bastion fringed with fire. (XV)

The derangement of the storm poem ends in dissolution. *In Memoriam* continually threatens itself with termination. 'But that large grief ... Is given in outline and *no more*' (V). Language allows grief to be expressed in no more than an outline, but the poem also categorically discontinues itself. It can utter grief 'no more'. And it brings itself to a halt. 'I held it truth ... That men may rise on stepping-stones/Of their dead selves' (I). Each isolated lyric is a precarious stepping-stone which might not lead to another when language breaks down.

> Dark house, by which once more I stand
>   Here in the long unlovely street,
>   Doors, where my heart was used to beat
> So quickly, waiting for a hand,
>
> A hand that can be clasp'd no more –
>   Behold me, for I cannot sleep,
>   And like a guilty thing I creep
> At earliest morning to the door.
>
> He is not here; but far away
>   The noise of life begins again,
>   And ghastly through the drizzling rain
> On the bald street breaks the blank day. (VII)

'On the bald street breaks the blank day.' Again, the poem can go no further. The day dawns or *fragments*, breaking like something brittle on or against the bald street. The poet, not belonging to the dawn, like the ghost in *Hamlet* (but unlike the ghost, guilty of his exile from life and the day rather than death and the night), fusing the 'blank misgivings' of Wordsworth's 'Immortality Ode' with the blank day, moves about in worlds literally not realised, because the day breaks ambiguously out of, or is only seen *through*, the obstructive drizzle of rain. Breaking day and the hard, resistant street exist in unreactive relation to one another, the light failing to transform the street, the street unresponsive to the day. Bald and blank repel the reciprocity the pairing alliteration attempts to assert. Language fails to establish the correspondence it claims, and offers only a mutual exchange of emptiness. The obstruction of rain, the barrier of the door '*where* my heart was used to beat', by which, and against which, *directly* (with extraordinary physical frankness) the heart-beat knocked to gain entrance, are metaphors of a condition expressed in the organisation of the language of *In Memoriam*. It sets up barriers. Like the self-retarding stanza form, it creates obstructions and blocks against itself. Though the poem longs 'to flood a fresher throat with song' (LXXXIII), and constantly remembers the 'Ode to a Nightingale', it rarely achieves Keats' easeful flow of lyric feeling, because it is halted, and sometimes almost disabled, by an ambiguous syntax which says one thing and its opposite simultaneously, a 'contradiction on the tongue' (CXXV), asserting and negating at one and the same time. Two sentences out of the same words. The double, coalescing Romantic grammar seizes up in contradiction. Parallelism subjects the poem to paralysis. The gaps and transitions which are the life of Romantic language make either voids or barriers. 'O sweet, new year delaying long ... *Delayest* the sorrow in my blood' (LXXXIII). The delaying spring is accused of the continuance of sorrow and yet at the same time is imperatively asked to delay, to keep sorrow in the blood. The paralysing and the creative energies of grief mutually retard one another.

The poem is most immobilised when it is not sure what form or what language to fix itself to, idealist or non-idealist, mind-moulded or 'matter-moulded' (XCV), actively shaped by the self, passively formed by an external world. It is not even certain whether the distinctions themselves are fixed.

> Old Yew, which graspest at the stones
>   That name the under-lying dead,
>   Thy fibres net the dreamless head,
> Thy roots are wrapt about the bones.
>
> The seasons bring the flower again,
>   And bring the firstling to the flock;
>   And in the dusk of thee, the clock
> Beats out the little lives of men.
>
> O not for thee the glow, the bloom,
>   Who changest not in any gale,
>   Not branding summer suns avail
> To touch thy thousand years of gloom:
>
> And gazing on thee, sullen tree,
>   Sick for thy stubborn hardihood,
>   I seem to fail from out my blood
> And grow incorporate into thee. (II)

'And grow incorporate into thee': and grow bodiless, as mind or spirit with the 'dusk' of the yew, or become physically embodied in it. Either way lies the loss of distinction. 'And *in* the *dusk* of thee, the clock/Beats out': external clock, external time, tolls in the shadow of the yew or else, like a heart *in* the dusk of the tree itself, a shadowy, mind-created symbol of unchanging grief, internally registers 'a thousand years of gloom' – darkness and *sadness*. Whether the yew refuses to 'avail' the branding sun of the objective world to touch it, or whether the concrete world itself cannot 'avail' to reach and touch it, are equal and opposite possibilities. The opposites result, not in conflict, but in paralysis.

'To *touch* thy thousand years of gloom': 'And learns... And finds I am not what I see,/And other than the things I *touch*' (XLV). The blocks occur when Tennyson is talking about perception and the relationship between the physical and mental worlds. Consider the connections made between touch and being in sections XLV and XCV: Created out of pronouns, 'I', 'me', the beautifully economical baby poem about the growth of identity uses verbs as stepping-stones to self-consciousness as the baby knows himself as object to himself and discovers the intransigent world of subject and object – 'this is I'.

> But as he grows he gathers much,
> And learns the use of 'I' and 'me',
> And finds 'I am not what I see,
> And other than the things I touch.'

But as 'he grows he gathers... And learns... And finds'. 'And learns the use of "I" and "me"': the baby gathers his growing, takes the knowledge of his growing as a fact of awareness, learns by its 'use' and finds what he uses. The emphasis is on an almost tragic imprisonment in the physical self and in the consciousness – 'the frame that *binds* him in' – which is a necessity for the definition of a separate identity which can relate to the world as other, the not-self, and a necessity for the growth of 'clear memory'. Strictly read, however, the ellipsis of the second parallelism reverses the first and becomes an idealist statement or hypothesis – 'And finds "I am not what I see,/And other than the things I touch"': 'And finds "I am *not* what I see, [And *I* am not] other than the things I touch".' Two possibilities obstruct one another. Isolation, perhaps, grows defined, like an outline, as the self is sealed off from the world, and independent memory evolves. Or perhaps isolation grows defined through an act of mind which includes the other in its definition of self-separation, fusing subject and object in the process of creating relationship. The ambiguous parallelism returns one to the first stanza of the poem. The baby, *pressing* his palm against the breast (pressing himself away from and *into* the breast) has never thought that 'this is I'. This, the pressing palm exerting itself against its first experience of a resistant physical world, the baby's physical entity and consciousness, is 'I' at the first act of awareness and self-consciousness at the breast as the baby comes to understand that it is other to what it feeds upon. On the other hand, the syntax allows that the breast, source of life and literally part of the baby because its milk is taken in by the child, can also be included as 'I': this, the breast, is 'I'. The circle of the breast is outside the suckling child, or baby and breast are included in a circle of interchange and reciprocal being where subject and object are both other to each other and as one.

This, one of the subtlest poems of *In Memoriam*, is perhaps a lyric which finds momentarily a way of transcending the obstructions it creates for itself. But *In Memoriam* is never stable. 'The dead man *touched* me from the past' (XCV): 'I [am not] ... other than the things I touch' (XCV):

> And strangely on the silence broke
> The silent-speaking words, and strange
> Was love's dumb cry defying change
> To test his worth; and strangely spoke
>
> The faith, the vigour, bold to dwell
> On doubts that drive the coward back,
> And keen through wordy snares to track
> Suggestion to her inmost cell.
>
> So word by word, and line by line,
> The dead man touched me from the past,
> And all at once it seemed at last
> The living soul was flashed on mine...
>
> Vague words! but ah, how hard to frame
> In matter-moulded forms of speech,
> Or even for intellect to reach
> Through memory that which I became:

The 'silent-speaking words' which broke on the poet are either the silent words of the dead friend's letter, or words silently re-iterated in the poet's consciousness. 'Love's *dumb* cry' cannot be differentiated as belonging to the poet or the writer of the letter, just as 'the faith, the vigour', could belong to each, expressed in written words, or generated in the poet's being. Neither speech, nor even intellect can reach 'Through memory that which I become.' Memory is either creative or passive. The intellect cannot recreate through or by means of memory, but the placing of the words allows a reading, 'that which I became through memory, or the creations of memory' – the 'clear memory' of the baby poem, perhaps, the shaping consciousness itself. Transcendental experience may be given from outside the self or it may be a creation of mind. Experience, and words, may be mind-moulded or they may be matter-*moulded*, formed from the material world. And language may be simply moulded by matter, mere printed marks.

'That which I *became*': 'Thy place is changed; thou *art* the same' (CXXI). The 'double' naming of the Hesper/Phosphor poem simultaneously offers an active and a passive self, a living or a static universe:

> Sad Hesper o'er the buried sun
>   And ready, thou, to die with him,
>   Thou watchest all things ever dim
> And dimmer, and a glory done:
>
> The team is loosened from the wain,
>   The boat is drawn upon the shore;
>   Thou listenest to the closing door,
> And life is darkened in the brain.
>
> Bright Phosphor, fresher for the night,
>   By thee the world's great work is heard
>   Beginning, and the wakeful bird;
> Behind thee comes the greater light:
>
> The market boat is on the stream,
>   And voices hail it from the brink;
>   Thou hear'st the village hammer clink,
> And see'st the moving of the team.
>
> Sweet Hesper-Phosphor, double name
>   For what is one, the first, the last,
>   Thou, like my present and my past,
> Thy place is changed; thou art the same.

'Thy place is changed' – by external conditions, fixed and final. Or, with the openness of a continuous present, thy place is continually in a state of change. What 'thou art', what being is, is defined simultaneously in two radically opposed ways. Hesper watches over 'a glory done', a glory over or a glory *being made*, a glory ended or self-creating and perhaps even made by the watching Hesper itself. The poem has a double name and a double structure, of antithetical, linear beginnings and endings or cyclical renewal. The second and fourth stanzas contrasting cessation and movement, night and day, death and life, are locked in equipoise, miniature pastorals which are virtually inverted images of one another – the team of horses, the boat, the closing door (stanza 2); the boat, the sound of activity, the team. Appropriately, the verbs describing activity and movement are passive in the night pastoral, active in the day pastoral. But paradoxically 'listenest' in the night stanza (like 'watchest' in the first), is a sharper, less involuntary perceptual verb than 'hear'st' and 'see'st' in the day stanza. The transforming agent of perception comes into prominence and questions the passivity of experience when it is most subject to necessity. The locked, antithetical opposition is also subverted by the intervening stanza. Phosphor arises 'fresher for the night', fresher for the quietude of night into dawn, and fresher to *encounter* the cyclical renewal of night which follows the 'greater light'. Both structures are subject to necessity – with delicate toughness the cyclical movement of renewal is the renewal of darkness – but one offers a self and a universe capable of transformation while the other does not.

The more fixed to form, the more miniaturist and precise the language of *In Memoriam* seems, the more ambiguous it actually is. The poem discovers the ambiguity of form – solid form, hollow forms, mere form. 'The hills are shadows, and they flow/From form to form' (CXXIII). 'Vague words! but ah, how hard to frame': to frame, to make a solid physical structure like the baby's 'frame' which binds him in, or to invent, to make something new – even with some duplicity. The work of the poem is to overcome the immobility which arises from the discontinuous and uncertain oscillation between an open, reflexive, mind-created world and a binding, subject/object account of experience. It does so by redefining its form. And this redefinition is inextricably bound up with the overcoming of grief, or the acceptance of it, and the liberation of energy. The project the poem discovers is not to recover so much as to construct an idea of death, which is an 'awful *thought*' (XIII) – death to a living man can only be a thought, an act of imagination. This constructing of death can only be done by an act of imagination, defining death against its opposite, life, and creating both anew, redefining 'my present and my past'. Reflexive, idealist language is ultimately the strongest in this project, for all the doubts about it, because it is found to be most capable of keeping words in play and enables the poem to grow. It grows by flowing from form to form, building itself out of itself, contemplating its past, the stepping stones for growth. It arises, above all, out of the collapse of its analogies, out of its dead self, which enables it to find a new account of analogy and metaphor. The struggle of the poem is with discord and concord. The contemplations of analogy finally lead to a redefinition of the idea of form. I turn to this process in the following discussion.

Section V, the first poem on language, begins the debate on analogy

> I sometimes hold it half a sin
>   To put in words the grief I feel;
>   For words, like Nature, half reveal
> And half conceal the Soul within.
>
> But, for the unquiet heart and brain,
>   A use in measured language lies;
>   The sad mechanic exercise,
> Like dull narcotics, numbing pain.
>
> In words, like weeds, I'll wrap me o'er,
>   Like coarsest clothes against the cold;
>   But that large grief which these enfold
> Is given in outline and no more.

This poem demonstrates the failure of analogy through the structure of its metaphors with brilliant, concise virtuosity, half-concealing, half-revealing the complexity it deals with. I return to it before examining particular sequences of *In Memoriam*. 'I sometimes hold it half a sin/To put in words the grief I feel ... In words, like weeds, I'll wrap me o'er ... But that large grief which these enfold/Is given in outline and no more.' Language is an external form to thought and Tennyson appropriately adapts the classical metaphors of the subject/object world – to 'put in words', to portray, as in the mimesis of drawing and outlining in words; like funeral 'weeds', words are the dress of thought. These are matter-moulded expressions. Half-concealed in the poem, however, and only half-recognised by it, is another account of language. To put grief *in* words, to fuse feeling and form, word and meaning, to structure experience through language rather than to match thoughts and words. With characteristic exquisiteness, 'weeds', the conventionalised archaism of poetic diction which masks and formalises, denoting the conventional dress of mourning, a form for a form, is exactly appropriate for the externality being described. So appropriate, that words might be said to create rather than to cover thought. They may be mind-moulded. But the governing metaphor of the poem collapses in spite of this alternative possibility. Tennyson exposes the fallacy of analogy by showing that one side of his comparison cannot be transformed. The categories of grief, garment, drawing, can only transfer their qualities if grief is accepted as solid body or matter, the literal side of the analogy coerced by the figurative into physical being. But it remains a feeling, escaping from its figurative term; it is *large* grief, into which the idea of limit, or definition or outline can hardly enter. The 'soul within' the self, within the word, escapes definition. Grief is pervasive, the 'cold', as well as the experience of the suffering subject being protected from the cold by words. The metaphor of outline cannot even become a metaphor for this metaphor, and strains almost to disintegration in the effort to 'picture' a grief which is outside and inside the self simultaneously. Equivalences and correspondences fail. They fall in 'half', the word used three times in this short poem. The 'use' of measured language is a psychological one, a 'mechanic exercise' which has nothing to do with truth. This is why it is 'half a sin', to put grief in words, as well as being a sin to express an excess of feeling which should not be made public. 'Measured language', metrical language, measures, tempers, equals out feeling, even represses it, by *being* mechanical, dissociated from meaning and feeling, 'Like dull narcotics, numbing pain'.

The poem might be said to reveal through language simply because it has explained itself and its contradictions and enabled what it explains to come into being. The external mechanic exercise numbs pain, like dull narcotics, but it is also, the syntax allows, like numbing *pain* as well as being like *dull* narcotics. Some feeling and awareness, if only the awareness of pain is created through the 'use' and practice of language. Just as narcotics are stimulants, awareness might be intensified by mechanic exercise itself. *In Memoriam* slowly and distrustfully discovers the possibilities half-revealed by this statement and by the whole poem. It tentatively abandons the fixed forms of objective analogy which mark 'the type' in favour of analogy discovered through self-reflection. Section V hopes that the given, permanent Types of the external world can be both the model and the content for language – words like weeds. Permanent likeness and difference enables generalisation, truth. The world and the pedetermined fixities of language are congruent, objectively matching word to thing, form to content, depending on the stable opposition of subject and object. But when the structure and the structuring of consciousness is the model for analogy (and Section V hints that this may be) the world will become an aspect of the self, the self an aspect of the other – I 'am [not] other than the things I touch'. Stable categories and a stable relationship between subject and object necessarily dissolve. Language constitutes the world. It is not predetermined by it any more than the self is. Section V initiates a dialogue between two kinds of metaphor-making which continues to the end of the poem, and this also has consequences for the idea of form. There is the analogy of predetermined matching of word and thing and the analogy which restructures relationship.

Two accounts of analogy, two accounts of form. And 'slowly forms the firmer mind' (XVIII): 'and sow/The dust of continents to be' (XXXV): 'the wave/In roarings round the coral reef' (XXXVI): 'the dust of change' (LXXI): 'the solid earth ... grew to seeming-random forms,/The seeming prey of cyclic storms' (CXVIII). The cyclical, internal dissolution of geological change dissolving to reform, reforming to dissolve, which so fascinated Tennyson, is a model for the cyclical form of *In Memoriam*. It is always subverting the classical, objective, linear account of form which the poem also maintains to its end. We 'ranging down this lower track' (XLVI), the pathway, the stepping-stone, progressing from beginning to ending, ordered externally by space and time, but forced to leap the impossible transcendental gap between time and eternity. The anniversary and Christmas poems mark time (and perhaps, since some of these over-selfconscious poems are inferior, mark time in another sense). Lyrics such as the second yew tree and dark house poems consciously register linear continuity and conflict with the cyclical movement of the poem.

Yet almost in spite of itself, and its fascination with the reforming of cyclic change, *In Memoriam* longs to be a narrative, 'truth embodied in a tale' (XXXVI), to achieve the permanence of myth-making which is embodied in biblical legend, to be another Type. And particularly in the earlier part of the poem the fixed form of the Type is associated with linear progress. The Lazarus story, which it meditates on (XXXI–III) before the section which considers truth embodied in a tale, is the Type of a permanent myth even though it is so full of questions about permanence. But finally lyric XXXVI is deprived of the consolation it seeks. Legend is accessible to the simple and the poor, it has 'breath'. As an enactment, a story, it is like 'deeds' and 'more strong than all *poetic* thought'. But, like the coral reef with which this poem ends – 'And those wild eyes that watch the wave/In roarings round the coral reef' – it dissolves and reforms its life. It is a form and can become a dead form. The poems about the wrecking of Nature's own forms by itself (LIV, LV, LVI) are a 'Type' of the poem in quite another sense than that of the permanent, unchanging Types of which they mourn the loss. They destroy the form which it longs to adopt. Nature is not 'careful of the Type'. The Lazarus poems in the earlier sequence (XXXI–III, XXXVI) explore the possibility of giving form to experience in Types, symbols, analogies, and give rise to a series of experiments with metaphors for death (XL–XLVII). They include the baby poem which aims to establish the after-life as the necessity of memory, and 'If sleep and death be *truly* one' (XLIII). The collapse of the Type in evolutionary form marks the exhaustion of those possibilities of continuity, an exhaustion which has already been recognised in Section XLVIII. This lyric asserts that it cannot 'close grave doubts', 'part and prove' any more than 'poetic song' can express truth in 'closest words' (XXXVI). It can only 'sport with words'. Permanent Types collapse, analogies collapse – 'a dream,/A discord' (LVI); and yet in spite of this apparent termination which, indeed, *was* the termination of one earlier version of *In Memoriam*, the dust of dissolution is sown for 'continents to be' (XXXV). For the poem concurrently recognises a quite other movement, another kind of form or forming than the concord that truth is 'fixed' to; it recognises the unstable, fluent 'tracts' (CXVIII) of experience which dissolve in order to reform. This is why, puzzlingly, the poem and the universe can be seen both as 'without ... an aim' (XXXIV) and as 'toil co-operant to an end' (CXXVIII). The poem returns on itself in the sequence on sleep (LXVII–LXXI) and redefines earlier accounts of sleep, preparing for its future and for the climactic transcendental moment of XCV by seeing the dream as a model of idealist experience which is unfixed to form. But the sleep sequence dissolves itself yet again, in spite of having silted up materials for the poem, and the poem rebuilds itself out of this destruction – 'Here rolls the deep where grew the tree (CXXIII)'. This dissolution and rebuilding continues to the end of the poem. The struggle of the two accounts of form with one another is implied in the ambiguousness of the stepping-stones metaphor in Section I. You go on by having experience behind you as a series of hard, separate entities, moving on to the next stage, developing, progressing. You leave, as Section LVII so painfully recognises, 'half my life ... behind' if you move on from grief. On the other hand, growth occurs on stepping-stones '*of* their dead selves'. Experience rises out of its own dereliction. The past is formative. The self includes its past or dead self generatively within itself because the 'dead' experience is actually the very means of its growth.

The gradual but increasing emphasis on self-reflexive analogy rather than one which is fixed to a static external world both enables the cyclical rather than the linear form of the poem and is enabled by it. Three sequences in particular show how Tennyson's exploration of metaphor-making enables the poem to continue, as these remember one another and reform themselves. No poem so obsessively remembers itself as *In Memoriam* does. I move to the sequence concerned with the funeral ship (IX–XIX), the sleep poems (LXVII–LXXI) and the poems about the departure from Somersby (C–CIII). These are linked by the re-emergence of the dim dawn poem (LXXII, XCIX).

Two kinds of poetic form, each a commentary on the other, exist concurrently in the 'fair ship' sequence, often within the same poem. One is linear, narrative, temporal and external, marking the progress of the ship carrying the dead man from Vienna to England. It uses formal, ceremonial 'measured language' of a consciously organised kind more noticeably than any other group in *In Memoriam*. This sequence is the willed, 'sad mechanic exercise' initiated in Section V. The other form is psychological, expressive lyric, non-temporal, marking the vicissitudes of subjective life. Each form criticises the other. Both forms use the barrier of poetic diction as a means almost of neurotic displacement to mask death and the body, the boat, the sea. Conventional, external poetic diction becomes the greatest source of irony, half-revealing and half-concealing the deepest concern of this sequence which is with the collapse of safe and guaranteed order, the dissolving relationship between the internal and external worlds. The kinds of analogy which can be constructed become a crucial preoccupation here. The sequence tries out both the analogy in which objective equivalents for experience are provided by the external world and the analogy in which relationship is constituted by mind. Both fail.

'The Danube to the Severn gave': Section XIX, the last poem in the sequence, is a last attempt to provide a precise and exquisitely fitting image of experience in objective fact which ostensibly matches and illustrates the retarding movement, the ebb and flow of grief which inhibits song. Yet it is a false analogy in spite of the delicate exactitude with which the parallel appears to be made.

> There twice a day the Severn fills;
>   The salt sea-water passes by,
>   And hushes half the babbling Wye,
> And makes a silence in the hills.
>
> The Wye is hushed nor moved along,
>   And hushed my deepest grief of all,
>   When filled with tears that cannot fall,
> I brim with sorrow drowning song.
>
> The tide flows down, the wave again
>   Is vocal in its wooden walls;
>   My deeper anguish also falls,
> And I can speak a little then.

Just as the flow of the brimming Wye is blocked at its fullest and highest point by the movement of the Severn, so the poet's grief rises, but is paralysed: his tears cannot fall even though they 'brim' at the brink of falling; he cannot give utterance to grief. 'I brim with sorrow drowning song.' In movement again, the Wye is 'vocal' (the equivalent of Tennyson's song) and 'My deeper anguish also falls,/And I can speak a little then'. The lie of the analogy turns on the word 'falls': tears overflow, if this 'falls' is to become congruent with the earlier 'fall' – 'tears that cannot fall' – but the Wye 'falls', not by overflowing, but by falling back to its natural level. The parallels between tears and Wye deviate just when they seem most to match. Again, the poem says two things at once. Poetry can be made possible by the release or overflow of feeling (this is a perfect account of expressive art) or by letting the 'deeper anguish' fall to a lower level of the consciousness (as the Wye falls to its bed), repressing the most powerful emotions and giving voice only to superficial feeling. The Wye is an 'exercise' which fails, and turns into a game with language, a game in which the rules of analogy are subverted so that contradictions emerge. The rigorous serenity of this poem masks the strain.

The antithetical storm and calm poems (XI, XV) try out the possibility of subjective analogy, another kind of consonance, by seeing how far the external world may be a replication of the self, structured by the subject and returning the forms of his consciousness to him as object to himself. Though the poems seem antithetical they are actually complementary. Different emotions, 'calm despair and wild unrest' (XVI), but the same collapse of relationship. The storm poem, I have suggested, discovers the derangement of idealist language. The storm is an objective analogy for psychological upheaval but becomes identified with it. The fusion of the mind of the perceiver is so complete that they become inseparable. When nothing falls outside the self relationship is dissolved, and distinction becomes meaningless. The extremities of incompatible verbs – 'rises' set against 'dropping' in the first stanza, 'looming' set against 'topples' in the last, mark the disappearance of proportion and concord. Everything becomes part of everything else, everything stands for everything else without distinction in the language of the non-objective world – the poem '*Mingles* all without a plan' (XVI).

To mingle. This verb is picked up from the calm lyric by section XVI, which attempts to analyse both it and the storm poem – 'Calm and still light on you great plain/That sweeps ... To *mingle* with the bounding main'. Plain and main mingle as rhyme words. The calm poem tries out the possibility of finding the world as an attribute of the self, but whereas the storm poem finds a threatening fusion of subject and object, the calm poem finds only the pathetic *fallacy*. It cannot evolve the external world from its moods.

> Calm is the morn without a sound,
>   Calm as to suit a calmer grief,
>   And only through the faded leaf
> The chestnut pattering to the ground:

Calm and deep peace on this high wold.
    And on these dews that drench the furze,
    And all the silvery gossamers
That twinkle into green and gold:

Calm and still light on yon great plain
    That sweeps with all its autumn bowers,
    And crowded farms and lessening towers,
To mingle with the bounding main:

Calm and deep peace in this wide air,
    These leaves that redden to the fall;
    And in my heart, if calm at all,
If any calm, a calm despair:

Calm on the seas, and silver sleep,
    And waves that sway themselves in rest,
    And dead calm in that noble breast
Which heaves but with the heaving deep.

'Calm is the morn... Calm and deep peace... Calm on the seas': each stanza repeats 'calm' like the self-mesmerising incantation of a lullaby as an exercise in self-induced serenity. 'Calm' oscillates between being a noun, a possession of the landscape, and an adjective, a psychological, affective state which 'mingles', creates an affinity between inner and outer worlds. But the calm is not penetrative. It is '*on* this high wold', '*on* yon great plain' or dissipated '*in* this wide air'. Finally, calm is refused metaphorical possibilities altogether. 'Dead calm', the customary metaphor for the sea, is transferred to the dead man and is a literal truth – 'And dead calm in that noble breast'. The euphemisms for death are transferred to the sea – 'silver sleep', 'waves that sway themselves in rest' – ironically pointing the sentimentality of attempts at psychological affinity. The dead language of poetic diction opposes the living, suffering 'heart' of the poet to the 'noble breast' of the dead man which 'heaves' but only with the mechanical life of the heaving deep. We normally think of the heaving breast as the sign of expressive feeling and emotion, heaving with sighs, but it is breathless here, deprived of anything but the inert physical weight of the body which is a dead form, appropriately described in a dead form of words – breast.[1] The psychological adjective, 'deep' – 'deep peace' – has been appropriated as a noun for the sea – 'the deep' – space without limit or shape. Calm is death. The calm lyric is an attempt to impose a psychological reading of the world but which poignantly recognises its imposture. The activity of the self and world are neither reciprocal nor fused. The universe, if not dead, continues its activity in dissociation from the poet, the chestnut 'pattering' where the poet discovers a morn 'without a sound', the main 'bounding' in independent life, leaping in the limitlessness of the present participle, but also the agent of limit and constricting, bounding, the plain. The sea in affinity with calm becomes death, which resists the understanding of the human imagination. The only fusion of self and universe occurs in the calm of death. The reiterated 'calm' becomes not soothing but an obliteration of energy. Repetition is death.

The haunting possibility that idealist analogy has no content is expressed in the extraordinarily analytical lyric (XVI) which follows and is enabled by the calm and storm poems. Sorrow is a 'changeling', inconsistent but, as the double note of 'changeling' suggests, transforming. Then follows the negation of transformation in what is probably the most despairing questioning of the non-objective world in the poem. 'Can sorrow such a changeling be?'

> Or doth she only seem to take
> 　　The touch of change in calm or storm;
> 　　But knows no more of transient form
> In her deep self, than some dead lake
>
> That holds the shadow of a lark
> 　　Hung in the shadow of a heaven?
> 　　Or has the shock, so harshly given,
> Confused me like the unhappy bark
>
> That strikes by night a craggy shelf,
> 　　And staggers blindly ere she sink?
> 　　And stunned me from my power to think
> And all my knowledge of myself;
>
> And made me that delirious man
> 　　Whose fancy fuses old and new,
> 　　And flashes into false and true,
> And mingles all without a plan?

The deep self, like some dead lake – deep and dead are changeling words, dead self, deep lake – only seems to register the 'touch' of an external world. But the self or lake create nothing else, and certainly no other, no object, in place of this illusory relationship. It 'knows' nothing of 'transient form', the living but ephemeral forms of the external world, or 'changeling', internally shaped forms of its own. Not to 'know' is not to know the means of creating knowledge. The dead lake simply 'holds the shadow of a lark/Hung in the shadow of a heaven'. 'Hold' is a verb almost as important as 'touch' in *In Memoriam*. Here the dead self, the deep lake, fixes its images and keeps them stationary. Hold and hung balance one another, the lark in virtual death, hung. The lark may be a static reflection held in the reflection of sky and clouds, passively received and replicated by the dead consciousness, or worse, as the lyric asserts, it may simply be a *shadow* on the surface held in the larger shadows of sky and clouds which move about it. In this case it is an indistinct, indirect and secondary form which has none of the suggestion of transference implied in the idea of reflection. These shadows are more like the insubstantial internal forms of consciousness in Section IV which cannot be released from the self and given external being – 'Such clouds of nameless trouble cross/All night *below* the darkened eyes'.

As if to endorse the failure of integration, the final parallelism describing the failure of unintegrated fancy is itself unintegrated. The fancy fuses 'old and new' and 'flashes into false and true'. The metaphor is drawn from gunpowder and chemistry. One disintegrates, the other blends. ('Flashes' is far away from the climactic Section XCV, where the living soul was 'flashed on mine'.) Old and new, false and true, are neither fused as equivalents nor arranged in meaningful opposition as the arrangement of the pairs would ostensibly insist, line above line, the old falsity, the new truth. The arrangement could equally denote the old truth, the new falsity. It is as unstable as the fancy. The statement about the inconsistency of fancy gives no guarantee even to the stability of the parallel it makes, which falls apart intellectually. What is left is a structure without a content which falls into incoherence, 'without a plan' – without a plan, a projection, a model, a metaphor.

The poems which try out self-reflexive metaphor are the most immediately startling and unsettling in this group. The more formal poems on the ship, suggesting the inexorable progress of a journey, a linear narrative, look conventional. The more formal poems, however, are equally if not more subversive and at the same time paradoxically freer than the purely 'subjective' poems. It is as if the mask of poetic diction grants the poem freedom to 'play' with possibilities which are unreachable by the 'subjective' poems because the formal poems are 'false' as consolation or more outrageous than the 'subjective poems' can ever be. The virtuosity of poetic diction in the Fair Ship series is astonishing. The consolatory, generalised forms of diction 'outlining' grief have a prolific inventiveness and ingenuity which revivifies conventional forms. The inertia of the body and mysteriousness of death for instance, is exquisitely suggested by these circumlocutions – 'a vanished life', 'dark freight' (X), 'mortal ark', 'A weight of nerves without a mind' (XII), 'the burthen' (XIII). But this masking diction is both ingenuous and disingenuous, half-revealing and half-concealing consolation, and a refusal of consolation. Poetic diction asserts the freedom of mind to create its objects with a liberation and equanimity unknown to the expressive, subjective lyric forms. In this diction, Phosphor, the morning star, really can 'glimmer' unimpeded 'through early light' and find its image returned back to itself on 'the dewy decks' (IX) in contrast with the obstructed, unreactive world of the dark house poem. The world can be a reflection of the subject in unperplexed concord. The mind can be released, with an outward projection of the imagination, 'to dart' and 'play' (XII): the fancies 'rise on wing' (XIII) or glance about the object of grief and bring it into being. The mind is liberated to fulfil that longing of the bereaved person, so shocking to the unbereaved, for the physical return of the dead. The single, continuous sentence of section XIV asserts, almost outrageously, that if the dead man got off the ship alive 'I should not feel it to be strange'.

The poetic diction *wishes*, and its artifice conceals its wishes, but outrage, shock, subversiveness, the reversal of conventional expectation, is also the mode of this elaborately euphemistic language. '*More* than my brothers are to me': the anti-social statement flagrantly undermining the conventional family priorities, violates the evenness of earlier more conventional parallelisms in Section IX – 'My friend, the brother of my love'. The widower of Section XIII finds in death 'A void where heart on heart reposed': a void in the place of the companion body and heart but, allowably, a void which was always present, unknown to the mourner even when the dead companion was alive. The funeral service and communion are expressed in the more elaborate circumlocutions – 'the ritual of the dead', the kneeling hamlet drains 'The chalice of the grapes of God' (X) – as if to indicate the *obsolete* formalism of a consolatory religious act of burial which merely makes us the 'fools of habit'. Most subversive of all, the syntax of this lyric goes on to tangle, expressing the possibility of suicide simultaneously with the act of religious consolation.

> So bring him: we have idle dreams:
>   This look of quiet flatters thus
>   Our home-bred fancies: O to us,
> The fools of habit, sweeter seems
>
> To rest beneath the clover sod,
>   That takes the sunshine and the rains,
>   Or where the kneeling hamlet drains
> The chalice of the grapes of God;
>
> Than if with thee the roaring wells
>   Should gulf him fathom-deep in brine;
>   And hands so often clasped in mine,
> Should toss with tangle and with shells.

For whom, poet or dead man, is it 'sweeter' 'To rest beneath the clover sod'? 'Than if *with thee* the roaring wells/Should gulf him fathom-deep in brine.' The delayed comparative 'than if with thee' strictly refers to the ship carrying the body who is last addressed nearly three stanzas away from this comparative. The delay inextricably tangles and exchanges pronouns, 'with thee', 'him', even 'us' in the search for a relationship less remote and nearer at hand. The pronouns become interchangeably the poet, Hallam. The last line is so severed from its syntactic relationships that it seems to express a preference for remaining dead and unburied. 'Should' becomes an imperative not a subjunctive – '*should* toss with tangle and with shells'. The poet can clasp the hand of the dead again by being dead too, and the syntax tangles to allow him the possibility of doing so.

The sleep sequence (LXVII–LXXI) moves beyond the 'play' of poetic diction in the Fair Ship sequence but is again blocked, retarded.

Section LVI ('So careful of the Type?') offers the dream as a model of the typeless universe – 'A monster then, a dream,/A discord' – and the cluster of poems on dreams and sleep explore the dream not only as a form of non-rational coherence but also as a form of idealist experience. Beginning with the liberation of 'When on my bed the moonlight falls' these poems become progressively less hopeful about the possibility of a subjective ordering of the world, and set up all over again the collapse of relationship in the non-objective world. Section LXX, the least hopeful of them all, remembers and conflates several earlier poems. 'When on the gloom I strive to paint/The face I know' returns upon the mimetic imagery of outline in Section V, but strives to represent an internal image on intangible gloom. The language of the phantom Nature (III) reappears in 'the hollow mask of night'. 'Cloud-towers by ghastly masons wrought': the internal 'clouds of nameless trouble' in Section IV ('To *sleep* I give my powers away'), the labouring breast of the dissipating cloud in the madness of the Storm poem (XV), fuse with the language of revolution which is derived from Carlyle and with the language of geological chaos in Section LVI. 'Dark bulks that tumble half alive,/And lazy lengths on boundless shores' returns upon and remembers the primeval chaos of the Type poem – 'A monster then ... dragons of the prime,/That tare each other in their prime'. Carlyle, Lyell, De Quincey's dreams and Dante's visions come together to create a psychological inferno. It is more extreme than its predecessor, the Storm poem, because the idea of the external world is obliterated altogether. Everything is internalised in 'shadowy thoroughfares *of thought*' entirely the experience of mind.

> I cannot see the features right,
>   When on the gloom I strive to paint
>   The face I know; the hues are faint
> And mix with hollow masks of night;
>
> Cloud-towers by ghostly masons wrought,
>   A gulf that ever shuts and gapes,
>   A hand that points, and pallèd shapes
> In shadowy thoroughfares of thought;
>
> And crowds that stream from yawning doors,
>   And shoals of puckered faces drive;
>   Dark bulks that tumble half alive,
> And lazy lengths on boundless shores;
>
> Till all at once beyond the will
>   I hear a wizard music roll,

And through a lattice on the soul
Looks thy fair face and makes it still.

The great difference between the dark bulks of LXX and the 'monster' chaos of the earlier LVI is that the monster, like the dragons and the dream there, is explicitly a metaphor for chaos. The images of this nightmare poem are referenceless. The aspect of comparison implied in metaphor is absent. The dream makes images without including a notion of their equivalences, which can only be understood if at all in the non-logical relation of one image to another. The dream cannot tell us what its content is. The threatening aspect of this dream is precisely the indeterminate imprecision of the images – 'dark *bulks*', 'lazy *lengths*'. Gulf, land, shapes, crowds, faces, are juxtaposed as discrete items, dissociated from one another, without relationship. They are sequential and simultaneous and become amorphously part of one another. They 'mix'. The mixing is created indiscriminately out of the fusion and discontinuity of images. The gulf which shuts and gapes, the 'yawning' door, create the breaks and gaps which consciousness is. No wonder this poem follows upon the dream of blight in the universe (anticipating a Hardy-like desolation) where the dreamer dreams that 'Nature's ancient power was lost' (LXIX). The dreamer wears a crown of thorns, identifying himself with Christ. But this dream is an allegory without a correspondence – 'The words were hard to understand'. Similarly, the saving form of the last stanza of LXX, 'Looks thy fair face' – is arbitrary, a lucky chance.

The dream landscapes of Sections LXVIII and LXXI are actually reduplications and conflations of earlier pastoral landscapes and *In Memoriam* (XXII, XXIII, XXVIII, XLVI, LXIV), but they 'remember' these linear, on-going walks and progresses in a limpid, crystalline form which holds them pure and static, radiant but immobile. 'I walk as ere I walked forlorn/When all our path was fresh with dew,/And all the bugle breezes blew/Reveillée to the breaking morn' (LXVIII): 'In walking as of old we walked/Beside ... The cataract flashing from the bridge,/The breaker breaking on the beach' (LXXI). Dreams have the wholeness and fulfilment of art ('That so my pleasure may be whole') but they create wholes which are incapable of movement. The cataract flashing, the breaker breaking, hold the landscape in a continuous static condition of repetition in an enclosed present tense which has a strange discrepancy with what is actually being talked about in the dream, 'The dust of *change*, the days that *grow*'. The dream cannot manage time; the language of these poems seizes up as time seizes up. 'I walk as *ere* I walk'd before': I walk as I did before the tragedy or, the syntax allows, I walk as I always did before now, forlorn. In spite of the creative displacements and inversions of dream work (with brilliant inventiveness in Section LXVIII the 'trouble' of the poet is displaced to the dream Hallam from the dreamer who is really experiencing it) the dream is incapable of introspection into itself. The *interpretation* of dreams belongs to the mediation of the waking consciousness which is by definition absent. 'But ere the lark had left the lea/ I wake, and I discern the truth' (LXVIII). The repeated 'ere' marks the passage of time outside the dream but simultaneous with it as the real dawn and soaring lark supervenes on the dream dawn and marks the temporal movement of which the dream is incapable. 'And I *discern* the truth' only in waking and in time. Sleep, 'Death's twin-brother' in this poem, paradoxically 'knows not death' as death cannot know itself, because with the wilful irresponsibility of the dream work it fuses past and present, ignoring the fact of death and is therefore unable to contemplate it as an experience.

What is gained from the sleep poems is not the potency of the dream, or the trance, both of which are allied to madness, but the potency of the mediation of the waking awareness and full consciousness. The dream as a model of idealist experience is abandoned but idealist experience is reclaimed in the form of the interpreting mind and the imagination aware of what it is *aware* of. 'I *know* that in thy place of rest... And then I *know* the mist is drawn' (LXVII). *Self*-consciousness. This is tentatively explored as the source of ordering, controlling the structuring of the universe in place of the naïve idealism of dreams and trance (and even madness). Dreams poignantly offer the pure, ingenuous fulfilment of lyric feeling in redeemed loss, but that is all.

> When on my bed the moonlight falls,
>   I know that in thy place of rest
>   By that broad water of the west,
> There comes a glory on the walls;
>
> Thy marble bright in dark appears,
>   As slowly steals a silver flame

> Along the letters of thy name,
> And o'er the number of thy years.
>
> The mystic glory swims away;
>   From off my bed the moonlight dies;
>   And closing eaves of wearied eyes
> I sleep till dusk is dipt in gray:
>
> And then I know the mist is drawn
>   A lucid veil from coast to coast,
>   And in the dark church like a ghost
> Thy tablet glimmers to the dawn.

Here the released play of liberated imagination is ambiguously an experience created out of thought (and creating thought) or one which is formed by the nature of the external world. But whether it is a reciprocal movement between self and world or not it could not come about at all without the creative intensity of the perceiver's imagination and self-conscious awareness. 'When on my bed the moonlight falls ... I *know* ... There comes a glory on the walls.' The parallelism is arranged as a virtual causal sequence. The moonlight *falls*, a glory consequentially *comes*, brought into being by the perceiver's knowing. 'A glory' may be intended as a synonym for moonlight, but moonlight is an objective fact; 'a glory' carries with it the sense of an evaluated, non-physical numinous *presence*, as the later 'mystic glory' suggests. It is both heavenly glory and one which is created out of spirit, the perceiver's spirit. The identification, in spite of the spatial gap between moonlight and glory, is subtly enabled by the parallelism 'on the walls', there, 'on my bed', here, 'in thy place of rest', there. The euphemistic poetic diction of 'place of rest', the grave, fuses the poet's imagination with the dead man but also distinguishes them, alive, dead. A 'place of rest' is circumlocution for grave and literally a bed. As if to assert the power of imaginative activity the causality is reversed when the moonlight fades – 'The mystic glory swims away;/From off my bed the moonlight dies' – as if the fading of the glory creates the fading of the moonlight. Again, poetic diction makes the glory active, living, autonomous – it *swims* away, becomes blurred, but also *moves* off. The literal, physical moonlight merely *dies*. The lighting up of the dead man's tablet by glory/moonlight is also expressed as if the light were capable of autonomous life. 'Thy marble light in dark appears' – in the place of rest? in the poet's mind? And does the marble *seem* to be, or does it *appear* substantively? The ambiguity of the nature of 'seeing' and appearance is reinforced by the recall of Shakespeare's Sonnet 43 in which the poet dreams of or imagines the appearance of the lover. The lighting up of the marble occurs with the intensity of a dream and the substantiveness of a fully perceived and *imagined* object. Perception requires imagination to be alive, illuminated. 'As slowly steals a silver flame/Along the letters of thy name.' The light or glory or both seem to *read* 'thy marble' and at last name, transforming experience by naming the nameless trouble of Section IV, renewing an imaginative knowledge of the dead and charging it with vitality. '*Thy* marble': the marble which commemorates the dead, the marble in which the being of the dead man is strangely fused, the symbol becoming what it symbolises, or possessing a mystical presence derived from the dead. The stepping-stones of the dead self in Section I, the stones which 'name the underlying dead' in Section II, are brought together here, transformed by the recreative imagination which knows itself as an act of imagination.

'And closing eaves of wearied eyes/I sleep... And then I *know*'. The physical obstruction of the eyelid is insisted upon by this elaborate circumlocution, and draws attention to the problem of seeing and knowing when the eye is closed. What form of knowing, what form of consciousness and its status, is brought into being? The question is reinforced by the syntax which asserts that you can 'know' in sleep or that the waking consciousness of the speaking poet can sustain its knowledge and knowing outside the condition of sleep. By association, the status of the first 'I know' in the poem is called into question, too. A knowing of the full consciousness or half-sleep? The questions are there, but so also is the imaginative intensity with which imaginative intensity is understood. The palpable barrier of the eyelid does not prevent the poet's imagination from moving beyond the 'lucid veil' (lighted and clear, transparent) of mist to recreate the dark church where the stone tablet 'glimmers' to the dawn. Sleeping or waking the materials of perception and imagination in the external world exist to be recreated in the mind. The stone tablet 'glimmers' to the dawn, receptive, giving back light like the stars which glimmer on the decks in Section LX and unlike the bald street in the dark house poem. The status of physical and mental forms and the mediation of the imagination have gathered complexities round them by this stage of *In Memoriam* and this lyric does not minimise them. But in this poem, momentarily, the obstructing door of Section VII, the veil of Section LVI – 'behind the veil, behind the veil' – have been redefined as the penetrative imagination breaks through the barrier of the substantive world without abolishing it and makes it belong to mental life. The mind fixes itself to form, marble and tablet, by recreating it. What is extraordinary about this movement of mind is that its process is achieved and implied without the use of metaphor, but simply through the *structural* correlation of parallelism – 'when *on* my bed', '*in* thy place of rest', 'the moonlight', 'a glory', 'I *know*', 'I *know*'. There are metaphors, like the delicate shift from moonlight to glory (the beauty of the shift is that 'glory' is a virtual synonym for moonlight but not necessarily a metaphor for it), the clusterings of poetic diction, the paradoxes ('lucid veil') which enable the experiences described to be ambiguously of the mind or of the world. But there is no metaphor for the process of imaginative projection, which is presented literally, as a structural relationship of which the mind is coextensively aware – I *know*.

In Memoriam never resolves anything. Even the notorious statement of certainty, 'I have felt' (CXXIV) never mentions the name of God and is put in the past tense as if it had been a recurrent experience of the past, rather than maintained as truth – 'a warmth *would* melt ... the heart *stood* up ... I have felt'. 'He, They, One, All; within, without.' These are either antitheses or inclusive categories. He and They can be set against one another and paired antithetically with One and All or the structure could maintain that He *is* They, One *is* All. And 'All' can be either within or without or both within and without. But Section XCV, the 'living soul' or Trance poem, is a lyric which indicates that the flow of the poem is on the turn. In a characteristically Tennysonian paradox, 'the *doubtful* dusk *reveal'd*': it reveals, even though the dusk is doubtful because it makes objective forms in the world ambiguous and the subject's perception of them uncertain. The revelation is partly about language. It is possible to 'frame in words' the ambiguities of experience. The poem 'frames' the mystical experience with the pictorial lines about the white kine and the trees which 'Laid their dark arms about the field', bonding and fixing a physical circle which 'contains' the mystical experience as if they represent the physical frame in which 'clear memory' and consciousness can be active. The dusk, or nature, does reveal, however ambiguously and returns upon the first poem about language (V), implicitly revising it. But language as picture, as representation or imitation, coexists with the language which is also able to 'frame', invent or create the 'doubtful' experience of trance itself. Words are not mere 'forms of speech' but formative. Language can construct experience as well as being external frame or clothing for it.

Section XCV liberates the poem into a freer and fuller play with possibilities. Rather than closing 'grave doubts' it discovers the energy to sport with words, as the revived wind swings the 'heavy-folded rose'. The final stanza discovers a metaphor for the continuity of life and death – 'East and West ... *Mixt* their dim lights... To broaden into boundless day' This is 'Like life and death', a resolution and an analogy which is too simple for the complexities of the poem, and which is later revised by the Hesper/Phospor lyric. If possible, the poem sports more wildly with possibilities as it nears its end, and with a sense of newly released energy. The liberation of the 'wild bird' lyric (LXXXVIII) 'remembers' and revalues the static, shadowy lark of Section XVI. It celebrates the wild extremes of contradictory feeling which 'meet' in the bird's song. The bird, correlative of the poem's condition, sings free and apart from it as if the denatured form of the lark is released from the dead lake of the poet's consciousness. 'A thousand pulses *dancing*', dancing *in spite* of or because of 'a contradition on the tongue' (CXXV). The scepticism is freeing, not obstructive. The poems play with the ambiguity of relationship, with the possibility of a non-objective world and the fragmentation of the self, as fully as they are prepared to make claims for the substantive but ever-reforming external world. As a result of this play of possibility another account of image-making emerges in the departure poems. It is image-making rather than analogy or metaphor. These poems adopt neither of the alternatives at work in the poem up to this point. They do not adopt the fixity of objective analogy which matches a stable world and correspondingly conceives of language as an external mould or form for pre-existing referents: nor do they assert the subject as its own object in which all metaphor creates the world as a replication of the self and language is conceived as autonomously creating experience. Instead the departure poems exploit the vital ambiguity of the relation between self and world returning continually to the reciprocity of self and other which establishes itself in spite of ambiguity. In consummate pastoral, with exquisite poise, equanimity and toughness, they explore the interchange and transformation of relationship between self and world.

The difference between the dim dawn anniversary poem which precedes the departure poems (XCIX) and the dim dawn poem which follows the sleep sequence (LXXII) is the difference between the same epistemology conceived in a vital and a static form. The 'streaming pane' of the earlier poem separates see-er and seen, blurring both itself and the perceiver's vision with the 'quick' (fast-falling and *living*) 'tears' of rain. The weeper's tears, the weather's tears. The identification of internal and external world (the day of Hallam's death 'blurred' the sun, literally and subjectively, is explicitly made as the self attempts to fuse with and appropriate the world as metaphor for its vision. But there is something wilful and forced in this activity. Consciousness insists upon constructing the world in its image. The day would have 'look'd the same', whether it had been stormy or not and is only stormy by a lucky consonance. The self-projection is static, coercing the materials of perception to its uses. The active, transforming interplay of agent and reflecting medium is quite different in the last dawn poem (XCIX) even though in its essentials the idea of the subject meeting its image in the object is the same. The dim dawn 'tremblest through thy darkling red/On you swollen brook that bubbles fast'. The dawn trembles through the red sky ('darkling' possesses the active force of a verb here) and trembles simultaneously, the syntax allows, through the red, fast-moving brook, day breaking reciprocally through sky and water, transforming one another as subject and object interact.

Tennyson uses that habitual and most potent Romantic image, reflection, for the ambiguous relationship of subject and object. Each element of the landscape in Section C 'reflects' a kindlier day, and in CI, the brook moves outwards from the garden and fragments the '*sailing* moon in creek and cove' into 'silver arrows', as the moon sails, the syntax allows, in sky *and* creek. Reflection is mobile, changing, reduplicative. Section CII poises the ambiguity of this relationship consummately in the affective 'embrace' of field, farm, self, in its last stanza.

> I turn to go: my feet are set
>   To leave the pleasant fields and farms;
>   They mix in one another's arms
> To one pure image of regret.

This 'pure' image, generalised and distilled by the unspecific pastoral of 'pleasant fields and farms', belongs both to landscape and mind. It is an external image, a picture and a living form, evoking feeling, and an internal image, a *representation* of pure feeling, pure regret. The doubleness of 'image of regret' allows that the image is created out of pure regret and created *by it* as well. It is also *pure* image, in the sense that it is created out of pure mind. The subtle movement between external and internal image is made particularly complex because the words, 'I turn to go' suggest either that the poet is glancing back at the actual pastoral scene or that he carries it, arrested, in his mind. External and internal image fuse, ambiguously, *mix*, in the poet's consciousness, just as the fields and farms 'mix', in one another's arms. 'My feet are *set*': he is prepared to leave and yet *rooted* in the landscape. Exactly the same double movement is in Section CI – 'Till from the garden and the wild/A fresh association blow,/And year by year the landscape grow/Familiar to the stranger's child'. The landscape 'grows' for the stranger's child, and it 'grows' in its own right. The poem forces a doubleness upon associationist psychology, making it bear the conventional reading of tie or connection between child and landscape, and an idealist reading in terms of a fresh *idea* or memory for the child. Both poems bear out Hallam's insight about the two-way movement of Tennyson's poetry, that it both evolves its mood from the external world, and fuses images in a medium of powerful emotion, an insight more subtle than Ruskinian pathetic fallacy. Both poems shift the implications of the baby poem towards an account of the growth of identity as reciprocal making by self and world. 'The baby, new to earth and sky'; earth and sky are new to the baby, the baby is new to them. Section CII remembers the baby poem – 'the well-belovèd place/Where first we gazed upon the sky'.

The departure poems remake the landscape of the earlier pastoral poems and, in doing so, remake the metaphors carried by the landscape. In this process the vital act of memory actually leads to the rejection of memory. The earlier pastoral poems, beginning with XXII and continuing in the next four poems, returning in XXXVIII and XLVI, never release themselves from the idea of a track defined by its ending and progressing inevitably to a break. The spatial model is the same, but expressed in terms of the relationship between high and low, in Sections XCI, XLIV, LXI, LXII, LXIV. In Section C ('I climb the hill'), the poet's eye moves over the landscape and the past simultaneously for the landscape breathes a 'gracious memory' of his friend, returning his experience to him. Syntax and perspectives go hand in hand as the sentence lists the extraordinary variety of the man-nurtured and man-nurturing pastoral landscape — grange, fold, stile, mead, wold, knoll, quarry, hill, rock, rivulet. A long sequence of expectation is set up over three stanzas by the construction of the sentence which seems to offer a linear account of experience, a track of amplification which ends the statement about memory, sealing it off in the past: 'No gray old grange... Or... Or... Or, Nor hoary knoll,... Nor... Nor'. But the sentence has actually *begun anew* and relates forward to 'But each has pleased a kindred eye'. It relates not to the first object, memory, but finds a new one. With a kind of victory over itself, looking forward, not backward, the sentence has created anew not memory but the dead man's experience, or that of others, 'kindred' quite unknown to him. The self-projection is towards empathy, not the subjectivity of the past.

> But each has pleased a kindred eye,
> And each reflects a kindlier day;
> And, leaving these, to pass away,
> I think once more he seems to die.

To 'pass away': a euphemism for death and a literal description of the continuance of a journey. The poet dies, because his immediate consciousness of the landscape of memory dies with its death (it also passes away), or absence. But, 'I *think* once more': the series of little deaths of consciousness are necessary to the series of recreations in the mind. To recreate experience of the dead man, even of his death (the awful *thought* of death) requires neither landscape nor the wasteful fixations of memory, but the energies of pure mind and imagination. 'And year by year *our* memory fades/From all the circle of the hills' (CI). Memories of us fade from the community ('circle') we lived in, or, like light dying, from the very landscape itself, the circle of hills. Correspondingly, and inevitably, 'our' own memory fades as their physical presence no longer gives perception a presence to work upon. The release from memory is the condition of the recreation of pure image. But continual recreation has its corollary in a series of deaths. The mediation of self and world collapses and falls into one-sidedness. The delicate equilibrium of the departure poems disintegrates, a disintegration evolved from the same language which created the equipoise. The poem is back once more with the unstable fragmented idealist self. And this means that it returns upon its past and redefines its language anew. 'And *dream* my *dream*, and *hold* it true (CXXIII). Sea displaces rooted tree, solid land displaces sea – 'There rolls the deep'. What is the status of the idealist 'dream' and what correlation does it have with this condition of flux?

In Memoriam is one of the last great triumphs of idealist language over itself. It both overcomes and founders upon the coalescing, ambiguous forms of Romantic syntax, using these forms to express the problem of articulation and relationship which they engender. It struggles, as earlier nineteenth-century poems do not, with a psychological account of expressive language and the pathetic fallacy which threatens to undermine the firm epistemological base of Romantic poetry. Repeatedly it builds itself out of its collapse by giving full play to the language which threatens its destruction. Classical elegy coexists with psychological, idealist lyric: pastoral landscape with mind-created images. The coexistence of these 'forms' is employed to expose the contradictions inherent in each. *In Memoriam* is a poem about death trying to be a poem about life. It is 'life', not pain, the expected moral truism, which forms the 'firmer mind' (XVIII). On the other hand, 'Doubt and Death' '*let* the fancy fly' (LXXXVI), let the liberated mind free and *allow* or create its freedom, actually bringing it into being. The poem recognises its need for simple longings and consolation while continually investigating and complicating these desires. And so *In Memoriam* can be described as a poem of great intelligence. Its sporting with words, its attempt to set the possibilities of metaphor in play, reveals the problems of idealist language. It exposes the collapse of relationship inherent in its structure and looks forward beyond the nineteenth century to the problems of language experienced by later poets. It is not surprising that a poem about bereavement, the self without an object, should recognise so acutely the dissolution of idealist language. It is both willing and unwilling to do so, because it is both willing and unwilling to come to terms with death. A world without relationships: to *In Memoriam* to accept idealist language is to accept death.

NOTE

1 This point is made by Alan Sinfield, *The Language of Tennyson's 'In Memoriam'*, Oxford, 1971. I have learned much from this study.

Conclusion

This is not a conclusion, perhaps, in the terminal sense of the word because it implies a further study. The nineteenth-century poets I have discussed are in the grip of a series of problems, problems which they were at least partly in possession of, and which extend themselves into the modern period. My intention has been to describe those problems, in which an almost hubristically cognitive account of poetic language slides over into one which is potentially disabling, denying poetry the capacity to create and transform categories virtually in the act of claiming that it does so and suggesting an incipient collapse of relationship. I have proceeded by exploring the connections between epistemology and the structure of poetic language, believing that each implies the other. Questions of epistemology and the structure of poetic language become implicitly elided with or into political and cultural concerns, not because poetic language is forced to reflect some pre-existing ideological pattern in its form, but because it ceaselessly generates complexities and contradictions which, whether directly or by extension and implication, become questions about the word and the world. The configurations of poetic language are thus actively forming and questioning paradigms of relationship and action which are implicitly to do with possibilities and choices, limitations and freedoms, and they play into the extra-linguistic world as much as it plays into them. It must be self-evident that a particular historical period limits the nature and kind of question that can be asked, and that a writer will never be in full possession of his questions or solutions because they themselves are a part of the complex of contradictions he is trying to solve. But it is how these questions are asked in their ceaseless complexity, their mode of existence in poetic discourse through the form and organisation of words, which tells us something about the way in which language and history become part of one another and about the moments at which poetic form and politics intersect. It is a strangely static account of literature (and of ideology) which assumes that a text is caught in a predetermined pattern rather than responding to it and indeed reordering it through the play of language. And if one is prepared to see the language of a text as a play with limit established in and through the ordering of the work itself, one is relieved of the dubious practice of abstracting a fixed set of ideas and procedures from the text and assuming tautologously that they have produced the text.

I have looked at the language of nineteenth-century poetry as a play with the possibilities and limits of idealism. Although the movement from *The Prelude* to *In Memoriam* suggests that the problems of idealist language become more and more acute with time, I have not stressed the historical evolution of poetic language so much as the nature of the difficulties shared by this group of poets. However, there is no doubt that, considered diachronically, there is an evolution, and that nineteenth-century poetry handed on a set of problems to modernism. What is interesting is the manner in which these were defined, and the form of interpretation they were given by twentieth-century poets. It is proper to end this book by indicating how twentieth-century poets confronted what they interpreted as the dissolution of poetic language. I shall do this by centring the discussion on Yeats' 'Among School Children'.

In Chapter 1 I said that in Hopkins is to be found the 'lonely began' of modernism. It is Hopkins who is one of the first poets to make a rigorous distinction between abstraction and concretion in poetry. This arose from his sense that language was being unfixed by other nineteenth-century poets and dissolved from its tetherage to the world of objects. The terrifying dismembering of language is a disremembering, an obliteration of the distinctions by which we make relationships and therefore an obliteration of memory. The solution was to return us to the world and to keep a hold on reality by insisting that words return to their relationship with things, or if not that, that they are uniquely individuated in such a way as to become virtually things in themselves. The same insistence is to be found even more emphatically in Pound. 'When their [poets'] work goes rotten ... when their very medium, the essence of their work, the application of word to thing goes rotten, i.e. becomes slushy and inexact, or excessive or bloated, the whole machinery of social and of individual order goes to pot.' 'Go in fear of abstractions,' he says elsewhere.[1] The function of literature in the state is to maintain order by maintaining the exactness of the application of word to thing.

The disturbing way in which Hopkins' conservatism has evolved into something far more extreme is too obvious to point out and the naïvety of this account of language is obvious too. What is striking is the assumption that the nature of poetic language must *necessarily* be discussed in terms of a distinction between abstract and concrete, and that the nineteenth century has disabled the language of poetry for the twentieth by being slushy, inexact and abstract. This is rather different from the grounds of Marx's critique of Hegel, although it has some affinities with it. The longing for a content experienced by the idealist consciousness, in which 'the object as such presents itself to consciousness as something disappearing' (Chapter 1, p. 43) is a much more intricate and sophisticated diagnosis than the simple distinction between abstract and concrete. However, both Marx and Pound deny a cognitive function on the one hand to idealism and on the other to abstraction, and this is what is important. Idealism has no cognitive base because it is deprived of 'content'. Abstraction has no cognitive function because it is inexact and unrelated to concrete experience. So Pound retreats from the cognitive account of poetry as transformation and change claimed by Romantic poetry and establishes a new cognitive area for poetry in which the abstract idea is not simply latent in the concrete, or hiding in the sensory, ready to be released; if it cannot be rinsed entirely out of irreducible concrete experience, it is indivisibly part of the concrete image. And since words for him are not signs but are indivisible from the things they represent, not substitutes for sensation (as T. E. Hulme, the great vulgariser of modernism, put it) but actually hand over sensations bodily, it seems that we have got rid of the possibilities of abstraction entirely. The concentration on 'thingness' also enables the modernist poet to relieve himself of the notion of the subject, and of subjectivity. It is almost as if things write poetry irrespective of the perceiving self and its emotions. The slushiness of Romantic 'subjectivity' – for no modernist seems to be able to credit Romantic poetry with a strict epistemological base – and its arrogant claims for a self-generating world of imagination, is avoided.

Interestingly, the distinction between abstract and concrete is alien to the Romantics I have discussed. Indeed, it is precluded by the terms of their poetics in quite this form. They did not think they were doing what Pound thought they were. They were unwilling to rest an account of poetry on onesided distinctions because such distinctions are precisely what poetry transforms. The synthetic power of imagination transforms and subsumes categories, healing the fracture between idea and the phenomenal world, the discursive reason and intuitive power, subject and object, by making each 'translucent', as Coleridge put it, in the other.[2] Ideally it mediates rather than mystifying relationship. It is from this that it achieves its cognitive power. (Perhaps only Keats, who felt that axioms of philosophy should be 'proved upon our pulses' (Letter to Reynolds, 3 May 1818), comes near to resting an account of poetry on the abstract/concrete distinction.) As I have argued in earlier chapters, however, the claim that language can create and transform categories can actually involve the disappearance of distinction and opposition, the essential oppositions and antitheses by which the world is construed. Romantic thinking can lead to the Nietzschian proposition that being is an empty fiction and that the 'apparent' world is the only one. This accounts for the hiatus between Romantic accounts of their own poetry and twentieth-century reinterpretations of the Romantic condition. And it is this sense of dissolution, as much as a concern with abstraction, which drives modernist poets to assert the primacy of the concrete. The irreducible concrete image provides a way of holding on to the 'real' world.

The return to the 'real' world, however, provides a new problem. The terms in which twentieth-century poets interpret the Romantics provide the basis for a new debate. The cognitive problem is reintroduced in a different form, and debate takes place around the nature of the image. For if poetry takes its stand upon the irreducible concretion of the image, which is to resist abstraction and is not to be effaced into the self-present idea, if it is not to mean but to be, how does meaning emerge at all? The sensory, immediate and self-enclosed image may partake in some sense of the world of phenomenal experience but how does it interpret itself? If it does not interpret itself it might as well be replaced by the sensory world, or else it can exist in a curious transcendent autonomy and self-referential independence, freed, it is true, from discursive forms, but existing at the margin in comparison with the centrality claimed for Romantic poetry. Its only protection is that it renews a sense of the particular and maintains a unique language, cut off from other discourses, but asserting some special privileged and untranslateable experience which is in some way profoundly necessary in a world taken over by forms of thought dominated by abstraction. The special status given to the irreducible objective image is really only the reverse of the special status given to the idealist subject in Romantic poetry, a special status often assumed by critics as unproblematical, but as I have argued, struggled with by the Romantics themselves. The image creates as many difficulties as it solves.

One can find debate about the image in many forms and contexts but I turn to Yeats and 'Among School Children' because of the intensity of his concern and because I think that the Romantic account of poetry as knowledge is one of the 'Presences' of the poem. I turn to the end of the poem:

> Labour is blossoming or dancing where
> The body is not bruised to pleasure soul,
> Nor beauty born out of its own despair,
> Nor blear-eyed wisdom out of midnight oil.
> O chestnut-tree, great-rooted blossomer,
> Are you the leaf, the blossom or the bole?
> O body swayed to music, O brightening glance,
> How can we know the dancer from the dance?

This final stanza is often seen rather blandly, and the interrogatives which end the poem are not seen to take the 'enterprise' of the poem back to the first line – 'I walk through the long school room *questioning*'. Perhaps it does seem as if Yeats has found his image for resolving the nature of the image: the self-born image no longer mocks man's enterprise by being transcendent and beyond it but as 'labour' becomes a process in unbroken continuity with itself and its products. The structure of the metaphor incorporates labour into the predicate in such a way that labour is not in equivalence or correspondence with blossoming and dancing but is inherent in them, expressing itself as blossoming and dancing in identity with them. Labour creates images for its own processes by which we know it and by which we create analogies for it. In a circular and reflexive way labour creates images which image it, and it is possible to affirm the identity of process and product, doer and deed, knower and known. The chestnut tree in organic unity with itself, the dancer inseparable from the dance (the abstract pattern of the dance is only realised in and through the activity of the dancer), suggest a moment of supreme fullness in which being and meaning, image and concept, word and what it represents, are one and indistinguishable. For a moment at least the poem posits that it is possible to be lifted out of the stress and divisiveness of experience beyond the condition in which blear-eyed wisdom bruises the body to pleasure soul. 'Blear-eyed wisdom', of course, recalls Keats' 'leaden-eyed despair' in the 'Ode to a Nightingale' and reminds the stanza of the condition 'where but to *think* is to be full of sorrow'. By asking questions, Yeats' poem does go on thinking to the very end, and if it did not, the resolution of the first stanza as I have described it could be accused of blandness and sentimentality. Indeed, it *is* bland and sentimental as I have defined it. To see that a resolution is not won so easily it is necessary to go back to the first stanza, particularly as the resolution of the poem as I have described it seems to leave out the school children with which the poem begins, and makes the title seem merely occasional.

The poem begins in the context of popular education. That Yeats is a Protestant, inspecting a Catholic Montessori School, should be remembered. 'Among School Children' appeared in *The Tower* in 1928, a volume which also contains 'Meditations in time of Civil War'. The institutionalised calm of this school room is to be seen in the context of Irish struggles not so long before the poem was written. It is not innocuous. It is also worth remembering that in spite of the specialness of this particular school (not stressed in the poem), popular education in Ireland had a long-standing history as far back as the 1830s. People at this time were beginning to enquire whether the rigid syllabus of Irish schools should accommodate Irish myths and legends and more imaginative material. The point of drawing attention to this is to stress that the first stanza places the question of education and living knowledge squarely at the forefront of the poem. The ordered neatness of the children's activities, registered in a sing-song monotone, reflects some constraint.

> The children learn to cipher and to sing,
> To study reading books and histories,

To cut and sew, be neat in everything
In the best modern way.

The poet's own reading books and histories, the Trojan story,
Plato's parable, the Quattrocento, Aristotle, Pythagoras, are not
irrelevant to the children, as, in the sweep of the poem through
private reverie, myth and metaphysics, learning is redefined as
labour. Labour is the process of giving birth and labour is work,
in the sense that both Hegel and Marx would have understood,
as the totality of the labour of the self upon the world. It is the
process of self-creation through relationship with the other, the
act of separation which is the prerequisite of cognition. There is
a moment of living labour as the children gaze 'in momentary
wonder' upon 'A sixty-year old, smiling public man', aware of
what is other to them. The wonder is ephemeral, but it seems to
light up their experience in a way the mundane activity of
learning does not.

The full meaning of labour is created through the enterprise of
the poem and is latent in the first stanza in the list of humdrum
activities – 'The children learn to cipher and to sing'. The
children do sums and have singing lessons, proleptically anticipating Pythagoras in stanza VI, perhaps, another mathematician
and singer. But 'cipher' is a curiously archaic word and oddly
paired with song, and one is alerted to a certain strangeness. In
Yeats' poetry, however, song is insistently his word for poetry. It
is characteristic that the possibility of this grace should be
lurking in the children's activities, but singing also takes on
further meaning, because it is linked with ciphering ambiguously as complementary to it and in opposition to it. Song, in
contrast with dealings in the abstractions and symbols of Arabic
numerals, looks forward to the image at the end of the poem, the
place where meaning and being are at one, the experience which,
in unity with itself, need not go beyond itself. The self-referring
world of music is an apposite embodiment of the image. A
cipher, on the other hand, is a code and also a key to a code,
possessing a secret or hidden meaning. It is a set of substitutions
or correspondences which represent a meaning beyond themselves but in that a code exchanges signs for signs it is secondary
and displaces an original. Hence other meanings of cipher as a
copy and a passive agent. Clustering round cipher are the implications of abstraction. Clustering round song are the

implications of the irreducible concrete image. The enterprise of the poem is to create a dialogue between them, which brings them closer together rather than forcing them apart. For a cipher at least reaches towards a referential meaning, in contrast to the self-enclosed world of music. Yet in that it is secondary, offering signs for other signs there is a severance between a code and meaning, in contrast to the unity of experience and meaning in music. The richness of the poem comes from its attempts both to bring them together and its recognition that the two are perhaps irreconcilable. The complexity of its enterprise is reflected in the way it tests out the possibilities of prepositions and relational particles, in, into, upon, of, enabling them to express different kinds of relationship: 'be neat in everything/In the best modern way', 'in momentary wonder'; 'Into a sphere', 'Into the yolk and white of one shell', 'Her present image floats into the mind'; 'I look upon one child', 'that colour upon cheek or hair', ' a shape upon her lap', 'Upon a ghostly paradigm', 'Upon the bottom of the king of kings', 'upon a fiddle-stick', 'Old clothes upon old sticks to scare a bird'; 'I dream of a Ledaean body', 'of a harsh reproof', 'And thinking of that fit of grief or rage', 'daughters of the swan', 'of every paddler', 'mess of shadows', 'of Ledaean kind', 'enough of that', 'There is a comfortable kind of old scare-crow', 'Honey of generation', 'the pang of his birth', 'O self-born mockers of man's enterprise', 'out of its own despair', 'out of midnight oil'. Generally 'upon' is used to express the external relationship of something with another and often desig-nates unrelatedness or contingent contact and a splitting apart. 'In', 'into' generally designates inherence and identity. It is as if the two extremes of cipher and image are represented here. But by far the most complex particle is 'of' which plays between the parameters expressed by 'into' and 'upon', since it can designate separation and belonging, ambiguously suggesting a partaking of and a severance from, production out of or construction out of, a possession belonging to or a thing apart that one is con-cerned about. It is not possible to look at every case of prepositional interplay, which in conjunction with an emphatic use of infinitives, gives the poem its extraordinary pressure, a rhetoric where the axes of prepositions swing things into con-junction and apart. The prepositions work to 'cut and sew' the poem, bringing Plato and paradigm, Aristotle and Alexander's bottom, Pythagoras and fiddle-stick, Old clothes upon a stick, into both conjunction and disjuntion, with a characteristic disrespect for concordance and an equally strong sense of the witty concord of these heterogeneous things. In all this interplay the swing of 'of' is paramount. It is important that 'of' relates to a vital ambiguity in labour itself, in which the thing born is part of the self and separate from it, 'out of' the self in two senses, or in which work done involves an extension of the self and a separation of the self and world.

The larger organisation of the poem is a series of cuts, disjunctions and conjunctions, all of which have the character of a non-sequitur, and all of which are held in some connection, one might say sewn together, rather obviously. The first cut is the movement to the privacy of reverie immediately after the first stanza. Memories of Maud Gonne, vicariously as a child and then directly as woman, are more intense and more present than the 'paddlers' with whom the poet is surrounded. The puzzle of the poem is how it gets from this through metaphysics to the worship of images by nuns and mothers and thence to its end. In memory one can see enacted the process and experience of imagining. 'Her present image floats into the mind', looks forward to the 'images' and 'Presences' addressed in the penultimate stanza, and makes the point that images do not need tangible presence to be generated. But on the whole it is the disconnection of this part of the poem which is most noticeable. Its vulnerable exposure to passion and intensity – 'And thereupon my heart is driven wild' – and its equally vulnerable self-involvedness and uneasily mocking self-disgust is like a small lyric poem inside a larger narrative of thought and action. The miniature lyric ends shockingly, not only expressing the poet's sense of lack of worth, but attempting to generalise a nihilism which must, by implication, include the school children as well as the poet: 'What youthful mother' would think her child a 'compensation' for the pains of birth 'Or the uncertainty of his setting forth' if she could see that child 'With sixty or more winters on its head'? The note on Porphyry seems to be an attempt to cover up a certain embarrassment on the part of the poet and to obfuscate the inclusiveness of the stanza's negatisms.

The shock of this question cuts into the solutions of Plato, Aristotle, Pythagoras.

> Plato thought nature but a spume that plays
> Upon a ghostly paradigm of things;
> Soldier Aristotle played the taws
> Upon the bottom of a king of kings;
> World-famous golden-thighed Pythagoras
> Fingered upon a fiddle-stick or strings
> What a star sang or careless muses heard:
> Old clothes upon old sticks to scare a bird.

'Upon' becomes the insistent preposition here, and in these masterly epigrams, activates the notion of 'play' which in turn invokes various aspects of ciphering. It is hard to know, in the account of Plato's thought, whether the spume of nature and the phenomenal world or the 'ghostly paradigm' of ideas is the cipher. Both seem abstractions, each dependent on the other. And however 'solid' Aristotle may be, he has his cipher in Alexander, the King of Kings. Pythagoras, who might seem to unite poetry and abstraction, seems a magnificent but ineffectual figure transposing, almost like a dilettante, what has already been transposed by the 'careless Muses'. The attempt to 'sew' the poem together is given up – 'Old clothes upon old sticks to scare a bird'. A scarecrow is a 'paradigm', and indeed a parody of a man, and abandoned.

Another attempt to 'sew' is mounted in the second stanza. The nuns of the first stanza and the mothers of the fifth reappear – 'Both nuns and mothers worship images'. (There is an interesting switch of gender and it is difficult to know what significance to give it. Nuns, even though they worship the static icons of marble or bronze, seem to come together with mothers not only as sufferers, but as people immersed in being in some way, in the middle of experience, like Maud Gonne's fit of grief or rage or her subsequently ravaging political life.) To worship an image, of course, in terms of conventional Christianity is blasphemous.

> Both nuns and mothers worship images,
> But those the candles light are not as those
> That animate a mother's reveries,
> But keep a marble or a bronze repose.
> And yet they too break hearts – O Presences
> That passion, piety or affection knows,
> And that all heavenly glory symbolise –
> O self-born mockers of man's enterprise;

This is the most elliptical stanza of the poem. It surges towards a resolution, but without, it seems, knowing where it is going, terminating invocation without a predicate in the passionate 'Labour is blossoming', which replaces the missing predicate without supplying it. There is a lacuna which is never filled in. Images and Presences are defined by relative clauses which come to the verge of a revelation but can only be explained in terms of themselves. Images, Presences, 'symbolise' and they are 'mockers'. That these 'break hearts' is the critical insight of this stanza. We can be helped to see how they do this first by looking at the uneasy semantic overlap of 'images', 'Presences' and 'symbolise' and then at the impacted syntax in which they exist. The three words balance around different relationships between the sign and what it represents and each puts different stress on the proxy or secondary, substitutive nature of the sign. An image is a substantive and visible thing and yet however iconic it may be an idea or 'shape' in the mind which would even constitute the visible thing as an image. 'Presences' are things brought into being, experienced inwardly as realities, and have eucharistic associations – the Word made flesh. The symbol is the visible sign of the invisible thing not present and indeed unknowable except through the sensible symbol. Passion, piety or affection 'knows' Presences (and images and by extension symbols). That is, Presences are known in and through these passionate states of being. Through them the symbolic or image-making act is born. We are helped to see how Presences 'mock' and 'break hearts' by remembering that by passions, pieties and affections Yeats did not mean only the nice passions, the intense and harmonious passions, such as love, child-birth, religious feeling; but, as the poem almost violently testifies and fully asserts to in what I have called the miniature lyric of stanzas II–IV, and in the shock of stanza V, he means the necessarily disruptive ravages of grief, political violence, sectarian hatred, civil war, all the energies of which surge in the rhetoric here as presences which drive the heart wild. All these things create images which mock. Images are mockers of man's enterprise in the sense that they become other and beyond, and seem *sui generis* and apart, self-born. Images are mockers in the sense that they are born out of the self and out of man's enterprise (the enterprise of passion, piety and affection which are and make men 'labour') and because they therefore *imitate* the enterprise, another sense of mock. The syntax allows both senses and brings into play again the idea of the cipher, the abstraction or the secondary thing which is nevertheless bound up with the self-present image. The paradox leads to the breaking of hearts because of the fatal tendency to equate and identify the image, Presence or symbol, whether domestic or political, with what it represents, which in turn produces fantasy, fanaticism, madness. The Irish conflict is not so far behind this stanza.

The lacuna between this penultimate and the last stanza should warn against the interpretation of the triumphant interrogatives of the last stanza in terms of an ultimate cognitive resolution of the cipher and the song. Rather, the poem continues to enquire how experience plays into image and image into experience by stressing the agonising gap between idea, cipher, paradigm, and experience. Somehow the heart driven wild, the materia, the phenomena, the unique intensity of experience need both paradigms and images to render them meaningful and indeed to be the cognitive agent of meaning, but both paradigms and images 'mock'. The great questions of the last stanza are often taken to be metaphorical questions, but they are rather literal questions about metaphor. 'O chestnut tree' is a perfectly good biological, teleological, epistemological question. Above all, it is a question about metaphor. What is the tree as image? How is it derived from the unique physical identity of the tree? The labour of metaphor both unifies and separates. Labour is an act of separation more than it is an extension of the self. It may be that an identity of experience and image, language and the world, is sought, but the process reveals the irremediable gap between them and the labour of metaphor creates the questions which arise out of the process. We *do* know the dancer from the dance and the urgency of the last stanza comes from the need to know how, and why it should be so necessary to do so. Metaphor does not heal separation by making correspondences which obliterate distinctions, but it preserves the gap and maintains separation in the process of making relationships and so enables us to ask questions about the act of making relationships. It keeps questioning alive.

Perhaps the feeling of resolution comes from the fact that these are happier, more triumphant questions than the earlier unhappy interrogatives out of which the poem is born, which were questions immersed in the sense that but to think is to be full of sorrow. The confidence of the last stanza is the confidence of asking meaningful questions. It is the energy of metaphor which brings this about. Here the energy of metaphor, and perhaps the primordial cognitive moment, is expressed in the brightening glance of the perceiver apart from what he perceives, a brightening partly created by the object of perception, the momentary wonder which is the prerequisite of enquiry and of figural thought, whether it initiates cipher or song. With this phrase, 'O brightening glance', the school children are reunited with poem, not sewn back into it, as one feels the nuns and mothers are, but re-incorporated. The poem vindicates its title, bringing into prominence another preposition used only once in the poem, '*Among* School Children', a preposition which can be respected without sentimentality.

I have emphasised the work of separation and the preservation of distinctions in the labour of metaphor here and in doing so have perhaps marked off Yeats and his preoccupations too sharply from the concerns of nineteenth-century poetry. It should be apparent, however, that 'Among School Children' is part of a continuing dialogue with the epistemological and human concerns of the earlier period. Its organisation and language make it belong generically to those concerns described aptly, not by a poet, but a novelist in the twentieth century, Virginia Woolf in *To the Lighthouse*. Mr Ramsay's son, answering Lily Briscoe's question about his father's work, replies that it is about 'subject and object and the nature of reality'.

NOTES

1 'How to Read', *Literary Essays of Ezra Pound*, T. S. Eliot (ed.), Faber and Oxford, 1960, pp. 21, 5.
2 *Biographia Literaria*, J. Shawcross (ed.), Oxford, 1907, Vol.II, p. 1. 'This power ... reveals itself in the balance or reconciliation of opposite or discordant qualities: of sameness, with difference; of the general, with the concrete, the idea, with the image, the individual, with the representative.'

Index

Page numbers in bold type indicate main sections of the book devoted to the name in the text. Lowercase n indicates the name in the notes at the end of each chapter.

219